Positive Psychology

Positive Psychology

Text Book For Graduation
and Post Graduation
Based on NEP and
Competitive Examinations

Dr. Reeta Kumari

University Dept. of Psychology
Ranchi University, Ranchi

**MOTILAL BANARSIDASS
INTERNATIONAL
DELHI**

Delhi, 2023

ISBN : 978-81-19196-59-3

Also available at
MOTILAL BANARSIDASS INTERNATIONAL
H. O. : 41 U.A. Bungalow Road, (Back Lane) Jawahar Nagar, Delhi - 110 007
4261/3 (basement), Ansari Road, Darya Ganj, New Delhi - 110 002
203 Royapettah High Road, Mylapore, Chennai - 600 004
12/1A, 2nd Floor, Bankim Chatterjee Street, Kolkata - 700 073
Stockist : Motilal Books, Ashok Rajpath, Near Kali Mandir, Patna - 800 004

Printed & Bound by
MOTILAL BANARSIDASS INTERNATIONAL

I dedicate this book

to

My beloved husband

Mr. Arun Kumar Sahu

and

Loving sons

Saheb and Louhit

Brief note about the Author

Dr. Reeta Kumari is the eminent teacher of Psychology in the University Department of Psychology, Ranchi University, and Ranchi. She has obtained her academic achievements from the Ranchi University. She has completed her Post Graduation in Psychologyand Hindi from Ranchi University, Ranchi. The degree of Ph. D. in Psychology has been conferred upon her in the year 2006 by the Ranchi University; Ranchi. She has submitted her final thesis to the Ranchi Universityfor the award of highest academic degree of D. Litt.

Dr. Reeta Kumari has demonstrated outstanding dedication and commitment to the field of Psychology through her exceptional contributions in writing textbooks,conducting research works and developing **Psychological Tools (Scales)** whichare useful for the research works.Her hard work and dedication towards research have been instrumental inenlightening of understanding of human behavior, cognitive process and mental health. Dr. Reeta has written highly appreciated bookson different topics of Psychology namely- **Introduction to Psychology, Uchchatar Manovaigyanik Parikchhan, Uchchatar Manovaigyanik Prayog, Applied Psychology, Health Psychology, Education Psychology, How to Write a Research Proposal, Social Issues, Play and Development Psychology, Elementary Computer Application and Environmental Studies.** Her coming book is **Positive Psychology**. Her written books have been widely acclaimed bystudents and teachers alike and have played a significant role in shaping the way we learn and teach.

Dr. Reeta has edited the books based on social issues such as **Human Trafficking in India, Dump before Death, Witchcraft: Critical Analysis, Honor Killing Shaping the Society through Educationand Child Abuse**.

The author has shown remarkable passion and skill in developing educational materials (Tools /Scales) that are both informative and engaging. She has developed **eight Psychological Research Tools (Scales)** which are very useful in conducting research works.

Dr. Reeta has successfully provided the guidance to **seven** Research Scholars for the award of Ph. D. degree and **eight** other Research Scholars are doing their research works for Ph. D. under her guidance. Her research works have been instrumental in advancing our understanding of key issues in the field of Psychology and have provided valuable insights that have helped to inform teaching practices

She has been the editor of a renowned research Journal **Resonance-National Journal of Value Education** for the last twelve years. She has served as a resource person in the Orientation and Refresher Programmes at UGC Human Research Development Centre, Ranchi. She has also served as Course Co-coordinator during the Orientation and Refresher Programmes in January 2016, February 2019 and July 2022 respectively.

She has successfully completed UGC sponsoredminor Research Project entitled **Marital Adjustment Stress and Depression among Working and Non-Working Married Women**. She has successfully conducted UGC sponsored National Seminar on the topic –**Shaping the Society through Education in the year 2017**. The author has presented **eight** research papers in the International Seminars and **35** research papers in the National Seminars. Her **59** research papers have been published in different journals. She has presented her research paper in the Oxford University, London (United Kingdom) in 2023

She has been awarded IPA Academic Excellence Award 2020 by the Indian Psychological Association for the presentation of a Research paper during the Indian Science Congress held at Bengaluru in 2020

The tireless effort, dedication and personal sacrifices made by Dr. Reeta Kumari have been recognized and appreciated by the peers, colleagues and students. Her work has inspired many young scholars to follow in her footsteps and pursue their passion for Psychology.

Dr. Reeta Kumari

FOREWORD

This book on Positive Psychology is a new approach within psychology that allows studying the dimension of the normal person without illness and their strengths and virtues. It is the scientific study of optimal human functioning which narrows its focus to health, wellness, achievement and quality of life. Positive psychology is a new branch of psychology whose objective is the rise, development and realization of human inner powers. The purpose of this is to take such a reference for the teachers, education and student of psychology which includes the theory, concepts of positive psychology as well as the latest realities, discoveries and trends.

Positive Psychology focuses on the modern line of psychology that aims to discover and cultivate talents to make normal life more satisfying, not just dealing with mental changes. This book on Positive Psychology is dedicated to improvement, not just a place for psychology to be used. Positive Psychology focuses on the positive events and effects in life, including: Positive experiences (such as happiness, joy, motivation, and love) and Positive states and traits (such as gratitude, characteristics, and compassion)

The Three Pillars: Positive psychology has three central concerns: positive experiences, positive personal characteristics, and positive institutions.

While Positive Psychology encompasses many disciplines and fields, many scholars and practitioners have focused on maximizing the benefits of five factors essential *for happiness and well-being: positive emotions, connectedness, meaning, relationships, and achievement (often referred to as PERMA).*

I think this book on Positive Psychology will be a mile stone in this field because this theme is in the limelight in present scenario. The 21ˢᵗ century and especially the time to come is filled with challenges of different kinds. The world is becoming a universal village where everything is digital and Positive Psychology will be a guiding force to come out of all such difficulties.

I wish the book a grand success.

Dr. Om Prakash Kesri Head
P. G. Dept. of Psychology
Maharaja College, Arrah

FOREWORD

It is with great pleasure I introduce a fantastic book on Positive Psychology written by Dr. Reeta Kumari. This book is an exceptional resource for undergraduate and postgraduate students who want to learn more about the science of happiness, well-being, and positive human functioning.

This book provides an in-depth comprehensive overview of Positive Psychology and its practical applications, including topics such as resilience, gratitude, optimism, and mindfulness. She explores the theories, research, and interventions that have emerged from this rapidly growing field. Each chapter includes reflection questions that help students apply the concepts they have learned to their own lives. By doing so, students can develop the skills and habits that lead to greater happiness, success, and fulfilment.

Dr. Reeta emphases on the intersection of Positive Psychology with other disciplines such as philosophy and spirituality. This holistic approach not only enriches the reader's understanding of positive psychology but also highlights its relevance to everyday life.

The book is accessible, engaging, and well-organized, making it an ideal resource for both students and teachers. Whether you are new to positive psychology or have some prior knowledge, you will find this book informative, insightful, and inspiring.

It is written in a clear and accessible style, making it easy to understand and apply. I highly recommend this book to anyone who wants to learn more about positive psychology and its practical applications. It will undoubtedly be a valuable addition to library and a source of inspiration and motivation for years to come.

Dr. Sheo Sagar Prasad
Director
Institute of Psychological Research & Service
Patna University, Patna

FOREWORD

Positive Psychology is a new concept in the field of psychology which has evolved in recent years. So most of the people do not have acquainted with this new area of psychology. Positive Psychology is all about the study of factors that make the human life worthy living. As it is new concept of psychology, there is lack of books related to the subject.

Positive Psychology is a good attempt by the author Dr. Reeta Kumari. The author has written many books in past according to the syllabus. This book is also based on the new syllabus of UGC as per the New Education Policy. The present book is divided in to six chapters which contain different topics of Positive Psychology such as — Introduction to Positive Psychology, Subjective Well-being, Positive Cognitive States and Processes, Application of Positive Psychology, Pro-social Behaviour & Positive Environments and Positive Schooling, Dr. Reeta has made her efforts to include all the required subjects in the book as per the UGC syllabus.

The book would be highly useful for the students. Teachers would also be benefitted by this book in enhancing their knowledge of Positive Psychology.

Best wishes to the author Dr. Reeta and the book as well.

Prof (Dr.) Ram Chandra Singh
University Dept .of Psychology
Maharaja College, Arrah
V.K.S.University,Arrah(Bihar)

FOREWORD

Now a days we have been hearing the word-Positive Psychology but many people do not have idea of this term. The Positive Psychology is a new development in the field of psychology. Positive Psychology is the scientific study of what makes life most worth living. It focuses on the positive aspects of life. But there is huge shortage of appropriate book on the subject.

The present book- Positive Psychology is the result of genuine efforts of the author Dr. Reeta Kumari. This book has been written as per the syllabus of UGC under New Education Policy. The book contains almost all the topics of Positive Psychology and would be very beneficial for the students and the teachers as well. This book will meet the requirements of the students in the field of Positive Psychology.

I wish every success for the book as well as for the author.

Dr. Sabiha Yunus (Head)
University Dept. of Psychology
Jamshedpur Women's College University
Jamshedpur

FOREWORD

Living with happiness is a complex process. It is contributed by several socio-psychological factors. It is based on both individual as well as societal well-being. The sole aim of an individual is nothing but leading a dignified life which is contributed by positive subjective experience, positive individual trait and positive institution. There is the domain for **Positive Psychology** *which deals with happiness, well-being and positivity. Psychologists like* **Dr. Reeta Kumari** *are trying to bring happiness is the life of common people by disseminating knowledge of positive psychology. The book-* **Positive Psychology** *written by Reeta contains several topics like introduction to psychology, subjective well-being, life satisfaction, peace and happiness, positive emotion and emotional intelligence, resilience, self-efficacy, positive cognitive states, hope, wisdom, creativity,* **spirituality, mindfulness, aging, stress, life skills etc.** *This book covers a vast spectrum of chapters. She has tried her level best to explain basic tenets of positive psychology. It will be of immense importance for the under graduate and post graduate students. It will be helpful for research scholars also.*

I congratulate Dr. Reeta Kumari for her effort to add knowledge in the entire academic discipline.

Dr. Sadique Razaque
Head,University Deptt. of Psychology &
Director-IQAC
Vinoba Bhave University, Hazaribag Jharkhand

Preface

Positive Psychology is new exciting field and I have pleasure to write this book even working on a tight deadline. This text is designed as a comprehensive introduction to the science and practice of Positive Psychology, and is intended for undergraduate and postgraduate students who seek to deepen their understanding of this fascinating subject.This book is designed as per new syllabus of UGC under new education policy and it provides enough material for NET and several competitive examinations. Positive Psychology is a relatively new field that has emerged over the last few decades, with the aim of promoting human strength, virtues, wellbeing, happiness, and resilience in individuals and communities. This field offers a fresh perspective on human nature, focusing on what is going right in people's lives and what they can do to improve their mental health and overall wellbeing.

This textbook provides an overview of the concepts,key theories and empirical findings in Positive Psychology. The book is organized into six main sections, each covering a different aspect of Positive Psychology. The first section provides an introduction to the field and covers the History, Characteristics, Theoretical Frameworks, and Research Methods of Positive Psychology. The second section explores individual-level factors that contribute to wellbeing, such as Life Satisfaction, Peace and Happiness, Emotions and Emotional intelligence, Resilience and Self-efficacy. The third section examines Positive Cognitive States that influence wellbeing, including Optimism, Hope, Wisdom, Character Strengths and Virtues, Spirituality and Mindfulness. The fourth section explores practical applications of Positive Psychology including education, ageing, health and sports. The fifth section hasPro-social Behaviour& Positive Environments including Empathy, Altruism, Gratitude and many more. The last section indicates usefulness of positive psychology in Positive Schooling. I feel that all these sections can help to build a deeper connection with the reader while giving them even more reasons why they should read this book and it provides a lens to view the concept of positive psychology.

The book is written in an accessible and engaging style, with numerous examples, and exercises to help students apply the concepts to their own lives. Each chapter includes probable questions that help readers engage with the material and apply it to their own lives, making it an ideal resource for both classroom use and independent study. I hope that this book will inspire you to explore the fascinating field of Positive Psychology and apply its principles to enhance your own well-being and that of others.

Despite all efforts there may be mistakes in the present book and I would be highly thankful to you if you bring mistakes to the cognition of the author. Your suggestion will be appreciated and mistakes pointed out will be corrected in the next edition.

Dr. Reeta Kumari

Content

Brief note about the Author   (vii)

Foreword   (xi-xvii)

Preface   (xix)

Chapter-1
Introduction to Positive Psychology   1-36
- Nature of Positive Psychology
- Historical Background
- Why Positive Psychology is needed
- Definitions
- Characteristics of Positive Psychology
- Aim and Objectives of Positive Psychology
- Levels of Positive Psychology
- Scope of Positive Psychology
- Concerns of Positive Psychology
- Approaches of Positive Psychology
- Benefits of Positive Psychology
- Goal of Positive Psychology
- Assumptions of Positive Psychology
- Culture of Positive Psychology
- Criticism of the Movement in Perspective
- Eastern and Western Perspectives
- Theoretical Prospective of Positive Psychology
- The PERMA Model
- Recent Trends of Positive Psychology
- Dimensions of Positive Psychology
- Life above Zero

Chapter-2
Subjective Well-being   37-117
- Well-being
- Concept and Indicators of Subjective Well-being

- Definitions
- Characteristics of Subjective Well-being
- Signs of Subjective Well-being
- Types of Subjective Well-being
- Components of Subjective Well-being
- Causes of Subjective Well-being
- Impact of Subjective Well-being
- Importance of Subjective Well-being
- Measure Subjective Well-being
- To Improve Subject Well-being
- Well-being Theory, Theories of Subjective Well-being
- Life Satisfaction
- Definition
- Importance of Life Satisfaction
- Components of Life Satisfaction
- Life Satisfaction Theory
- Measuring Life Satisfaction
- Factors Associated with Life Satisfaction
- Improvement of Life Satisfaction
- Difference between Happiness and Life Satisfaction
- Quality of Life
- Definition of Quality of Life
- Peace and Happiness
- Peace and Happiness
- Indian Perspective on Happiness
- Theory of Happiness
- Causes of Happiness
- Happiness and Well-being
- Carroll Ryff Model of Positive Psychology
- Positive Psychology and Happiness
- Components of Happiness
- Strategies to Enhance Happiness
- Keys to Happiness
- Positive Emotion and Emotional Intelligence
- Positive Emotion
- Management of Emotion
- Enhancing of Positive Emotions
- Emotional Intelligence
- Definitions
- Emotional Competencies

- Goleman's Model of Emotional Intelligence
- Models of Emotional Intelligence
- Mayer and Salovey's 'Ability Model of Emotional Intelligence
- The Advantages of Emotional Intelligence
- Impact of Emotional Intelligence
- Importance of Emotional Intelligence
- Positive Thinking and benefits of Positive Thinking
- Resilience, Self-efficacy
- Resilience
- Definitions
- Characteristics of Resilience
- Factors which Effect Resilience
- Patterns of Resilience
- Enhancement of Resilience
- Importance of Resilience
- Types of Resilience
- Theories of Resilience
- Signs of Resilience
- Key Factors in Resilience
- Resilience Building Approaches
- Difference between Resilience and Positive Psychology
- Similarities between Resilience and Positive Psychology
- Self-efficacy
- Definition
- Characteristics of Self-efficacy
- Sources of Self-efficacy beliefs
- Types of Self-efficacy
- Dimensions of Self-efficacy
- Bandura's Theory of Self-efficacy

Chapter-3
Positive Cognitive States and Processes 118-182

- Introduction of Cognitive State
- Optimism
- Definitions
- Optimism and Pessimism
- Theories of Optimism
- Types of Optimism
- Unrealistic Optimism
- Types of UnrealisticOptimism

- Cognitive Mechanisms of Unrealistic Optimism
- Group of UnrealisticOptimism
- Benefits of Optimism
- Drawback of Optimism
- Hope
- Definitions
- Theory of Hope
- Importance of Hope
- Types of Hope
- Benefits of Hope
- Hope therapy
- Enhancement of Hope
- Wisdom
- Introduction
- Definitions
- Theories of Wisdom
- Properties of Wisdom
- Components of wisdom
- Creativity
- Components of Creativity
- Types of Creativity
- Traits of Creativity
- How to increase Creativity
- Characteristics of the Creative Personality
- Courage
- Introduction
- Definitions
- Types of Courage
- Character Strengths and Virtues
- Measurement of Character Strengths
- Characteristics of Character Strength
- Development of Character Strength
- Build Your Character
- Flow and Spirituality
- Characteristics of Flow
- Universal factors of Flow
- Stage of Flow
- Spirituality
- Types of Spirituality
- Spiritual Practices

- Spirituality in India
- Difference between religion and spirituality
- Savoring, Types, Levels and Benefits
- Mindfulness
- Concepts of Mindfulness
- Definitions
- Achieving Mindfulness
- Advantage of Mindfulness
- Benefits of Mindfulness
- Applications of Mindfulness
- Mindfulness Techniques
- Theories and Principles of Mindfulness
- Enhancement of Mindfulness
- Model of Mindfulness
- Uses of Mindfulness
- Foundations of Mindfulness

Chapter-4
Application of Positive Psychology

183-230

- Introduction
- Application in Education
- Contribution of Positive Psychology in Education
- Characteristics of Positive Psychology in Education
- PERMAFramework and Tool
- Positive Psychology in Ageing
- Strategies to Enhance Positive Aging
- Theoretical Perspectives of Ageing
- Positive Approach to Ageing
- Positive Psychology in Health
- Characteristics of Positive Health
- Positive Interventions of Mental Health Treatment
- Advantage of Positive Psychology in Health
- Factors of Positive Health and Well-being
- Application Positive Psychology in Sports
- Theories of Positive Psychology in Sports
- Importance of Positive Psychology in Sports
- Meeting Life Challenges
- Life Challenges and Adjustment
- Stress
- Behavioural Effects of Stress

- *Nature of stress*
- *Signs and symptoms of Stress*
- *Types of Stress*
- *Sources of Stress*
- *Effects of Stress*
- *Stress Management Techniques*
- *Causes of Stress*
- *Stress vs. Anxiety*
- *Impact of Stress*
- *Life Skill*
- *Types of Skill*
- *Basic Life Skills*
- *Importance of Life Skills*
- *Examples of Life Skills*
- *Stress as a Response*
- *Coping with Stress*
- *Positive Psychology in Work*
- *The PERMA Model*
- *Importance of Positive Psychology in Workplace*

Chapter-5
Pro-social Behaviour& Positive Environments   231-271
- *Empathy*
- *Definitions of Empathy*
- *Signs of Empathy*
- *Uses for Empathy*
- *Impact of Empathy*
- *Types of Empathy*
- *Altruism*
- *Characteristics of Altruism*
- *Types of Altruism*
- *Categories of Altruism*
- *Impact of Altruism*
- *Enhancing Altruism*
- *Causes of Altruism*
- *Empathy-Altruism Hypothesis*
- *Gratitude*
- *Definitions of Gratitude*
- *Stages of Gratitude*
- *Types of Gratitude*

- Perspectives on Gratitude
- The Effects of Gratitude / Social Effect
- Signs of Gratitude
- Influence of Gratitude
- How to Practice Gratitude
- Impact of Gratitude
- Forgiveness
- Benefits of Forgiveness
- Types of Forgiveness
- Forgiveness as Technique of Positive Living
- Models of Forgiveness
- Steps to True Forgiveness
- Applications of Forgiveness
- Attachment
- Stages of Attachment
- Factors that Influence Attachment
- Attachment Styles / Types of Attachments
- Characteristics ofAttachment
- John Bowl by theory of Attachment
- Secure and Insecure Attachment
- Causes of insecure Attachment
- Indian Perspective on Attachment
- Attachment and Love for Flourishing Relationships
- Relationship
- Characteristics of Relationships
- Problems in a Relationship
- Build a Healthier Relationship
- Theories of Love
- Flourishing Relationships

Chapter-6
Positive Schooling

272-285

- Concept of Positive Schooling
- Characteristics of positive classroom environment
- PERMA's key Elements of Positive Classroom
- Components of Positive Schooling
- Coping Strategies in Positive Education
- Causes of Academic Stress
- Student strategies for Coping with Academic Stress
- Types of Coping Strategies

(xxviii)

- *Gainful Employment*
- *Characteristics of Gainful Employment*
- *Implications (Benefits) of Gainful Employments*
- *Skill Development to Ensure Gainful Employments*
- *The value of self-control*
- *Characteristics of Self-Control*
- *Benefits of Self-Control*
- *Disadvantages of Self-Control*
- *Goals of Self-Controlled Person*
- *Rule of Goal Setting*
- *Self-regulation*
- *Components of Self-regulation*
- *How Self-Regulation Develops*
- *Qualities of Self-Regulators*

Chapter-I

Positive Psychology

Nature of Positive Psychology

Traditional Psychology in the earlier days was considered mainly as a technique or treatment to cure mental illness. Due to the prevalence of many mental disorders, psychology adopted methods of science to cure those diseases. It deals greatly in identifying proximal causes of mental illnesses and creating effective therapies for those who are already suffering from disorders. Ironically, traditional psychology focused on the resources solely for the treatment of those who are already ill but we have fallen short in identifying distal buffers to mental illness, such as personal strengths and social connections and prevention aimed at the larger population. We never care for the prevention of these very illnesses in those who are not ill. Before the movement of positive psychology, mainstream psychology focused heavily on the negative aspects of life, such as anxiety, stress and depression. Before World War II, psychology had three main missions: 1. to understand and cure mental illness; 2. to improve the lives and productivity of individuals; and 3. to identify and nurture high talent. During the period of World War II, all available psychology resources were directed toward researching and treating psychological disorders and left the issue to identify and nurture high talent. The failure to study talents, strengths, and other positive aspects of life left a gap in the field of psychology. Any science that deals with the fundamental questions of human life is incomplete if it only focuses on the negative side. Positive psychology was born out of the need to scientifically study the positive aspects of life. The theory of positive psychology has evolved greatly over the last few years which have been uncovering the building blocks of happiness and wellbeing. In order to give concept of positive psychology Martin Seligman found that people were aware of and using their strengths like courage, persistence, and wisdom which greatly impacted the quality of their lives. However, positive psychology is nothing else but psychology, adopting the same scientific methods. It simply studies different topics and asks slightly different questions, such as - what works?'rather than -what doesn't?' or - what is right?' rather than - what is wrong. Psychology should not be just about illness or health; it also is about work, education, insight, love, growth, and play. And in this quest for what is best, positive psychology does not rely on wishful thinking, self-deception, or hand waving; instead, it tries to adapt what is best in the scientific method. Positive Psychology is not just the study of disease, weakness, and damage; it also is the study of strength and virtue. Treatment is not just fixing what is wrong; it also is building what is right.

Positive psychology is a recent branch of psychology to find and nurture genius and talent. The field is intended to complement, not to replace traditional psychology. This branch of Psychology emphasizes the importance of using the scientific methods to determine how things go right. Positive psychology means initiation of the positive feelings and behaviors. It is a science of positivity which includes positive subjective experience, positive individual traits, and positive institutions to improve the quality of life. Positive psychology is the scientific study of human strengths and virtues. It uses psychological theory, scientific research and evidence-based interventions to understand and improve human well-being. It is the study of the conditions and processes that contribute to the flourishing or optimal functioning of people, groups, and institutions. At its best, it has been able to give the scientific community, society and individuals a new perspective providing empirical evidence to support the phenomenon of human flourishing. The most important thing to understand about positive psychology is that it is indeed science. It is a subfield of psychology, and although it is sometimes derided as a "soft science" or a "pseudoscience," it is still based on the scientific methods of evaluating theories based on the evidences.Originally, there was three pillars of positive psychology according to Seligman, 2002 like positive subjective experience, positive individual characteristics (strengths and virtues), and positive institutions and communities. So far, positive psychology has produced a great deal of new research into the first two areas but much less into the third.

Historical Background

The roots of positive psychology can be traced to the thoughts of ancient Greek philosophers. Aristotle believed that there was a unique daimon, or spirit within each individual, that guides us to pursue things that are right for us. Acting in accordance with this daimon leads one to happiness. Positive psychology did not emerge suddenly but it began in 1998/1999. It has, in fact, been suggested that positive psychology has always been there in the discipline of psychology. But it has never been viewed as a holistic and integrated body of knowledge. Broadly, positive psychology has a lot of commonalities with humanistic psychology.Prior to the Second World War, psychology had three tasks to cure mental illness, improve normal lives and identify and nurture high talent. However, after the war the last two tasks somehow got lost, and to concentrate on the first one. Psychology after World War II became a science largely devoted to healing. It concentrated on repairing damage using a disease model of human functioning. This almost exclusive attention to pathology neglected the idea of a fulfilled individual and community. Psychology as a science depends heavily on the funding of governmental bodies after World War II. During the period, facing a human crisis on such an enormous scale, all available resources were poured into learning about and the treatment of psychological illness and psychopathology.

Defined in this way, positive psychology has a long history, like William James's "healthy mindedness" in 1902, to Allport's interest in positive human characteristics in 1958, to Maslow's advocacy for the study of healthy people in lieu of sick people in 1968, and to Cowan's research on resilience in children and adolescents in 2000. Moreover, the term positive psychology dates back at least to 1954, when Maslow's first edition of Motivation and Personality was published with a final chapter titled : Toward a Positive Psychology. Positive psychology places a lot of emphasis on being a new and forward thinking discipline. The roots of positive psychology can be traced to the thoughts of ancient Greek philosophers. Aristotle believed that there was a unique daemon, or spirit within each individual, that guides us to pursue things that are right for us. Acting in accordance with this daemon leads one to happiness. The question of happiness has since been picked up by prominent thinkers, and gave rise to many theories, including Hedonism, with its emphasis on pleasure and Utilitarianism, seeking the greatest happiness for the greatest number. In the 20th century, many prominent psychologists focused on the subject matter of positive psychology. Amongst them was Carl Jung with his individuation. Maria Jahoda, concerned with defining positive mental health and Gordon Allport, interested in individual maturity. Since then, the matters of flourishing and wellbeing were raised in the work on prevention and wellness enhancement. The most notable of positive psychology's predecessors in the year 1950s and reached its peak in the 60s and 70s which was the humanistic psychology movement. This movement placed central emphasis on the growth and authentic self of an individual. The most famous ones were Carl Rogers, who introduced the concept of the fully functioning person, and Abraham Maslow, who emphasized self-actualization. In fact it was Maslow who was the very first to use the term positive psychology. This is where positive psychology believes that humanistic psychology, because of its skepticism of an empirical method, is not very grounded scientifically. Contrary to the humanists, whilst rejecting the mainstream psychology preoccupation with negative topics, positive psychology embraces the dominant scientific paradigm. Positive psychology thus distinguishes itself from humanistic psychology on the basis of methods, whereas the substance and the topics studied are remarkably similar. Rightly or wrongly, positive psychology tends to present itself as a new movement, often attempting to distance itself from its origins. The recent positive psychology movement grew out of recognition of this imbalance and a desire to encourage research in neglected areas.

The second aspect of psychology that came into existence was the identification and nurturing of talent especially in young children. When these children were shown proper direction and encouragement, they were found to be more productive and intelligent. This identification process was done using psychology. The third dimension that was added to psychology was to make people's life more fulfilling than just the mere fulfillment of their immediate needs. Psychology was aimed to make people transcend from a negative emotional state to a state of neutral emotion but the induction of positive emotion or feeling was never given a consideration until recently.

Positive psychology began as a new area of psychology in 1998 by Martin Seligman, who was considered the father of the modern positive psychology. He urged psychologists to continue the earlier missions of psychology of nurturing talent and improving normal life. Seligman's research in the 1960s and 70s laid the foundation for the well-known psychological theory of "learned helplessness. Positive psychology grew as an important field of study within psychology in 1998 when Martin Seligman chose it as the theme for his term as president of the American Psychological Association. "Research on positive psychology topics is not new, but the time was right for a correction and an organized positive psychology movement. In India, the positive psychology concept aroused in 2500 years ago from the earlier of Vipassana meditation. Mindfulness is not a state of doing but a state of being in which you are fully aware of the present moment and do not evaluate your inner or outer environment. Mindfulness applications include somatic problems including chronic pain, fibromyalgia, and psoriasis, behavioral problems such as eating, parenting, and addiction; disorders such as depression, bipolar disorder, and borderline personality disorders; emotional problems such as stress and anxiety.

The positive psychology movement is not without its challengers and critics. Many criticisms seem to arise from the assumption that if there is a positive psychology, then the rest of psychology must be negative psychology, and if we need a positive psychology, it is because this so-called negative psychology has taught us little. This interpretation is unfortunate and, more important, untrue. In fact, it is because psychology has been so extraordinarily successful that the imbalance, the lack of progress on positive topics, has become so glaring.

Positive psychology is a young field. Even in its short history it has focuses on many aspects of happy and healthy living. However, there are some areas that have yet to be explored in depth. One of such areas is the intersection between culture and positive psychology. Positive psychology is often criticized for taking a western perspective. It is also said that the concepts and theories of positive psychology apply more to developed countries who are now in a post-materialistic era. Hence, positive psychology must take in from other cultures, concepts of good life and the factors affecting happiness. During the past 20 years, the number of scientific studies on positive psychology has increased tremendously. In addition, countless interventions have been developed to increase people's wellbeing and positive psychology has moved ahead in a variety of new directions.

However, the historical development of positive psychology can be summarized as under:

Martin Seligman & Mihaly Csikszentmihalyi (2000) : define positive psychology as the scientific study of positive human functioning and flourishing on multiple levels that include the biological, personal, relational, institutional, cultural, and global dimensions of life.

Sheldon and King (2001) define positive psychology is nothing more than the scientific study of ordinary human strengths and virtues.

Gable and Haidt (2005) defined positive psychology is the study of the conditions and processes that contribute to the flourishing or optimal functioning of people, groups and institutions.

Peterson, (2008): Positive psychology is the scientific study of what makes life most worth living.

According to American Psychological Association (APA), Positive Psychology is a field of psychological theory and research that focuses on the psychological states (e.g., contentment, joy), individual traits or character strengths (e.g., intimacy, integrity, altruism, wisdom), and social institutions that enhance subjective well-being and make life most worth living.

Seligman's (2003) three pillars of positive psychology

1. Positive subjective experiences (such as joy, happiness, contentment, optimism, and hope)

2. Positive individual characteristics (such as personal strengths and human virtues that promote mental health);

3. Positive social institutions and communities that contribute to individual health and happiness

Why Positive Psychology is needed

The science of psychology has made great strides in understanding what goes wrong in individuals, families, groups, and institutions, but these advances have come at the cost of understanding what is right with people. For example, clinical psychology has made excellent progress in diagnosing and treating mental illnesses and personality disorders. Researchers in social psychology have conducted groundbreaking studies on the existence of implicit prejudice and negative outcomes associated with low self-esteem. Health psychology has shown us the detrimental effects that environmental stressors have on our physiological systems and cognitive psychology has illuminated the many biases and errors involved in our judgments. These are all important findings in our field, but it is harder to locate corresponding work on human strengths and virtues. Positive psychology focuses on wellbeing, happiness, flow, personal strengths, wisdom, creativity, imagination and characteristics of positive groups and institutions. Furthermore, the focus is not just on how to make individuals happy, but on happiness and flourishing at a group level as well. Positive Psychology looks at how individuals and groups thrive and how increasing the wellbeing of one will have a positive effect on the other. Positive psychology is not simply the focus on positive thinking and positive emotions. It's much more than that. Indeed, the area of positive psychology is focused on what makes individuals and communities flourish, rather than languish.

Positive psychology focuses on the positive events and influences in life, including:

1. Positive experiences (like happiness, joy, inspiration, and love).

2. Positive states and traits (like gratitude, resilience, and compassion).

3. Positive institutions (applying positive principles within entire organizations and institutions).

Positive psychology concentrates on positive experiences at three time points: (1) the past, centering on wellbeing, contentment and satisfaction; (2) the present, which focuses on concepts such as happiness and flow experiences; (3) the future, with concepts including optimism and hope. Not only does positive psychology distinguish between wellbeing across time points but it also separates the subject area into three nodes:

- **The subjective node**, which encompasses things like positive experiences and states across past, present and future (for example, happiness, optimism, wellbeing);

- **The individual node**, which focuses on characteristics of the good person' (for example, talent, wisdom, love, courage, creativity); and

- **The group node**, which studies positive institutions, citizenship and communities (for example, altruism, tolerance, work ethic)

Definitions of Positive Psychology

Positive psychology has been described in many ways and with many words, but the commonly accepted definition of the field is this:

Positive psychology is the scientific study of what makes life most worth living (Peterson, 2008).

However, positive psychology is a scientific approach to studying human thoughts, feelings, and behavior, with a focus on strengths instead of weaknesses, building the good in life instead of repairing the bad, and taking the lives of average people up to great instead of focusing solely on moving those who are struggling up to normal. Moreover, following are also important definitions:

Sheldon and King (2001) defined positive psychology as "nothing more than the scientific study of ordinary human strengths and virtues," one that "revisits the average person".

Peterson, (2008): Positive psychology is the scientific study of what makes life most worth living ".Positive psychology is a scientific approach to studying human thoughts, feelings, and behavior, with a focus on strengths instead of weaknesses, building the good in life instead of repairing the bad, and taking the lives of average people up to "great" instead of focusing solely on moving those who are struggling up to "normal".

Gable, Shelly L., Haidt, Jonathan*: Positive psychology is the study of the conditions and processes that contribute to the flourishing or optimal functioning of people, groups, and institutions.*

Wikipedia: *Positive psychology is the branch of psychology that uses scientific understanding and effective intervention to aid in the achievement of a satisfactory life, rather than merely treating mental illness.*

Seligman and Csikszentmi-halyi, (2000): *Positive psychology* is simply psychology that focuses its interest on the analysis of what is good in life from birth to death.

Positive Psychology is the scientific study of human flourishing, and an applied approach to optimal functioning. It has also been defined as the study of the strengths and virtues that enable individuals, communities, and organizations to thrive

Paul Wong: The underlying theme of positive psychology is that life can be made better for all people if certain conditions are met

Martin Seligman: *Positive psychology is the scientific study of human strengths and virtues*

Hugo Alberts: *Positive psychology is the scientific and applied approach to uncovering people's strengths and promoting their positive functioning.*

SephFontanePennoc: *Positive psychology studies what is going right with the human mind and behavior and how to foster these types of wellbeing on both the macro-, group-, and individual-level"*

Characteristics of Positive Psychology

There are many traits or characteristics associated with a positive mindset or positive psychology

1. **Optimism**: Positive people have a desire, a willingness to make an effort and do things instead of being unsure of themselves. A positive person will take a chance and bargain on being successful rather than the other way round.

2. **Acceptance:** Never think that nothing bad happens to positive people, nor that thinking positively will protect you from the facts of life. Yet, having positivity can be a bit like faith and enable you to acknowledge when things don't turn out.

3. **Resilience**: It means bouncing back from adversity, disappointment, and failure instead of giving up. Be resilient when faced with adversity, sadness, loss, disappointment or failure is a trait you will find in a positive thinker.

4. Gratitude: It provides actively, continuously appreciating the good things in your life. One of the key characteristics of a positive person is the gratitude they feel and show for the good in their lives.

5. Mindfulness: It's impossible to practice positivity without having a level of awareness of how your mind is functioning. Even when times are tough, positive thinkers won't let their minds turn on them and will remain conscious and mindful, shifting their focus onto the silver lining.

6. **Integrity:** This trait is being honorable, righteous, and straightforward, instead of deceitful and self-serving. Integrity is very important for positive person. Along with seeing the good in others, you should too practice being honorable.

Aim and Objectives of Positive Psychology

The aim of positive psychology is to study what is good in life and why it is worth living. The aim of positive psychology is to study the other side of the coin - the ways that people feel joy, show altruism, and create healthy families and institutions. The aim is not to erase or supplant work on pathology, distress, and dysfunction. Rather, the aim is to build up what we know about human resilience, strength, and growth to integrate and complement the existing knowledge base. Further, the aim of positive psychology is to catalyze a change in psychology from a preoccupation only with repairing the worst things in life to also building the best qualities in life. To redress the previous imbalance, we must bring the building of strength to the forefront in the treatment and prevention of mental illness. The field of positive psychology is about positive subjective experience like well-being and satisfaction (past); flow, joy, the sensual pleasures, and happiness (present); and constructive cognitions about the future - optimism, hope, and faith. The aim of positive psychology is to catalyze a change in psychology from a preoccupation only with repairing the worst things in life to also building the best qualities in life.

Levels of Positive Psychology

Positive psychology is often referred to as having three different levels:

- **Subjective level:** focuses on feelings of happiness, well-being, and optimism, and how these feelings transform your daily experience

- **Individual level:** a combination of the feelings in the subjective level and virtues such as forgiveness, love, and courage

- **Group level:** positive interaction with your community, including virtues like altruism and social responsibility that strengthen social bonds

Scope of Positive Psychology

Some of the major scopes of interest in positive psychology which include:

- Character strengths and virtues
- Flow
- Gratifications
- Gratitude
- Happiness/pleasures
- Helplessness
- Hope
- Mindfulness
- Optimism
- Positive thinking
- Resilience

Happiness

Happiness is experienced from small happy moments. Happiness is a moment of subjective satisfaction, it is conceived of as an aim or end, as an ideal welfare state and is stable that one attains.

Creativity

The ability to perform, to produce various and valuable things. It is the ability of the brain to reach new conclusions and solve problems in an original way. It is a skill that can be learnt.

Flow / Flow

Developed by psychologist Mihaly Csikszentmihaily, who defined it as a state in which a person is completely absorbed in an activity for its own pleasure and enjoyment, during which flies and without pausing actions, thoughts and movements follow the other. The person uses his skills and abilities to the peak.

According to Mihaly Csikszentmihaly there are seven flow states:

- A feeling of ecstasy, of being out of everyday reality.
- Inner clarity, knowing what to do and how well to do it.
- It is possible to know the activity, that the abilities are adequate and worrying or boring.
- The feeling of sentience, the feeling of rising beyond the limits of the ego, does not concern itself with itself. The ego feels that transition in a way that I didn't think possible.
- Opportunity, completely focused on today, does not feel the passage of time.
- The intrinsic motivation that creates the "flow" becomes its own reward.

Flexibility / Toughness

The ability of an individual or group to deal with adversity, overcome them, and be strengthened by experience. It can be an analogue of personal strength, how a person overcomes bad events and even manages them to improve their present and future.

Optimism

External personality traits that lie between external events and the individual's interpretation of them. Believing that preconceptions portend favorable future achievements. Optimism is the value that helps us to face difficulties with a good spirit and perseverance, by searching people and situations positively, trusting in our abilities and the possibilities that we can achieve.

Humor

Babies laugh an average of 300 times a day. An adult does between fifteen and one hundred. Laughter is a powerful healing tool, reducing stress, tension, aggression and depression. It releases endorphins (the "happiness" hormone). Develop creative thinking and communication skills. Improves quality of life. A good laugh strengthens the body's immune system and lowers the hormones that can cause stress.

Emotional Intelligence

It is the ability that human beings have to experience, express and control their own emotions, in addition to being able to understand the emotions of others. Estimate your happiness.

Personal Strength

According to Seligman (2003), strengths and virtues act as a barrier against adversity and psychological disorders and may be important for enhancing the capacity for recovery:

1. **Knowledge and wisdom**: creativity, curiosity, openmindedness, love of learning, perspective, innovation.
2. **Courage:** Courage, firmness, integrity, vitality. Humanity and Love: Love, Kindness, Social Intelligence.
3. **Justice**: Citizenship, Justice, Leadership.
4. **Temperance:** Forgiveness and mercy, humility, discretion, self-control.
5. **Transcendence**: Appreciation of beauty and excellence, gratitude, hope, humor, spirituality.

Concerns of positive psychology

Positive Psychology has the following three central concerns:

1. **Positive Emotions**:

Understanding positive emotions includes contentment with the past, happiness in the present, and hope for the future, positive views about self and others.

2. **Positive Individual Traits**:

Understanding positive individual traits consists of the capacity for love and work, courage, compassion, resilience, creativity, curiosity, integrity, self-knowledge, moderation, self-control, and wisdom.

3.   Positive Institutions:

Understanding positive institutions includes justice, responsibility, civility, parenting, nurturance, work ethics, leadership, teamwork, purpose, tolerance, and strengths. Relating to the study, these positive institutions will increases academic achievement and problem solving activities.

Positive Emotions

Positive emotions are emotions that are enjoyable to experience. The Oxford Handbook of Positive Psychology defines it as "pleasant or desirable situational responses... distinct from pleasant feelings and indistinguishable positive effects" (Cohn & Fredrickson, 2009). This definition means that positive emotions are pleasant responses to environment.Positive emotions include the response to situations pleasant or desirable, ranging from concern and contentment to love and joy, but different from pleasant feelings and irrespective of positive effects. These emotions are markers of overall well being or well being, but they also help enhance future development and success. This has been demonstrated in work, school, relationships, mental and physical health, and performance improvement. The extensive and constructive theory of positive emotions shows that all positive emotions lead to expanded thoughts and actions and that the expansion helps to build resources that contribute to a Successful Future.

Positive Individual Traits

Positive Individual Trait is a blend of biological factors and environmental factors. We all have parameters set by our genetics, and our experiences determine how we act. The positive traits of an individual focus on a person's strengths and qualities. Following are a few examples of positive psychological traits:

- Honesty and responsibility for one's actions are admirable qualities.

- Adaptability and compatibility are great traits that can help to get along with others.
- Motivation and determination will help to keep on going no matter what.
- Compassion and understanding help to have good relationships with others.
- Patience is a good personality trait.
- Courage helps to do the right thing in difficult situations.
- Loyalty is a must-have quality that makes others trusts.

Positive Institutions

Positive institutions is a "structured cultural or social organizations and practices that enhance and develop highest human strengths, combining and refracting our strongest points outward in ways that benefit the world, ultimately leading to a flourishing fullspectrum world". (Cooper rider and Godwin, 2014). Positive institutions are those organizations that cultivate civic virtue, encouraging people to behave like good citizens while promoting the collective good. Understanding positive institutions entail the study of the strengths that foster better academic achievements, problem solving technique and well being of adolescents.

Approaches of Positive Psychology

Positive Psychology focuses on those aspects of human behaviour and experiences that represented optimal functioning and positive emotions. Some of the critical approaches of positive psychology are given below:

1. Happiness and its causes
2. Psychology of Flow,
3. Hope and Optimism
4. Positive self-esteem
5. Self-efficacy

Benefits of Positive Psychology

There are most impactful and influential outcomes of positive psychology as under:

1. Positive psychology teaches us the power of shifting one's perspective.
2. Positive psychology also lends itself to improvements in the workplace
3. Positive emotions actually increases our chances of success
4. Positive psychology movement is a more well-defined idea of what "the good life" is
5. It increases the experience of positive emotions;
6. It helps to identify and develop strengths and unique talents;
7. It enhances the goal-setting and goal-striving abilities;
8. It builds a sense of hope into the perspective;
9. It cultivates the sense of happiness and wellbeing;
10. It nurtures a sense of gratitude;
11. It helps to build and maintain healthy, positive relationships with others;
12. It encourages to maintain an optimistic outlook;
13. It helps to learn to savor every positive moment.

Goal of Positive Psychology

1. A primary goal of the positive psychology movement is to be a catalyst for change in the focus of psychology from a preoccupation with repairing the worst things in life.
2. To provide preventive function that buffers against future psychopathology and even recovery from illness.
3. **To refocusing** the entire field of psychology.
4. **To restore balance** within the discipline of Psychology which was too much focused on negative aspects.
5. **To improve understanding of positive human behaviors**

to balance the negative focus of much mainstream research & theory.

6. **To develop an empirically-based conceptual understanding** and language for describing healthy human functioning that parallels our classification and understanding of mental illness

7. **To boost present well being**

8. **To prevent future problems**

9. **To make life worthwhile**

10. **To find elements of positive psychology** represented in so many different areas of psychology, from physiological to clinical psychology

11. **To take interest in subjective experiences such as subjective wellbeing/happiness, flow, joy, optimism and hope.**

12. **To identify, study and enhance those qualities that improve on the positive subjective experiences and adaptive personality traits of individuals**

Assumptions of Positive Psychology:

The most basic assumption of positive psychology is that human goodness and excellence are as authentic as disorders and distress and therefore deserve equal attention from mental health practitioners. The discipline of positive psychology is primarily focused on the promotion of the good life. The good life refers to those factors that contribute most predominately to a well lived life. Qualities that define the good life are those that enrich our lives, make life worth living and foster strong character. Seligman (2002) defines good life as a combination of three elements: Positive connection to others or positive subjective experience; Positive individual traits and; Life regulation qualities. Positive connection refers to aspects of our behavior that contribute to positive connectedness to others. It is the positive subjective experiences that includes the ability to love, forgive, and the presence of spiritual connections, happiness and life satisfaction that combine to help and create a sense of deeper meaning and purpose in life. Positive individual traits may include such things as a sense of integrity, the ability to be creative, and the presence of virtues such as courage and humility. Life regulation qualities are those qualities that allow us to regulate our day-to-daybehavior in such a way that we can accomplish our goals. Some of these qualities include a sense of individuality or autonomy, a high degree of a healthy self-control and wisdom to guide behavior. According to positive psychology, the good life must also include the relationship with other people and the society as a whole.

1. A major assumption of positive psychology is that the field of psychology has become unbalanced.

2. Human goodness and excellence are as authentic as disorders and distress and therefore deserve equal attention from mental health practitioners

3. The discipline of positive psychology is primarily focused on the promotion of the good life.

4. This includes the ability to love, forgive, and the presence of spiritual connections, happiness and life satisfaction

Culture of Positive Psychology

There are different approaches within the field of positive psychology and Bacon presents the idea that there are two "cultures" or two "schools of thought"in positive psychology, or two different ways to view the positive psychology construct of personal strengths:

1. **Focus culture**: In focus culture, individuals are focused on developing and expressing their personal strengths.

2. **Balance culture**: Balance culture is instead oriented towards balancing and bringing harmony within oneself and among others.

Bacon argues that individual will have different in their life experience and life path to the focus culture and balance culture. Bacon believes that the strengths can be categorized into these two cultures and goes into depth, explaining why creativity is the prototypical strength in the focus culture and why wisdom represents an ideal strength in the balance culture. Bacon and others argue that there are two different cultures, or schools of thought, within positive psychology. These two cultures reflect a new way to categorize strengths.

Criticism of the Movement in Perspective

1. Research findings are often invalid, overstated, and misleading
2. There is too much emphasis on self-report and cross-sectional survey data
3. Positive psychology has a cultural and ethnocentric bias
4. The field is too individualistic
5. Positive psychology is just a promotion of a "Pollyanna" personality type, not an authentic exploration of the good life

Eastern and Western Perspectives

There are two perspectives strength of Positive Psychology as under:

1. Western perspectives and
2. Eastern perspectives

The Western Perspective

Athenian

The Greek philosophers Plato and Aristotle discussed virtues and human strengths. Aristotle described the details of moral virtues: courage, moderation, generosity, munificence, magnificence, even temper, friendliness, truthfulness, wit, justice and friendship. In addition to these, he also described intellectual virtues (Solomon, 2006). Aristotle also believed that the government should take the responsibility of the development of virtues in the society through early education. In the Old Testament, the virtues of faith, hope, and charity are highlighted. These were later discussed as part of the Seven Heavenly Virtues by Thomas Aquinas. According to historians, Aquinas listed these virtues as fortitude, justice, temperance, wisdom, faith, hope, and charity. Similarly other scholars also cite the Ten Commandments given by Moses in the Old Testament as directives for cultivating certain strengths within the Jewish tradition.

Athenian view from discussion of virtue and human strength emphasizes the importance of a political community, or "polis", and states that people with good human virtue arrange themselves into a society and model good behaviour.

Judeo-Christianity

The Judeo-Christian approach discusses the importance of the virtues of faith, hope, charity, fortitude, justice, temperance, and wisdom. It states that laws and rituals serve to cultivate strengths within society.

Key Western Values (Individualism)

- Autonomy/personal freedom
- Competition
- Personal achievement
- Self-oriented
- Future-oriented
- Hope
- Uniqueness (seen through commodities, names, attitudes, performances, attributes, etc.)

The Eastern Perspective

1. **Confucianism:** Confucius stated that leadership and education are central to morality. He emphasized morality as the cure for evils. The teachings are quite similar to those laid down by Aristotle and Plato regarding the responsibility of the leaders. Attaining virtue lies at the core of Confucian teachings. Five main virtues laid down are: humanity, duty to treat others well,

etiquette and sensitivity for others 'feelings, wisdom and truthfulness.

2. **Taoism:** Lao-Tzu, the creator of the Taoist tradition states that his followers must live according to the Tao (the way). Tao is the energy that surrounds everyone and is a power that envelops surrounds and flows through all things. Understanding will flow from experiencing the way for oneself by fully participating in life. Hence, experiencing both good and bad events can lead to a greater understanding of the way. According to the Taoist philosophy, the most important goal is spontaneity and naturalness.

3. **Buddhism:** Throughout the teachings of the Buddha, the good of others is emphasized. Buddha also teaches that suffering is a part of being and that this suffering is brought on by desire. Nirvana is considered the state in which the self is freed from any kind of desire. Both premarital and post mortal states are proposed. Buddhism gives a very important place to virtues, Brahma Viharas. These virtues include love (maitri), compassion (karuna), joy (mudita), and equanimity (upeksha). Hence, the Buddhist philosophy entails dissociating from desire to put an end to suffering. Buddhism spread from India to China and also to other countries in Asia, such as Korea, Japan, Thailand, Myanmar (Burma), Sri Lanka, Cambodia, Laos, and Vietnam over the years.

4. **Hinduism:** In comparison to the three eastern philosophies mentioned above, the Hindu tradition differs in the sense that it does not have a specific founder and it is not clear when this tradition began. The main teachings of this tradition emphasize the interconnectedness of all things and emphasis is on the personal improvement. The goal is to live one's life correctly so that one can go to afterlife without repeating life's lessons in a reincarnated form. The quest of one's life is to attain ultimate self-knowledge and to strive for ultimate self-improvement. This is known as Karma. Hence, the good life in this tradition encompasses continually doing good actions. The idea of a harmonious union among all individuals is woven

throughout the teachings of Hinduism that refer to a single unifying principle underlying all the earth.

The different thought processes between Western and Eastern cultures impacts the positive psychology that they seek in their own lives. For example, in seeking happiness, Westerners give priority to "life, liberty. and the pursuit of happiness" as well as goal-directed thinking. Easterners, on the other hand, may be more accepting in their situation, and put more weight on inner life balance.

Key Eastern Values (Collectivism and individualism)

- Seeks to cultivate interdependence
- Sharing/cooperation
- Conformity/desire to fit in
- Promote harmony/avoiding conflict
- Going with the flow
- Loyalty to family and friends
- Past-oriented
- Group-oriented
- Compassion

Differences between Eastern Perspective and Western Perspective

1. **Value systems:** The cultural differences between the West and the East can be understood by looking into their value systems. Most western cultures are individualistic while most Eastern cultures are collectivistic. In individualistic cultures, the individual is the main focus whereas in collectivistic cultures, the group is valued above the individual. For instance, Western cultures value autonomy and personal freedom. Where as in Eastern cultures cooperation is given more importance.

2. **Orientation to time:** There are differences in the western and eastern cultures in terms of time orientation. The western

culture is more oriented to the future, where asthe Eastern culture gives greater focus on and respect for the past.

3. **Thought processes:** There is some major difference between people in western and eastern culture. The easterners have a more circular thinking style. In most western cultures priority is given to right to life, liberty and the pursuit of happiness. The goal of the easterner is to achieve balance.

4. **Differences in routes to attain positive outcomes:** There is difference between western and eastern cultures in terms of the routes to attain positive outcomes. Westerners focus more on the individual goal(s) while easterners focus more on group or community goals. Westerners focus more on hope while easterners focus more on compassion and harmony.

5. **Collectivism: Compassion and harmony:** In the main eastern philosophical traditions, compassion and harmony are repeatedly mentioned. In eastern cultures harmony is considered to be crucial for happiness. The concept of nirvana in Buddhist teachings also refers to a state of harmony, balance and equilibrium. But in western culture it is not found.

Theoretical Prospective of Positive Psychology (Hedonic and Eudemonic Happiness)

Well-being is an intangible, multi-faceted, complex, and sociological phenomenon. Hence, there is also no general agreement on the definition and measurement of well-being. In psychology, there are two popular conceptions of happiness: hedonic and eudemonic. Hedonic happiness is achieved through experiences of pleasure and enjoyment, while eudemonic happiness is achieved through experiences of meaning and purpose. Eudemonic is defined in this volume as: Flourishing, realization of potentials reflecting the true self. Happiness comes from the pursuit of virtue/excellence.

A significant conceptual contribution of positive psychology is to define core features of psychological well-being. Well-being is a complex construct of optimal experience and functioning. The theories of psychological well-being are derived from two general perspectives:

1. **The Hedonic**: focuses on happiness and defines well-being in terms of pleasure, comfortable states and pain avoidance

2. **The Eudaimonic**: focuses on meaning and self-realization and defines well-being in terms of the degree to which a person is living a good life and being fully functioning.

Hedonic Well-being

The hedonic dimension of psychological well-being has been called 'subjective well-being' and includes both affective and cognitive ingredients. Affective components of subjective well-being include positive effect like experiencing pleasant emotions and moods and negative effect like experi-encing unpleasant, distressing emotions and moods. This balances the overall equilibrium between positive and negative effect. High levels of hedonic well-being do not imply the absence of negative emotions, but it means that negative emotions are still there although they are less frequent and prominent than positive ones. Life satisfaction and satisfaction with specific life domains are considered cognitive components of subjective well-being.

EudaimonicWell-being

Eudaimonic well-being would come from actions that are coherent with personal values that imply a full commitment with which people feel alive and real. Thus, well-being consists in the harmonious development of an individual's capacities which would lead to a virtuous life. This perspective of the nature of eudaimonic well-being is one of the reasons why the identification, development, and putting into action psycho-logical strengths has become a central target in positive psychology. A fulfilled life is one in which we have the opportunity to express and develop our maximum po-tentials which would bring benefits not only for ourselves but also for society at large. It argues that healthy psychological functioning is based on: (1) an adequate satisfaction of basic psychological needs (basically, autonomy, relatedness, and competence); (2) a system of consistent and coherent goals (i.e., intrinsic goals, better than extrinsic ones) and (3) goals which are consistent with the person's interests and values. Self-determination theory asserts that when these needs are satisfied, motivation and well-being are enhanced, and when they are limited, there is a negative impact on our well-functioning.

One of the most controversial issues in the study of positive psychology is the disagreement between hedonic and eudaimonic perspectives regarding concepts to well-being. The hedonic well-being arises in Greece and is understood as the pursuit of sensation and pleasure. Here, subjective well-being is the most widely used approach, encompassing three core components: life satisfaction, the presence of positive mood, and the absence of negative mood. On the other hand, the eudaimonic perspective has its roots in Aristotle's postulations, and presents well-being as the realization of one's true potential. The psychological well-being is one of the most accepted approaches of eudaimonic wellbeing and according to Ryff's,there are six distinct aspects of human actualization: autonomy, personal growth, self-acceptance, life purpose, mastery, and positive relatedness. However, there is common view among positive psychologists is that we would do better to aim at 'eudaimonic happiness' rather than 'hedonic happiness. But each one denotes important and complementary aspects of wellbeing.

The PERMA Model

Recently, Seligman(2011) has proposed new version of model of well-being. According to his new concept, the latest model of well-being is the PERMA model. This model of well-being has several measurable elements: Positive emotion (P), Engagement (E), Positive relationships (R), Meaning (M), and Accomplishment (A).Each of these elements has three properties: contributes to well-being; People pursue it for their own sakes, and It's measured and defined independently from the other elements. Each of the five elements can be con-sidered as indicators of well-being and they typically involve both hedonic and eudaimonic components. Future research should tackle the issue of which model provides the best in-dexes of validity.

1. **Positive Emotions:** This explains thatpositive emotions can build our physical, intellectual, and social abilities. People who experience positive emotions make more connections, create more inclusive categories, and have heightened levels of creativity.

2. **Engagement:** This explains the flow, which is an experience of optimal psychological functioning, that slightly exceeds our skill level, and therefore, requires us to stretch to a new level of performance. Our head also quiets down when experiencing flow. The area of the brain responsible for cognitive processes such as self-reflection and self-consciousness shows less activation during states of flow. We know that happiness isn't something that simply happens but it is the product of individual facing challenges that are neither too demanding nor too simple for one's abilities.

3. **Relationships:** This explains that human being is happy and healthy only because of good relationship. We have a need for connection, love, and physical and emotional proximity to others. The connection begins at birth as human babies depend on others to care for them because they are unable to survive on their own. In addition, humans develop and learn about life and navigating the world through interactions with other people and the perspectives they offer.

4. **Meaning:**Seligman argues that one's level of wellbeing is affected by choices, attitudes, and behaviors whereas positive emotions are necessary for a healthy life which requires an exploration of meaning. *Meaning* provides us strengths and virtues in the service of something much larger than we are. When we only chase pleasure for our own sake and fail to use our strengths toward something meaningful, we might squander our potential. But when we apply and develop our unique strengths and virtues toward something bigger than ourselves, we experience a deeper sense of satisfaction.

5. **Accomplishments**: This explains that people who feel personally involved in achieving their goals indicate higher levels of wellbeing and are in better health than people who lack a sense of direction in their lives. We often pursue accomplishment for its own sake, even if it doesn't translate into an increase in positive emotions, meaning, or the quality of relationships.

Recent Trends of Positive Psychology

Positive psychology studies have advanced into mainstream in psychology during the past decades and have significantly developed since Seligman's first publication in 2000. Since then, representatives of positive psychology approaches from all over the world have begun to integrate positive and constructive perspectives into psychology. The pioneers of positive psychology have used their research to bring a new perspective to bear on the problem-oriented discourses of analytic and mainstream psychology in order to measure human strengths focus on human capacity and increase the view on constructs such as mental health, happiness, hope, and well-being. A more recent positive psychology approach aims to advance previous discourses and give positive psychology a new direction. Positive psychology emphasizes a new approach to life and meaning by working through both sides of situations, the negative and the positive, and nature of the good life. More specifically, it is argued that positive psychology is epitomized by an appreciation of the fundamentally dialectical nature of well-being. As a holistic and integrative approach to the shadow and light sides of life, it has successfully been used to in psycho-biographical research which explores the lives of extraordinary individuals. Because psycho-biographical studies have found that extraordinary people frequently have deeply negative and painful aspects in addition to deeply positive and creative sides. It explores the 'dark' side of life while emphasizing its role in our positive functioning and transformation as human beings even aims to transform the terror of death. According to the third wave of positive psychology is broadening the discourse towards complexity which means in this case that it goes beyond the individual, looking more deeply at groups and systems in which individuals are embedded, becoming increasingly multicultural, interdisciplinary and methodologically richer. However, if this is third wave in positive psychology needs further discussion because it is highly complex and inclusive with regard to aspects on microand macro-levels:

Positive psychology is a science concerning on positive features such as human virtue and strength that make life worth living. The field of positive psychology at the subjective level is about positive subjective experiences. This includes the experiences of wellbeing, satisfaction, flow, joy, and happiness. It also includes having constructive cognitions about the future that is hope and optimism. Positive psychology, as a discipline, can be viewed both at the individual and the group level. At the individual level, positive psychology emphasizes on positive personal traits. This includes the capacity for love, courage, interpersonal skills, aesthetic sensibility, perseverance, forgiveness, originality, future mindedness, high talent, and wisdom. At the group level, positive psychology focuses on the civic virtues and the institutions that move individuals towards being a better citizen, which includes responsibility, nurturance, altruism, civility, moderation, tolerance, and work ethic.

Following are the Recent Trends of Positive Psychology

Positive psychology is not simply the focus on positive thinking and positive emotions butit is much more than that. Indeed, the area of positive psychology is focused on what makes individuals and communities flourish, rather than languish. The field of positive psychology at the subjective level is about positive subjective experience, well-being and satisfaction (past), flow, joy, the sensual pleasures, and happiness (present) and constructive cognitions about the future optimism, hope, and faith.

1. Psychology growing evidence of the importance of "positive" phenomena in basic psychological processes such as perception and memory.

2. Great interest in understanding how to achieve and promote lasting behavior change

3.   An accelerated growth in the application of positive psychology in schools, that is, positive education.

4.   A rapid growth in the clinical applications of positive psychology and the evidence that can sustain them.

5.   Technology at the service of research on wellbeing and its promotion, big data studies and apps that enhance happiness.

6.   A sustained growth and greater sophistication in the study of character strengths and how to work with them in different contexts.

Dimensions of Positive Psychology

Positive Psychology has the following three central concerns:

1.   **Positive Emotions**: Understanding positive emotions includes contentment with the past, happiness in the present, and hope for the future, positive views about self and others.

2.   **Positive Individual Traits**: Understanding positive individual traits consists of the capacity for love and work, courage, compassion, resilience, creativity, curiosity, integrity, self-knowledge, moderation, self-control, and wisdom.

3.   **Positive Institutions**: Understanding positive institutions includes justice, responsibility, parenting, nurturance, work ethics, leadership, teamwork, purpose, tolerance, and strengths. Relating to the study, these positive institutions will increases academic achievement and problem solving activities.

Positive Emotions

Positive emotions are emotions that are enjoyable to experience. It can be defined as "pleasant or desirable situational responses... distinct from pleasant feelings and indistinguishable positive effects". This definition means that positive emotions are pleasant responses to environment. Positive emotions include the response to situations pleasant or desirable, ranging from concern and contentment to love and joy, but different from pleasant feelings and irrespective of positive effects. These emotions are markers of overall well being, but they also help enhance future development and success. This has been demonstrated in work, school, relationships, mental and physical health, and performance improvement. The extensive and constructive theory of positive emotions shows that all positive emotions lead to expanded thoughts and actions and that the expansion helps to build resources that contribute to a Successful Future. Adolescents experience and express a variety of emotions every day. Focusing on positive emotions is one way to help them build the skills they need to focus on in the classroom as well as ups and downs of life

Positive Individual Traits

Positive Individual Trait is a blend of biological factors and environmental factors. We all have parameters set by our genetics, and our experiences determine how we act. The positive traits of an individual focus on a person's strengths and qualities. Following are a few examples of positive psychological traits:

1. Honesty and responsibility for one's actions are admirable qualities.
2. Adaptability and compatibility are great traits that can help to get along with others
3. Motivation and determination will help to keep on going no matter what.
4. Compassion and understanding help to have good relationships with others.
5. Patience is a good personality trait.
6. Courage helps to do the right thing in difficult situations.
7. Loyalty is a must-have quality that makes others trusts.

Positive Institutions

Positive institutions are a "structured cultural or social organizations and practices that enhance and develop highest human strengths. Positive institutions are those organizations that cultivate civic virtue, encouraging people to behave like good citizens while promoting the collective good. Understanding positive institutions entail the study of the strengths that foster better academic achievements, problem solving technique and well being of adolescents

Positive Psychology Techniques

Positive psychology is solely focused on the solution. It is more than mere repair and is limited to offering a solution when something goes downhill. Positive Psychology is that discipline of psychology that focuses on psychology techniques through positive experiences, positive emotions, positive personality traits and positive social interactions. Positive psychology techniques focus upon psychological states, personal characteristics and strengths and cultural institutions which make living most valuable. Positive psychology techniques are scientific, different exercises and activities, which can be used with anyone for well being, Problem solving ability and Academic achievement in personal and professional life.

Definitions

Positive Psychology Institute (2012) defined Positive Psychology technique as the scientific study of human flourishing and an applied approach to optimal functioning. It is the study of strengths and virtues that enable individuals, communities and organizations to thrive.

Jonathan (2013) defined positive psychology technique as the study of the conditions and processes that contribute to the flourishing or optimal functioning of people, groups, and institutions.

Hugo Alberts (2014) defined positive psychology technique as the scientific and applied approach to uncover people's strengths and promoting their positive functioning.

PERMA technique

The PERMA model is widely recognized and influential in positive psychology. Seligman (2011) proposed this model to help explain and define welfare more deeply.

"PERMA" stands for the five dimensions of happiness according to Seligman:

P - Positive Emotions: While just looking for positive emotions is not an effective way to boost health, experiencing positive emotions is still an important factor. Part of happiness is enjoying at the moment that is, experiencing positive emotions.

E - Engagement: Having a sense of engagement means take time and be completely absorbed to excel in is an important part of happiness. It is hard to have a sense of happiness if not involved in whatever is being done.

R - Relationship: Humans are social creatures, and rely on connections with others to truly thrive. Having a deep, meaningful relationship with others is important for good well being and mental health.

M - Meaning: Even a cheerful person may not develop a sense of happiness if don't find meaning in life. Devoting selves to a cause and, we experience a sense of meaning that has no substitute.

A - Achievement: All thrive when succeed, achieve goals, and improve. Without the motivation to accomplish and achieve, we are missing out on one of the pieces of true happiness.

This model provides with a comprehensive framework for understanding well being as well as a foundation for improving health. There are ways to enhance one's true feelings of happiness and well being and the following are the things one should focus on

1. **Experience more positive emotions**: by doing more of the things that create happiness and enjoyment in daily routine.

2. **Work to enhance engagement** : pursue interests that engage the subject, develop skills and find a job that better matches your passions.

3. **Improve the quality of one's relationships with others**: make an effort to build more positive and supportive relationships with one's friends, family and another important person.

4. **Seeking meaning**: if one does not find it through your work, look for it in volunteer opportunities, personal interests or recreational activities, or act as a mentor to others.

5. **Stay focused on achieving goals**: try to keep your ambition in balance with all the other important things in life.

These five aspects of the PERMA pattern are measurable and are also important for overall feelings of happiness. This pattern overrides the older model of true happiness when considering more than just happiness or positive emotions. Of course, positive emotions are important - they're part of the PERMA model, after all - but focusing solely on the positive emotions.

Life above zero

Zero is the line that divides illness from health, abnormal to normal and unhappiness from happiness. Below zero side life is full of pain, suffering, and full of problems, stress, diseases, hence unhappy life. Below zero indicates disorder, dysfunctions and illness. Whereas, life above zero is full of meaningful, purposeful, satisfying, and healthy. Normal, in all its glorious understanding life pushes us to fit in to move from a negative to a neutral or zero and from zero to positive side of life. Traditional psychology has taught us much about life full of pain and suffering i.e., below zero. Positive psychology is all about the personal qualities, life circumstances, individual choices, life activities, relationships with others, transcendent purposes, and socio-cultural conditions that define a good life. By combining these factors with the criteria positive psychologists have used to define a good life. Hence, positive psychology is the study of life on the positive side of zero. Life above zero covers a large area of positive aspects of behaviour such as mindfulness, resilience, happiness, hope, trust, and empathy, these are component of positive psychology. Positive psychology focuses on developing strengths of people, so that they can go ahead, and lead a flourishing and meaningful life. Resilience, creativity, kindness, courage, and wisdom are a few strengths to name among many others. This way, positive psychology emphasizes life is above zeroi.e., presence of positive, not just absence of negative. There is a life above zero and everyone deserves to live it.

Following are the ways to increase positivity in life which includes:

- Identifying personal strengths and using them.
- Employing an optimistic attitude, seeing the bright side and meaning of your daily life.
- Savoring the activities of your life, thereby enjoying the meaningfulness of your experiences.
- Volunteering your time sinceyou are priceless, your time given to others is immeasurable and yields long-term happiness returns.

Questions

1. What is Positive Psychology? Discuss its nature.

2. Define Positive Psychology. What are the aims of Positive Psychology?

3. Describe the objectives of Positive Psychology.

4. Define Positive Psychology. Why it is needed.

5. Describe in short the historical background of Positive Psychology.

6. Discuss the characteristics of Positive Psychology.

7. What is Positive Psychology? Discuss its scope/field.

8. What do you mean by Positive Psychology? Discuss its benefits.

9. Discuss critically the movement in perspective of Positive Psychology.

10. What is the assumption of Positive Psychology? Explain.

11. Describe the goal of Positive Psychology.

12. Discuss the culture of Positive Psychology.

13. Discuss the Eastern and Western perspectives.

14. Describe the theoretical prospective of Positive Psychology.

15. What is PERMA modal? Explain.

16. What is a recent trend of Positive Psychology?

Chapter-II

Concept / Nature and Indicators of Subjective Well-being

Positive psychology is concerned with how people can do well, be well, feel well, and flourish over the long term. But subjective wellbeing is one way to understand what this means to different people. Subjective well-being, also known as self-reported well-being, refers to how people experience and evaluate different aspects of their lives. It is often used to measure mental health and happiness, and it can be an important predictor of individual health, wellness, and longevity. This isa way to assess how people feel about their lives.

Subjective well-being (SWB) is the personal perception and experience of positive and negative emotional responses and global and domain specific cognitive evaluations of satisfaction with life. It has been defined as "a person's cognitive and affective evaluations of his or her life

Ed Diener (1984) introduced a model of subjective well-being made up of three components which were related aspects of how people perceive their own well-being:

- **Frequent positive affect**: This involves experiencing positive emotions and moods on a frequent basis.

- **Infrequent negative affect**: This involves not experiencing negative feelings or moods often.

- **Cognitive evaluations**: This aspect of the model relates to how people think about their lives and overall life satisfaction.

These three factors control how people experience the quality of their lives. It also encompasses the emotional reactions people have and the cognitive judgments they make about their own life experiences.In the mid-1980s, subjective well-being as a measure of overall life satisfaction, happiness, and well-being has become increasingly common. It is frequently used as a measure in psychological research and as a marker of individual health.

Subjective well-being emerged as a measure of happiness and life satisfaction in 1984. It is now widely used today as a way to gauge self-perceived individual and societal health.Diener found that those who reported the highest levels of subjective well-being had satisfying social lives and were rarely lonely.

When we think about and appraise our lives, we compare our perceived status against our own standards of desirability. This is the subjective element of cognitive appraisal.

Definition ofSubjective Well-being

Diener (2000, p. 34), subjective well-being is "people's cognitive and affective evaluations of their lives."

Veenhoven (1997, p. 34) describes it similarly: "how good [life] feels, how well it meets expectations, how desirable it is deemed to be, etc.

Characteristics of Subjective Well-being

Subjective well-being is composed of several major components, including global life satisfaction, contentment with specific life domains, the presence of frequent positive affect (pleasant moods and emotions), and a relative absence of negative affect (unpleasant moods and emotions). The field of subjective well-being has several cardinal characteristics (Diener, 1984).

1. **Respondent response**: It is concerned with well-being from the perspective of the respondent; hence, importance is granted to the respondent's own views of his or her life.

2. **Long term satisfaction**: Long-term levels of satisfaction will be for stable and permanent changes in mood and life satisfaction.

3. **Healthy personality variables**: These variables are responsible, not only negative states such as depression and anxiety but also experiencing life satisfaction and pleasant emotions. Transient factors such as current mood and even current weather conditions affect judgment of life satisfaction, however, despite these temporary perceptions, subjective well-being is moderately stable across situations and across the life span.

Hence, as a person move through life their goals and needs change but subjective well-being remains somewhat stable. Campbell et al.,(1976) found that the demographic factors e.g. age, sex, income, race, education, and marital status accounted for less than 20% of the variance in subjective well-being. It is concluded that personal reactions to life's circumstances are more important than the events themselves and that personality affects the reactions. In fact, personality is one of the strongest and most consistent predictors of subjective well-being.

Signs of Subjective Well-being

- Being accepting of other people
- Being socially engaged
- Belongingness and being accepted by others
- Community support and resources
- Experiencing a sense of meaning and purpose
- Feeling independent
- Feeling like your life is close to what you think of as the ideal life
- Feeling as if the conditions of your life are excellent
- Feeling satisfied with your life
- Feeling that you have gotten the things that you want in life
- Having more positive emotions than negative ones
- Having opportunities to engage in spiritual practices
- Mastering areas that are important to you

- Physical wellness such as feeling like you are getting enough sleep, exercise, and nutritious food
- Self-acceptance

Types of Subjective Well-being

Broadly, Diener found that there were two types of subjective well-being as under:

Experienced Well-being

Experienced well-being refers to how often and how strongly people have feelings of happiness and joy. This type of well-being is also often referred to as hedonic well-being. It encompasses both affective and cognitive appraisals of overall well-being.

This type of well-being can also play a powerful role in health. For example, research has found that people who experience positive emotions more frequently tend to have stronger immune systems.[5]

Eudaimonic Well-being

Subjective well-being primarily focuses on experienced well-being. However, another type of well-being that can contribute to how people appraise their life and happiness is known as eudaimonic well-being. Eudaimonic well-being stems from living a meaningful life. Working toward goals, caring for others, finding a sense of purpose, and living up to your own personal ideals are important components of this type of subjective well-being.

Components of Subjective Well-being

Subjective well-being refers to how people experience and evaluate different aspects of their lives. It is often used to measure mental health and happiness, and it can be an important predictor of individual health, wellness, and longevity. A person who has a high level of satisfaction with their life, and who experiences a greater positive effect and little or less negative effect, would be deemed to have a high level of subjective well-being or in very happy. The concept of SWB falls within the 'hedonic' perspective that defines well-being or happiness as being fundamentally about maximizing pleasure and avoiding or minimizing pain.

Subjective well-being has three components:

1. **Life satisfaction** (LS): This aspect of the model relates to how people think about their lives and overall life satisfaction.

2. **Positive affect** (PA): This involves experiencing positive emotions and moods on a frequent basis.

3. **Negative affect** (NA): This involves not experiencing negative feelings or moods often.

These are independent factors that should be measured and studied separately. Thus, the presence of positive affect does not mean the absence of negative affect and vice versa.

Causes of Subjective Well-being

Subjective well-being is influenced by a number of different factorsthose that are internal, such as personality, or external, such as the environment or culture in which a person lives. There are some key causes that play an important role in overall subjective well-being:

- **Basic resources**: Having what you need in life, whether it is money, housing, or healthcare, is an important part of your subjective sense of well-being.

- **Personality and temperament**: Your inborn temperament can affect your happiness levels throughout life. Your personality is another key component. Traits such as extroversion tend to be linked to more positive feelings about life, while neuroticism tends to be connected to a more negative outlook.

- **Mindset and resilience**: People who maintain a positive mindset and who possess a strong sense of resilience tend to feel more optimistic even when facing difficult life events.[7]

- **Social support**: Research has shown that having social support has a powerful impact on both physical and mental well-being.[8]

- **Societal factors**: Characteristics of the society in which you live, including whether it is affected by problems such as crime, war, poverty, or conflict, can also influence how you feel about your life.

There are several internal and external factors in people's happiness as under:

Internal Causes:

- **Inborn temperament and personality:** Our genes and learned behaviors have an impact on our happiness. For example, you can inherit a trait like self-confidence, or you can rewire your brain to become more confident. This can help you experience the world around you in a more positive way, leading to higher subjective well-being.

- **Outlook on life:** Some people have a tendency to interpret things either positively or negatively. And, as we know, those with more positive thoughts and emotions experience higher subjective well-being.

- **Adaptation and resilience:** Things around us change all the time. Life events can influence an individual's subjective well-being, driving an improvement or deterioration. Resilience and adaptation to these changes is a crucial component of subjective wellness, allowing individuals to return to their baseline levels of happiness.

External Causes:

- **Material resources:** Research shows that we need enough income to meet our basic needs, like food and housing. Beyond meeting those needs, however, a higher amount of money does not increase happiness further.

- **Social resources:** A trusted and supportive network of friends, loved ones, and family is necessary for subjective wellness, though the amount of social contact needed to feel supported may vary.

- **The circumstances in which you live:** The society in

which we live influences our happiness. Living in a society of war and hunger lowers levels of happiness, while living in an economically developed society, in peacetime, with good social resources and healthcare, increases levels of happiness. Similarly, a workplace that fosters belonging and inclusion will be associated with higher levels of happiness, while a toxic work environment will be associated with higher levels of stress and anxiety.

Impact of Subjective Well-being

Subjective well-being doesn't just help you feel good about your life; it also has a powerful impact on your wellness in both the short and long term. In fact, subjective well-being may be one of the most powerful predictors of overall health and happiness.

Health benefits

People who have a more positive subjective well-being tend to be healthier and live longer.

- Subjective well-being may play a protective role in health. It was associated with decreased mortality and increased longevity.
- Positive emotions and well-being are also linked to stronger immunity and reduced inflammation.
- While stress and negative emotions can take a toll on your health, then subjective well-being can provide a buffer against these effects and may even undo some of the damage. Because positive emotions lower stress and promote healing, you may be better able to recover after coping with a stress-inducing situation.

Other benefits

People who experience positive emotions frequently are more likely to be productive and creative. They tend to earn more money, cooperate more with others, and engage in fewer risky behaviors.

They also have better social relationships and engage in more pro-social behaviors.

Concept of Subjective Well-being

A person who has a high level of satisfaction with their life, and who experiences a greater positive affect and little or less negative effect, would be deemed to have a high level of SWB [or in simpler terms, be very happy. The concept of SWB falls within the 'hedonic' perspective that defines well-being or happiness as being fundamentally about maximizing pleasure and avoiding or minimizing pain.

Importance of SubjectiveWell-being

There are many reasons why subjective wellbeing matters to individuals and society as a whole.

Quality of life

1. Our affective experiences and overall emotional wellbeing are central to our quality of life as individuals.
2. People who feel satisfied with their lives and frequently experience good feelings such as joy, contentment, and hope are more inclined to be seen as enjoying a high quality of life.
3. Measures of SWB can be used to inform policy decisions, academic curricula, and social initiatives that contribute to a better quality of life for citizens and communities across the world.

Human Progress

Gross domestic product (GDP) alone is not an adequate measure of life quality at the national level, but has some impact on SWB through various mechanisms.

Subjective well-being falls under one of the three basic orientations that facilitate wellbeing

1. The pleasant life – a hedonic orientation concerned with positive affective experiences

2. *The meaningful life* – a eudaimonic orientation that focuses on working toward a higher purpose

3. *The engaged life* – engagement with flow-eliciting activities (a psychological wellbeing orientation)

To Measure Subjective Well-being

Subjective well-being is often measured by self-report assessments of three types of happiness. Each is independent and should be measured separately.

There are three main types of happiness:

1. **High life satisfaction:** High life satisfaction is when we think our life is great. For example, when we are in a great romantic relationship, we often feel more contentment from our family and friendships, and we love our work.

2. **Frequent positive feelings:** Frequent positive feelings happen when we enjoy life. Possible causes of this happiness include supportive friends and family, a regular mindfulness practice, or a mindful approach to life.

3. **Infrequent negative feelings:** Infrequent negative feelings happen when you have very few concerns or worries and you rarely feel unpleasant emotions, such as anger. Possible causes to this happiness may include an alignment with your values and goals, and low neuroticism.

To Improve Subjective Well-being

Subjective well-being has such profound effects on both individual and societal health, there has been considerable interest devoted to ways to help people become happier and more satisfied with their lives.

Some specific strategies that have been shown to be effective include mindfulness and cognitive behavioral interventions.

- **Mindfulness** is a practice that involves learning how to focus on and appreciate the present. Instead of worrying about the past or future, people learn how to live in the moment and pay attention to the things that bring them joy and peace in the here and now.

- **Cognitive behavioral approaches** focus on helping people recognize negative thought patterns that interfere with happiness. Replacing these automatic ways of thinking with more positive, helpful patterns can lead to greater optimism and happiness.

Well-being Theory

In the year 2012, Seligman developed the Well-being theory also known as PERMA theory emphasizes on the core element flourishing. Positive emotion, engagement, meaning, positive relationships, and accomplishments comprise of five components of wellbeing theory. Increasing positive emotion about the past through cultivating gratitude and forgiveness; present through favoring pleasures and mindfulness; and the future through building optimism and hope are the main concern of positive emotion. Engagement involves fully indulging in skills, strengths, and concentration for a task. This involvement produces flow experience which is so reinforcing and satisfying that people engage in it without expecting anything in return. In a flow state an individual's attention is wholly seized in the moment, alertness wanes, and is not aware of instance. Relationships are elementary to wellbeing which braces life with purpose and meaning and strengthen the joyfulness, meaning, amusement, a feeling of belonging and pride. A sense of meaning and purpose refers to belonging to and serving something bigger than the self. Religion, folks, science, political views, work organizations, righteousness and community enables sense of meaning.

Theories of Subjective Well-being

The two basic types of theories of subjective well-being, which are *life circumstance theories* ("bottom-up" theories) and *dispositional/construal theories* "top-down" and construal theories)

1. Life Circumstance Theories

Life circumstance theories propose that your subjective well-being is mainly the result of the number of positive and negative events and circumstances in your day-to-day life experiences and favorable or unfavorable demographic factors such as socio-economic status, education, and physical health. From this perspective, people who were born into advantageous circumstances like financial security and stable family life will have greater subjective well-being than less advantaged, less fortunate people. In addition, life circumstance theories propose that overall subjective well-being and life satisfaction are the result of satisfaction or dissatisfaction with a variety of life in which positive and negative events and emotions may occur. For example, a married person's satisfaction with his or her marriage predicts his or her overall life satisfaction, but not vice versa. In addition, satisfaction with housing, financial situation, and social life predicts overall life satisfaction, but not vice versa. Employment, satisfaction with employment, and loss of employment also can have powerful effects on subjective well-being. Finally, a change in satisfaction with specific life domains predicts a change in overall life satisfaction. It isobserved that increases in subjective well-being due to positive life events and decreases in subjective well-being due to negative life events.

2. Dispositional/Construal Theories

Dispositional theories propose that subjective well-being is primarily the result not of life circumstances but of the biological or temperamental factors that influence how we interpret and judge life circumstances and events. The evidence is strong for genetic influences on predispositions; we perceive or *construe positive* and negative life events. For this reason, dispositional theories are also *construal theories* because they propose that cognitive construal's like beliefs, perceptions, and interpretation of life events and circumstances are the most important influences on subjective well-being. A large body of research on the heritability of personality and the strong relationship between personality and mental health and subjective well-being also supports dispositional/construal theories. Most of this the research has been conducted on the so-called "Big Five" personality traits: neuroticism, extraversion, agreeableness, conscientiousness, and openness to experience.

Summary

Subjective well-being refers to how you feel about your life and is often used as a measure of happiness. The concept emerged in the 1980s and is characterized by frequent positive emotions, infrequent negative emotions, and positive thoughts about life. Factors that contribute to how people feel about their lives include access to resources, personality, and social support. Higher levels of subjective well-being are linked to better health, lower stress levels, and longer life.

Life Satisfaction

Human is creature always evaluating his life situation. He will feel no satisfaction until he gains his goals. Perhaps, it can be said that the final aspiration of every human being is to attain his goals and desires and this attainment leads to life satisfaction. Therefore, Life Satisfaction is ultimate goal and every human being strives to achieve this goal throughout the life. Life satisfaction is a bit more complex than it seems; the term is sometimes used interchangeably with happiness, but they are indeed two separate concepts. Life satisfaction is the evaluation of one's life as a whole, not simply one's current level of happiness.Life satisfaction is the degree to which a person positively evaluates the overall quality of his/her life as a whole.

Definitionof Life Satisfaction

Satisfaction is a Latin word that means to make or do enough. Satisfaction with one's life implies contentment with or acceptance of one's life circumstances, or the fulfillment of one's wants and needs for one's life as a whole. Life satisfaction is a subjective assessment of the quality of one's life.

Diener, (1984): Life satisfaction is an overall assessment of feelings and attitudes about one's life at a particular point in time ranging from negative to positive. It is one of three major. Indicators of well-being: life satisfaction, positive effect, and negative effect.

Ellison and colleagues (1989):A cognitive assessment of an underlying state thought to be relatively consistent and influenced by social factors

Pavot& Diener, (1993): Life satisfaction has been identified as a distinct construct representing a cognitive and global evaluation of the quality of one's life as a whole

Hamilton (1995) Life satisfaction is the degree of contentment with one's own life style.

Ruut Veenhoven (1996): Life satisfaction is the degree to which a person positively evaluates the overall quality of his/her life as a whole. In other words, how much the person likes the life he/she leads

Cribb, (2000): Life satisfaction is referred as an assessment of the overall conditions of existence as derived from a comparison of one's aspiration to one's actual achievement.

Buetell, (2006): An overall assessment of feelings and attitudes about one's life at a particular point in time ranging from negative to positive."

JussiSuikkanen (2011): The life satisfaction is an intriguing one: a person is satisfied with her life when "a more informed and rational hypothetical version of her" would judge that her life fulfills her ideal life-plan.

Importance of Life Satisfaction

1. Life satisfaction makes us feel happier and simply enjoy life more, it also has a positive impact on our health and wellbeing

2. Life satisfaction is strongly correlated with health-related factors like chronic illness, sleep problems, pain, obesity, smoking, anxiety, and physical activity

3. Life satisfaction is actually related to a reduced risk of mortality. In addition, frequent fluctuations in life satisfaction

have been shown to be particularly harmful for health and longevity

Life Satisfaction Theory

There are two main types of theories about life satisfaction:

1. Bottom-up theories: life satisfaction as a result of satisfaction in the many domains of life.

2. Top-down theories: life satisfaction as an influence of domain-specific satisfaction

Bottom-up theories hold that we experience satisfaction in many domains of life, like work, relationships, family and friends, personal development, and health and fitness. Our satisfaction with our lives in these areas combines to create our overall life satisfaction.

On the other hand, top-down theories state that our overall life satisfaction influences (or even determines) our life satisfaction in the many different domains. This debate is ongoing, but for most people it is enough to know that overall life satisfaction and satisfaction in the multiple domains of life are closely related.

The Main Contributing Factors to Life Satisfaction

1. **Life chances**: In the life chances category, you will find societal resources like economic welfare, social equality, political freedom, culture, and moral order; personal resources like social position, material property, political influence, social prestige, and family bonds; and individual abilities like physical fitness, psychic fortitude, social capability, and intellectual skill.

2. **Course of events**: In the course of events category, the events can involve factors like need or affluence, attack or protection, solitude or company, humiliation or honor, routine or challenge, and ugliness or beauty. These are the things that can confront us as we go through our daily life, causing us to lean more in one direction or the other: towards greater satisfaction or greater dissatisfaction.

3. **Flow of experience**: The flow of experience category includes experiences like yearning or satiation, anxiety or safety, loneliness or love, rejection or respect, dullness or excitement, and repulsion or rapture. These are the feelings and responses that we have to the things that happen to us; they are determined by our personal and societal resources, our individual abilities, and the course of events.

4. **Evaluation of life**: The evaluation of life is an appraisal of the average effect of all of these interactions. It involves comparing our own life with our idea of the "good life," and how the good and the bad in our life balances out.

Measuring Life Satisfaction

Although life satisfaction is correlated with variables like income, health, and relationship quality, every individual may weight these variables differently than others. But it is also possible a person with low income, poor health, and few close relationships has higher life satisfaction than someone with wealth, a clean bill of health, and many friends. There is no objective way to measure life satisfaction from the outside

Components of Life Satisfaction

There are main five components of life satisfaction as under:

1. Career status, 2. social status, 3. financial status, 4. physical health, and 5. community support

Factors Associated with Life Satisfaction

Lio et.al. (1990) analyzed nine life satisfaction variables such as satisfaction with relations, hobbies, place of residence, satisfying life (happy or dull), health conditions, physical fitness and health and overall satisfaction with one's life situations.

Cribb (2000) found in his study the people become more satisfied with their lives, as they get older. This could be that as we age, we come to realize that most of the important things in life are not for sale. Among these are work satisfaction, friendship, pleasures of sol ary thought, reading and other forms of non-commercial leisure.

A man would be completely happy if he is satisfied in all aspects of life A life that involves the satisfaction of simple desires, gives many pleasures.

Factors affecting life satisfaction can be divided into two categories as follows:-

1. **Personal Factors**: Leisure Activities, Marital Status, Sports Participation, Mental and Physical Health, Positivity of Emotions - Coping Abilities, Ego Identity, Economic Status – Satisfaction with housing and living conditions, with income's purchasing power and with financial solvency Personality of the Individual

2. **Environmental Factors:** Social Circle/Friendship – satisfaction with friends and with availability of time to spend with them. Physical/Geographical Environment- Good Residential Facilities, Occupational Facilities – such as promotion, recognition, freedom, salary, job-security, work itself, job status, and friendliness of head, relationship with employees, achievement and working conditions enhances the life satisfaction. Community Environment – satisfaction with community services such as trash collection, public transport-road conditions, public lights, neighborhood safety and trust in local authorities

Improvement of Life Satisfaction

There are many factors by which life can be satisfied like relationships with loved ones, fulfillment from work, satisfaction with your physical health, happiness with your romantic life, and contentment with your sense of spirituality or religion.

Dr. Leslie Becker-Phelps offers five questions to boost life satisfaction.

1. Do you try new experiences? Trying new things and breaking out of your routine is a great way to improve your satisfaction with life.

2. Do you try your hardest in everything you do? Committing yourself to whatever you do 100% (or as close as you can get) will give you a sense of fulfillment and satisfaction that mindless work and passive pleasures simply can't deliver.

3. Do you enjoy spending time with other people? "No man is an island," after all! Even the most introverted among us need at least a few quality connections and occasional social interactions to feel happy with their life.

4. In your everyday interactions, do you approach people with a desire to get along? Related to getting out and meeting people, it's important that those interactions are positive. Make an effort to be more positive and agreeable to ensure that you have the right kinds of interactions.

5. Are you easily upset by different kinds of problems? Struggling with frequent anxiety, sadness, guilt, shame, or anger can easily drag you down. Set a goal to become a happier, more resilient person and work towards it. If you're not sure how to go about it, set up some time with a therapist or counselor to discuss (Becker-Phelps, 2012).

Difference between Happiness and Life Satisfaction

Happiness is an immediate, in-the-moment experience and enjoyable. A healthy life certainly includes moments of happiness, but happiness alone usually does not make for a fulfilling and satisfying life.Life satisfaction is more stable and long-lived than happiness.There are many factors that contribute to life satisfaction from a number of domains, including work, romantic relationships, relationships with family and friends, personal development, health and wellness, and others.

Quality of life

Life can be lived secretly, publicly and privately. We live our life as per our choice but with limitation and information. Quality of life depends upon place of birth, our families, and also community in which we live. Our opinions about quality of life can be determined by individual and collective memories and our background. Concept of quality of life should be like good life is much more than a commodity to be produced, distribute and consumed. Quality of Life has been defined by the World Health Organization as "an individual's perception of their position in life in the context of the culture and value systems in which they live and in relation to their goals, expectations, standards and concerns'. It is a broad ranging concept incorporating in a complex way the person's physical health, psychological state, level of independence social relationships, personal beliefs and their relationship to salient features of the environment. This definition reflects the view that quality of life refers to a subjective evaluation, which is embedded in a cultural, social and environmental context. As such, quality of life cannot be simply equated with the terms "health status", "life style", "life satisfaction", "mental state", or "well-being". Rather, it is a multidimensional concept incorporating the individual's perception of these and other aspects of life. Quality of Life is an overarching label that includes all of the emotions, experiences, appraisals, expectations, and accomplishments that figure into the good life. Quality of life is personal satisfaction or dissatisfaction with the cultural or intellectual conditions under which you lives. recreational interests, social functioning in friendships and relationships access to health care resources, standard of living and general well-being.

The QOLI provides information that will help you a personal growth program aimed at greater meaning, satisfaction and fulfillment in life. Fifty to eighty percent of overall happiness or satisfaction is composed of the the areas of life measured by QOLI. A person's satisfaction with a particular area of life is made up of four parts:

1. The objective characteristics or circumstances of an area,

2. How a person perceives and interprets an area's circumstances,

3. The person's evaluation of fulfillment in an area based on the application of standards of fulfillment or achievement, and

4. The value or importance a person places on an area regarding his or her overall happiness or wellbeing. CASIO model of life satisfaction as a blueprint for quality of life and positive psychology interventions.

The objective characteristics of an area of life contribute to satisfaction judgments such as when a person's satisfaction with work is based on the work itself, pay, relationships with co-workers and bosses, the work environment, and job security.

Definitions of Quality of Life

Szalai (1980)pointed out the similarity between the current concept of quality of life and the old age. Several questions are used in different societies in the interest of the health, welfare and prosperity of the person addressed.

Schalock (1989)suggests that the first people are willing to answer such questions and, second, that it gives proof of the capability of human beings to keep it evidence the life..

Diener and Larsen (1984)researched in this field that satisfaction was temporally and cross-situation despite affect changes. This stability is occurred because the internal standard of their life is subject to modification. Individuals may adjust their personal standards like self-esteem with the result that satisfaction levels are relatively consistent across time. This indicates that satisfaction measures may be insensitive to changes by planned interventions.

Cheng (1988)narrated that there is a basic difference between fateful measures and appraisal measure of overall happiness. He further suggested that people can experience to increase the positive emotions to negative emotions. Correlations between positive or negative feelings and life happiness have been unexpectedly low. Numerous researchers have done to measure a cognitive component because of this and the other theoretical difficulties associated with using positive and negative afflatus to form an overall index of SQL,

Bradburn (1969)has done work on equate subjective well-being with "avowed happiness". He defined happiness as an individual has an excess of positive over negative affect. Positive and negative affect were assessed by asking respondents how of they had experienced certain positive and negative feelings during the past few weeks.

Campbell, (1981) worked in this issue and narrated that subjective approach would maintain the direct source of information on the feeling about a life. The literature on SQL is concerned with people experience their lives in positive ways, including cognitive judgments and affective reactions.

Henshaw, (1973) suggested that the conditions of satisfaction and happiness are clearly dependent onthe ability to survive,a reasonable state of health, and on a multiplicity of things that permit or cause the achievement of desires or aspirations.

Schalock and others (1989): Quality of life is associated with the well-being of mental health and physical health. Various writers on the other hand have defined the concept of Being, belonging and becoming as the important domains of good Quality of life. Quality of Life is generally a related with factors such as social, health, economic and environmental conditions. These factors generally affect human and social development. Quality of Life is the outcome of physical and mental health of persons wellbeing.

Peace and Happiness

Positive Psychology is concerned with positive human experiences such as happiness, hope and optimism, fulfillment, positive relationships, and more generally with what makes life worth living. Peace and happiness concepts are related to positive psychology, which includes peace psychology as well.Peace and happiness have been described as **a positive human experience**. Positive Psychology seems naturally well positioned to inform a psychology of peace. Peace is an important condition, as well as a reflection, of positive human experience **and it is** associated with terms such as serenity, harmony, happiness, freedom, love, and well-being.In more peaceful societies people tend to find more value in harmony and higher levels of satisfaction with life.Peace has been defined not only as the absence or minimization of violence but also as the presence or development of harmonious relationships and social justice.Thus, there are some straightforward links between Positive Psychology and peace.

Peace Psychology is the psychology of peace, it seeks to (1) mitigate and prevent violence and borrowing from the field of peace and conflict studies (2) promote the ongoing pursuit of social justice. The first aim is related to "negative peace" and the second aim is related to "positive peace.

Positive emotions, personal well-being, and resilience may impact peace at different levelsranging from the personal and interpersonal to community, national, and global peace.

Peace has multiple meanings. It is a word with several dimensions used in varying macro as well as micro contexts.Global peace (peace treaties between countries or the harmonious relationship between societies) is an example of macro context usage. Personal peace (interpersonal peace and inner peace) is an example of micro-context usages. In general, peace of mind or inner peace refers to a deliberate state of either psychological or spiritual calmness.

Ward, (2010): Inner peace refers to emotional self-regulation and the ability to achieve a state of dynamic emotional equilibrium and competence.

Barua, (2014): Inner peace refers to a state of being mentally and spiritually at peace, with enough knowledge and understanding to keep oneself strong in the face of stress.

Gogava et al., (2018):A state of calm, serenity and tranquility of mind that arise due to having no sufferings or mental disturbances such as worry, anxiety, greed, desire, hatred, ill-will, delusion and/ or other defilements.

Happiness

The happiness is inherent to the human being. Everybody is interested in attaining the maximum level of well-being;thus, study of happiness has been one of the main requirements in disciplines like philosophy, sociology or psychology.Happiness is a highly valued in present day society. Not only the people do aim at happiness in their own life but there is also growing support for the idea that we care for the happiness of other people. Happiness is typically associated with the concepts of life satisfaction and subjective wellbeing.The word happiness is synonymous with 'quality of life' or 'well-being'. In this meaning it denotes that life is good, but does not specify what is good about life.According to psychology, happiness is about more than simply the experience of a positive mood.In other words, happiness is "people's evaluations of their lives and encompasses both cognitive judgments of satisfaction and affective appraisals of moods and emotions". Happiness is usually defined in terms of a good life, or flourishing. Positive psychologists often refer to two types of happiness: **hedonic** and **eudaimonic**. Briefly, *hedonic happiness* refers to how happy you feel whereas *eudaimonic happiness* involves being true to your authentic self.The hedonic approach offers a more parsimonious account for defining happiness. A simple definition of *hedonic happiness* is the positive balance of one's emotional experiences. If you have more pleasant than unpleasant emotional experiences, then you are considered to be a happy person. There are several advantages to the eudaimonic tradition of happiness. According to Aristotle life simply filled with consumptive pleasure is not a happy life. Cows may have all the pleasure of eating grass and grain but are they really happy? No. Aristotle would claim that the authentically happy life is also the virtuous life.

Happiness is a concept "the meaning of which everybody knows but difficult to define it. However, happiness is defined as happiness is a state of mind that includes the experience of joy, contentment, or positive well-being, combined with a sense that one's life will be good, meaningful, and worthwhile. According to subjective conception happiness can be defined as it is an individual over any period of time is their nice feelings (positive affective feelings) and less their negative feelings over that period time and duration.

Indian Perspective on Happiness

The philosophy of Chaarvaaka is a materialist view which states that the fulfillment of desires leads to pleasure. This view is subjective and this view aims for the wellbeing of everyone in the universe.

The Vedic and Upanishadic texts defined the ultimate truth with reference to permanent and impermanent. To realize the Atman and to know that Atman and Brahman are the same was considered as the path to liberation or moksha.

Views of Happiness

There are two important views of happiness: (a) happiness is enduring (it's not just that I feel pleased in the moment), and (b) happiness is global (I'm satisfied with my life as a whole, not just with select domains in my life).

Theory of Happiness

There are three ways that psychologists study happiness:

1. **Need and Goal Satisfaction Theories:** Need and goal satisfaction theories focus on the idea that the reduction of tensions, satisfaction of needs, and moving towards a valued goal leads to happiness. These theories suggest that happiness results from striving to achieve appropriate goals and meeting one's fundamental human needs.

2. **Genetic and Personality Predisposition Theories:** These propose that wellbeing is influenced by genes, and is associated with the personality traits of extraversion and neuroticism. This implies that wellbeing does not change much over time.

3. **Process/Activity Theories** Process/activity theories argue that well-being may be improved by participating in activities that are engaging and require effort. Process or activity theories state that engagement in an activity provides happiness. It is suggested that *people are happiest when they are engaged in interesting activities that match their level of skill.* This is called the state of "flow".

There are three clear well defined paths to happiness:

1. **Positive Emotion and Pleasure**: Happiness exists when positive emotions are dominant with the experience of negative emotion minimal. The so-called 'pleasant life' is one which involves enjoyable and positive experiences.

2. **Engagement**: Engagement refers to being fully involved in a task that is at hand and feeling absorbed by it. According to Seligman, the 'good life' is a result of a person developing and then demonstrating their 'signature' strengths and virtues in relationships, work, and leisure.

3. **Meaning**: Meaning exists when we have a higher purpose than ourselves. The 'meaningful life' sees a person using their signature strengths to work towards the greater good.

These three elements combine to result in authentic and stable happiness. Authentic happiness results from identifying and developing 'signature strengths' and virtues.

Causes of Happiness

A number of factors that contribute to happiness are as follows:

1. *Personality traits and happiness:* Personality studies of happiness show that happy and unhappy people have distinctive personality profiles. Happy people in western cultures are found to be extraverted, optimistic, having high self-esteem and an internal locus of control. In contrast, unhappy people are found to be high on neuroticism. However, a significant relationship has not been found between intelligence and happiness.

2. *Genetic and environmental basis for personality traits:* *Evidence* shows that 50 per cent of the variance in major personality traits such as extraversion and neuroticism may be accounted for by genetic factors. Whereas children with high activity levels and positive effect become extraverted, and hence more likely to be happy, children who are highly irritable and fearful show high levels of neuroticism in later life and so are more likely to show negative effectivity.

3. *Heritability of a happiness set-point:* About half of the variance in current happiness or subjective well-being is due to genetic factors. However, the set-point for happiness is about 98 per cent determined genetically.

4. *Culture and Happiness:* Specific cultural and socio-political factors have also been found important role in determining happiness. Subjective well-being is greater in individualist cultures than in collectivist cultures. Happiness is also associated with important features of government institutions. Subjective well-being is higher in welfare states; in countries in which public institutions run efficiently: and in which there are satisfactory relationships between the citizens and bureaucracy members.

5. *Marriage:* Married people have been found to be happier than unmarried people. Marriages in which people communicate clearly and respectfully and forgive each other's faults are usually associated with higher levels of satisfaction.

6. *Kinship:* Close ties between parents and children, between siblings, and between extended family members enlarge the social support network of an individual. Social support enhances subjective well-being and we are to derive happiness from this contact with our kinship network.

7. *Friendship:* Maintaining a few close confiding relationships with friends has been found to correlate with happiness and subjective well-being.

8. *Religion and spirituality:* There is association between happiness and involvement in religious activity. This could be due to the following reasons: *First*, religion provides a belief system through which people do find meaning and hope. *Second*, the involvement in religious activities like visiting the place of worship, doing charity etc provides people with social support. *Third*, involvement in religion leads to a healthier lifestyle.

9. *The Environment and Happiness:* More pleasant physical environments are associated with happiness. Geographical

location, housing, weather and the availability of music can all have short-term positive effects on well-being. Well being has been found to be associated with being in natural rather than artificial environments. People report positive feelings in geographical locations where there is vegetation, water and panoramic views

10. **Health**: The immune systems of happy people work more effectively than those of unhappy people

11. **Work**: Employment status is related to happiness. Employed people are happier than those who are unemployed, and people in professional and skilled jobs being happier than those in unskilled jobs. Job satisfaction and happiness have a correlation of with the work status.

12. **Education**: Education level is positively correlated with happiness and this relationship is particularly strong for low income groups.

13. **Goal attainment**: People report greater happiness on days when they achieve highly valued goals than on days when they achieve less valued goals.

Happiness and Well-being

The basic tendency of human being is to express the emotions in his environment towards the stimulus. Basically, we express our emotions in two ways as positive or negative form. Happiness is a mental or emotional state of well-being characterized by positive or pleasant emotions ranging from contentment to intense joy. Happiness as a concept seems to be readily embraced by the majority of people and appears to be more valued than the pursuit of money, moral goodness or going to heaven. When we feel pleasure experience in our environment we express positive emotions and when we feel sad experience in our environment we express negative emotions. The mental state of expression of positive emotions in a pleasure form may be called happiness. Expression of positive emotions depends on the positive functioning of physical, psychological and social functioning. In other words we can say that happiness is the combination of physical, psychological and social well-being.

A Philosopher and Religious thinkers often define happiness in terms of living a good life, or flourishing, rather than simply as an emotion. A Sociologist defines happiness in social aspects and relationships in the society. A Medical professional defines happiness as a state of complete physical health rather than simply as an emotion. An Economist defines happiness as a state of good economic condition rather than simply as an emotion. A Psychologist defines happiness as a good mental health and psychological well-being. As a scientific enterprise, positive psychology focuses on understanding and explaining happiness and subjective well-being and accurately predicting factors that influence such states. However, positive psychology is concerned with enhancing subjective well-being and happiness, rather than remediating deficits. A variety of biological, psychological, religious and philosophical approaches have striven to define happiness and identify its sources. When we analyzed these approaches we find that happiness and well-being is a state of mind developed by three basic interlinked elements such as physical or structural health, psychological or mental health and social health. These three elements are interlinked and affect each other. If we find complete ourself on physical element, we reach to second element as mental health and in the last after completing both physical and mental health; we will reach to the social element which is known as social health.

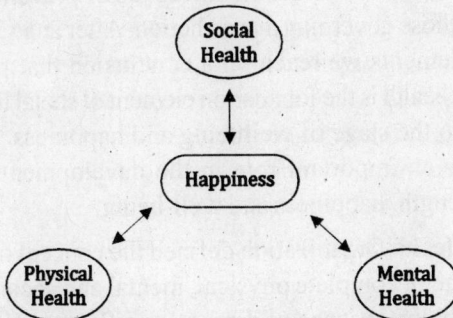

Happiness and well-being may be defined with the three basic elements which are as follow:

Physical Health:

Physical or Structural health can be determined by considering someone's height/weight ratio, their body mass index, their resting heart rate and recover time after exercise. Physical health has been the basis for active living campaigns and the many nutrition drives that have swept the industrialized world.

Mental Health:

Psychological or Mental health is a state of well-being in which we realize our abilities, can cope with life's normal stresses, and can work regularly and productively. If someone is suffering from mental health difficulties, they may attend counseling or psychotherapy to unlock' previous emotional turmoil and then actually use their past emotional trauma in order to grow and develop their emotional intelligence, thereby improving their overall emotional health.

Social Health:

Social determinants of health are the economic and social conditions and their distribution among the population that influence individual and group differences in health status. According to some viewpoints, these distributions of social determinants are shaped by public policies that reflect the influence of prevailing political ideologies of those governing a jurisdiction. After analyzed the basic interlinked elements we reach on a conclusion that physical and psychological health is the foundation element of social health. Social health leads to the stage of wellbeing and happiness. These three elements play an important role in the development of positive emotions, strength, happiness and well-being.

World Health Organization defined the concept of health that Health is a state of complete physical, mental and social well-being and not merely the absence of disease or infirmity (WHO, 1948).

Hierarchy of Happiness & Well-being

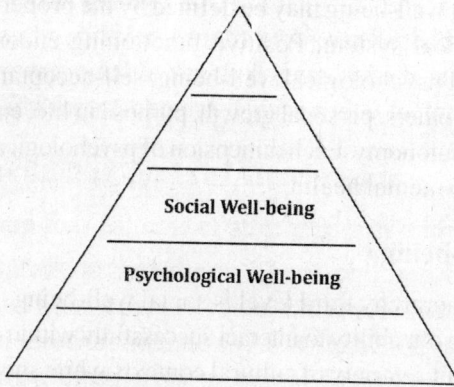

Maslow's hierarchy of needs concept assumes that lower level needs must be satisfied or at least relatively satisfied before higher level needs become motivators. These needs, which Maslow often referred to as basic needs, can be arranged on a hierarchy or staircase, with each ascending step representing a higher need but one less basic to survival.

After analysis the Maslow's model we find that only satisfaction of needs is not enough but the gain of total wellbeing also. Need and goal satisfaction theorists argue that the reduction of tension and satisfaction of biological and psychological needs and goals will cause happiness.In other words, happiness is a desired end state toward which all activity is directed.

Physical Well-being:

In the hierarchy the first level is physical well-being. Physical wellbeing has been defined by measuring health status, functional outcome, or quality of life. Physical health relates to anything concerning our bodies as physical entities. Physical health has been the basis for active living campaigns. Another term for physical health is physical well-being. Physical wellbeing is defined as something a person can achieve by developing all health-related components of his/her lifestyle.

Psychological Well-being:

In the hierarchy the second level is psychological wellbeing. Psychological well-being may be defined by the proper functioning of psychological system. Positive functioning encompasses six dimensions of psychological well-being: self-acceptance, positive relations with others, personal growth, purpose in life, environmental mastery, and autonomy. Each dimension of psychological well-being contributes to mental health.

Social Well-being

In the hierarchy third level is social well-being. Social Well-being refers to our ability to interact successfully within a community and throughout a variety of cultural contexts while showing respect for ourselves and others. Social well-being encompasses our interpersonal relationships, social support networks and community engagement. Thus, social well-being is defined as a positive functioning includes social challenges and tasks, and proposed five dimensions of social well-being. Thus, the triad comprising mental health includes the subjective feeling and functional states of emotional, psychological, and social well-being.

Well-being

In the hierarchy fourth level is well-being. Positive psychological definitions of well-being generally include some general characteristics such as the active pursuit of well-being, a balance of attributes, positive effect or life satisfaction, pro-social behaviour, multiple dimensions and personal optimization. Thus, well-being may be defined as a combination of positive functioning of physical, psychological, emotional, social, spiritual, economical system.

Happiness

In the hierarchy fifth level is happiness. It is the level where positive emotions arise. Positive emotions associated with the future include optimism, hope, confidence, faith and trust. It is the level of being happiness. Happiness is a mental or emotional state of well-being characterized by positive or pleasant emotions ranging from contentment to intense joy.

Carroll Ryff Model of Positive Psychology

Ryff (1989) conceptualized psychological wellbeing as comprised of self acceptance, personal growth, life purpose, environmental mastery and positive relationships with others. These skills are focused on the concepts of empathy, love and closeness. To experience well-being, an individual has to exhibit high levels of these six dimensions. That is, through fulfilling or actualizing ones potential an individual can experience well-being. To be precise, six dimensions of well-being can contribute to success. According to Ryff, the characteristic of a person having autonomy is practicing independence and adjusts his behaviour free of external pressures. Environmental mastery indicates the sense of expertise in taking care of daily matters and environmental factors. When a person is open to experiences and develops accordingly it contributes to personal growth. Positive relation is maintaining good interpersonal relations. A strong conviction and orientation of life is represented by the purpose in life and self acceptance is the well feeling about his or her self.

Positive Psychology and Happiness

An attempt has been taken to review a range of theories of positive psychology related to happiness with due focus on key elements are presented below:

Learned Optimism Theory: Learned optimism theory was one of the Seligman's (1990) contributing models to the development of happiness and wellbeing. Optimists attribute problems experienced as temporary and caused by external causes. They do not feature them as blameworthy or failures. Even in times of events not favourable, these individuals stand optimistic. Consciously challenging negative self-talks is the core basis of optimistic theory. It involves learning to talk through personal defeat. There is sense of accomplishments and can actively celebrate it. This theory of learned optimism was the foundation for Seligman to put up positive psychology and it led to the formulation of theory of Authentic Happiness.

Authentic Happiness

Theory Seligman (2004) proposed the authentic happiness theory with Positive emotions, engagement, and meaning as the core themes of the theory. Positive emotion is what a person feels and experience and life led fruitfully around this element is pleasant life. The second element engagement which involves being with the flow. Engagement makes the person feel loss of consciousness during an absorbing activity like time stopping. The meaningful life is the third element of happiness which is serving that is most important for the person. Thus, authentic happiness theory is regarding happiness in three elements. All three elements in right proportion leads to life satisfaction. After few years Seligman developed the theory further and proposed the wellbeing theory in the shift in thinking that the topic of positive psychology is wellbeing and not happiness.

Set Point Theory of Happiness

Set point theory of happiness is proposed by Lyubormirksy (2008). The main focus of the theory is that genes play a part in determining the general level of happiness. That is an individual has a set point which determines his level of happiness. Its central value is within the individuals range. The set point of happiness is determined genetically and is fixed and stable. Heritability of subjective well-being is found to be around 50% and the capability to feel contentment is programmed by genes. There is a tendency for the happiness levels to return to base line as it's a default nature. This means that happiness can be enhanced overtime but the set point cannot be changed as its constant.

Components of Happiness

The components of happiness include high positive effect, absence of negative affect and high life satisfaction. Thus the affective factors represent the emotional experience of joy, elation, contentment, positive emotions and cognitive factors represent cognitive evaluation of satisfaction. There are three components of happiness:

1. **Momentary mood:** how you feel right now
2. **Life satisfaction:** your overall evaluation of life
3. **Assessment of specific life domains:** work, relationships, finances, health, etc.

Strategies to Enhance Happiness or Enhance Pleasure

Normally, our society teaches us to chase: success, wealth, fame, power, good looks, and romantic love. But these are not really the keys to happiness. These do not give long-term happiness. Most people would like to be happier, or at least more content and relaxed. Positive psychology strives to help us understand how to increase happiness, more optimistic, and resilient. However, researchers in the field of positive psychology have found that you can genuinely increase your happiness and overall satisfaction with life and it doesn't require a winning lottery ticket or some other drastic change of circumstances. Character strength is not a fixed state but we can develop our strengths through deliberate practice. Practices for character strength includes identifying the focus value for the Integrity and then writing a daily diary about how well I have done in practicing that value. Positive Psychology shows us how to increase happiness by focusing on the positives and training our brains to use our strengths. Some strategies for increasing happiness:

1. Focus upon problem-solving, not just venting
2. Take time to build quality relationships with supportive people
3. Count your blessings and practice gratitude
4. Take time to engage in random acts of kindness
5. Respond actively and constructively, celebrating when others share good news with you

6. Attend to others mindfully, and practice compassion and empathy

7. Be kind to yourself, rather than overly self-critical or perfectionistic

8. Savor experiences because this will intensify and prolong your enjoyment of them

9. Set meaningful goals for yourself that provide structure and purpose, give a sense of identity and increase self-esteem

10. Build intrinsic motivation, rather than just relying upon doing things to please others

11. Seek healthy challenges, stretching your abilities just a bit beyond your comfort zone to realize your potential

12. Appreciate what you already have rather than focusing only upon what you still desire

13. Avoid the temptation to complain and reinforce negativity; instead, cultivate optimism and practice positively reframing your circumstances

Positive Psychology is useful to Increase Happiness

1. **Gratitude**: Gratitude is one of the most popular positive psychology approaches to increase happiness. People who practice gratitude regularly "experience more positive emotions, feel more alive, sleep better, express more compassion and kindness, and even have stronger immune systems."

2. **Humor:** There's a reason that videos of laughing babies and goats in pajamas are so popular that they make us feel better by quickly shifting our focus onto something fun, hopeful, and uplifting. We all know from experience that laughter is good medicine and research also confirms that laughter reduces physical pain, improves mood, counteracts stress, and increases resiliency.

3. **Smile more:** The simple act of smiling can shift your mood from negative to positive. Smiling not only increases happiness and emotional well-being but also reduces stress, makes more

likable and appear more competent. Since smiling is contagious, try to spend more time around others who smile often.

4. **Visualize success:** Visualization exercises help to relax the body and mind. This creates a mental picture of success which strengthens confidence and reinforces positive or optimistic thinking. They create a sense of calm and well-being that can translate into greater confidence and focus and less stress and tension.

5. **Self-compassion.:** Self-compassion is the natural antidote for self-criticism. We're judgmental and critical, finding fault with every little imperfection. By fixating on and amplifying our mistakes and flaws, we train ourselves to focus on the negatives. This damages our self-esteem and self-confidence, mood and this interferes with our ability to enjoy positive experiences and events in our lives.

Keys to Happiness, Self related Process of Enhancement of Happiness

People are born with certain happiness and genetics do play a role in happiness with it contribution only 50% in our life. Around 10% happiness develops due to life circumstances. Remaining, 40% is determined by your behavior, actions and choices. There are some tips to be happy by virtue of behavior, action and choices:

1. Training brain to be more positive: It is true that we can't change our nature, but we can train our brains to be more positive because negative things fuels unhappiness and plays a big role in depression and anxiety. Therefore, positive thinking gives happiness and so appreciation, and anticipates goodness is a powerful happiness booster.

Express gratitude: The research shows that gratitude helps you experience more positive emotions, decrease depression, feel better about yourself, improve your relationships, and strengthen your immune system. There are a number of simple exercises you can practice to increase and cultivate an attitude of gratitude, as under:

1. **Give sincere thanks to others:** When someone or does something to make your day easier, then give thanks and appreciation. It makes the person feel good, at the same time, it will feel also happiness.

2. **Keep a gratitude journal (Diary):** Research shows that keeping a gratitude journal is a powerful technique that instantly makes you feel happier and more connected to others.

3. **Count your blessings:** Focus on the blessings both big and small, from the people who love you.

4. **Write a letter of gratitude:** Martin Seligman recommends reading the letter in person for the most dramatic increase in happiness. So, write letter of appreciation to persons who did something that changed your life for the better.

5. **Find the positive in a negative event from your past:** Reevaluate a negative event from your past with an eye for what you learned or how you became stronger, wiser, or more compassionate. When you can find meaning in even the bad things you've experienced, you will be happier and more grateful.

2. **Nurture and enjoy your relationships:** Relationships are one of the biggest sources of happiness in our lives. The happier persons havehas a large supportive circle of family and friends and thriving better social life. That's why nurturing your relationships is one of the best emotional investments you can make. If you make an effort to cultivate and build your connections with others, you will get the rewards of more positive emotions.

1. **Make a conscious effort to stay connected.** Make an effort to stay connected to the people who make your life brighter. Take the time to call, write, or see each other in person. You'll be happier for it.

2. **Invest in quality time with the people you care about.** People who are in happy relationships talk a lot. They share what's going on in their lives and how they feel. Follow their example and carve out time to talk and enjoy each other's company.

3. **Offer sincere compliments.** As a practice of gratitude, it will also make you value the relationship more and feel happier.

4. **Seek out happy people.** Make an effort to seek out and spend time with happy people.

5. **Take delight in the good fortune of others.** Pay attention to your relationship when the other person is excited and and express your excitement for him or her.

3. Live in the moment and savor life's pleasures: When you focus on the present moment, you are much more likely to feel happy and at peace. So how do you start to live more in the moment and savor the good things life has to offer.Mindfulness meditation is a powerful technique for learning to live in and enjoy the moment. When practiced regularly, meditation appears to decrease activity in the areas of the brain associated with negative thoughts, anxiety, and depression. At the same time, it increases activity in the areas associated with joy, contentment, and peace. It also strengthens areas of the brain in charge of managing emotions and controlling attention.

2. Focus on helping others and living with meaning: There is always better in helping others. Here are some ways to live a more altruistic, meaningful life:

1. **Volunteer.** Happiness is just one of the many benefits of volunteering. It can be believed that this will contribute in a meaningful way in your life.

2. **Practice kindness.** This can give you pleasure to do a favor for a friend.

3. **Play to your strengths.** There are many different kinds of strengths, including kindness, curiosity, honesty, creativity, love of learning, perseverance, loyalty, optimism, and humor. Happiness will develop by using such strength.

4. **Go for the flow.** Research shows that flow, a state of complete immersion and engagement in an activity, is closely associated with happiness. Anything that completely captivates you and engages your full attention can be a flow activity.

3. Take better care of your health: Exercise and sleep are particularly important when it comes to happiness. Exercise has a powerful effect on mental well-being. People who exercise regularly are happier and they're also less stressed, angry, anxious, and depressed. Getting quality sleep every night directly affects your happiness, vitality, and emotional stability during the day. According to sleep scientists, the average person needs at least 7.5 – 9 hours each night.

Positive Emotion and Emotional intelligence

Positive Emotion

Emotions are a part of our daily life and existence. They form the very fabric of our life and interpersonal relations. Charles Darwin was the first to recognize the value of emotions. He noted that the emotional system energizes behavior needed to stay alive. Emotions cannot be stopped, they happen instinctually and immediately in response to situations and people. Emotion is a state of psychological arousal, an expression or display of distinctive somatic and autonomic responses. It is a complex psychological and physiological phenomenon involving an individual's state of mind and its interaction between that individual and her/his environment. Emotions can be experienced in three phases - cognitive, affective and conative. Cognitive refers to the knowing aspect, affective refers to the feeling aspect and conative refers to the striving aspect. Emotions are generally considered uncontrolled disruptions which are barely more than a state of mind or a feeling. Thus, several experts have suggested that emotions can be controlled by a rational and intelligent mind. Emotion is a subjective feeling and the experience of emotions varies from person to person. There are at least six emotions which experienced and recognised everywhere. These are: anger, disgust, fear, happiness, sadness, and surprise. Izard has proposed a set of ten basic emotions, i.e. joy, surprise, anger, disgust, contempt, fear, shame, guilt, interest, and excitement with combinations of them resulting in other emotional blends. All other emotions result from various mixtures of these basic emotions.

Emotions vary in their intensity (high, low) and quality (happiness, sadness, fear). However, women experience all the emotions except anger more intensely than men. Men are prone to experience high intensity and frequency of anger.

Joy, sorrow, hope, love, excitement, anger, hate, and many such feelings are experienced in the course of the day by all of us. The term emotion is often considered synonymous with the terms 'feeling' and 'mood'. Feeling denotes the pleasure or pain dimension of emotion, which usually involves bodily functions. Mood is an affective state of long duration but of lesser intensity than emotion. Both these terms are narrower than the concept of emotion. Emotions are a complex pattern of arousal, subjective feeling, and cognitive interpretation. Emotions, as we experience them, move us internally, and this process involves physiological as well as psychological reactions. Positive emotions mean guiding and understanding one's behavior and experience. Positive emotions can lead to enhanced well-being over time. Positive emotions and emotional intelligence are associated with multiple successful outcomes in the domains of mental health, social relationships, and work.

Positive emotions do not merely reflect momentary happiness or satisfaction, but more importantly serve the evolutionary adaptive function of widening a person's scope of attention and cognition as well as expanding the array of possible behaviors. Positive emotions facilitate creative and flexible thinking as well as effective problem-solving and coping skills. Positive emotions exhibit wider visual search patterns as well as more flexible mindsets and also report higher levels of feelings of self-other overlap. They buffer the deleterious effects of negative emotions and thereby contribute to psychological resilience and flourishing. Positive emotions often precede and predict positive outcomes in the domains of mental health, social relationships, and work.Positive emotions provide us with vital information for making sense of our inner experiences and navigating our social environment.

Management of Emotion

In daily life, we are often faced with conflicting situations.

Under demanding and stressful conditions, a lot of negative emotions like fear, anxiety, disgust, etc. develop in an individual to a considerable extent. Such negative emotions, if allowed to prevail for a long time, are likely to affect adversely the person's psychological and physical health. The major focus of emotion management techniques is the reduction of negative emotions and enhancing positive emotions. Effective emotion management is the key to effective social functioning in modern times.

The following tips are useful for achieving the desired balance of emotions:

1. **Enhance self-awareness**: Be aware of your own emotions and feelings. Try to gain insight into the 'how' and 'why' of your feelings.

2. **Appraise the situation objectively**: It has been proposed that emotion is preceded by evaluation of the event. If the event is experienced as disturbing, your sympathetic nervous system is activated and you feel stressed. If you do not experience the event as disturbing, then there is no stress. Hence, it is you who decides whether to feel sad and anxious or happy and relaxed.

3. **Do some self-monitoring**: This involves constant or periodic evaluation of your past accomplishments, emotional and physical states, real and vicarious experiences. A positive appraisal would enhance your faith in yourself and lead to enhanced feeling of wellness and contentment.

4. **Engage in self-modeling**: Repeatedly observe the best parts of your past performance and use them as an inspiration and motivation to perform better in the future.

5. **Perceptual reorganization and cognitive restructuring**: Restructure your thoughts to enhance positive and reassuring feelings and eliminate negative thoughts.

6. **Be creative**: Find and develop an interest or a hobby. Engage in an activity that interests and amuses you.

7. **Develop and nurture good relationships**: In the company of happy and cheerful friends you will feel happy in general.

8. **Have empathy**: Make your relationships meaningful and valuable. Seek as well as provide support mutually.

9. **Participate in community service**: Help yourself by helping others.

Enhancing of positive emotions:

1. Personality traits of optimism, hopefulness, happiness and a positive selfregard.

2. Finding positive meaning in dire circumstances.

3. Having quality connections with others, and supportive network of close relationships.

4. Being engaged in work and gaining mastery.

5. A faith that embodies social support, purpose and hope, leading a life of purpose.

6. Positive interpretations of most daily events

Emotional intelligence

In our day-to-day life we interact with a variety of people for various reasons. We are social animals and as a part of our social life we manage workplace relationships, friendships and family relationships. Some of us are quite good at managing relationships and as a result not only lead happy and satisfied lives, but also thrive at workplace. While some others are not so good at it, and often face discontentment and struggle. It is their emotional competencies, or their skillfulness in applying their emotional intelligence in managing their own emotions and of those around them. Emotional intelligence is not a new concept. It is present from the Vedic times and even in Bhagwat Gita in different forms. The Upanishads, the Epics, the Vedas - discuss in detail the nature of human mind and the significance of controlling it. Emotional intelligence has its roots in the concept of social intelligence which was first identified by E.L. Thorndike in 1920. Traditionally, intelligence had generally been viewed as a goal-directed activity characterized by the ability to solve problems efficiently, ponder and analyze objectively and the capacity for effective abstract thought. Emotions have a vital function in daily life and further emotions are generally considered uncontrolled disruptions which are barely more than a state of mind or a feeling. As a concept, emotional intelligence describes the relationship between emotion and intelligence. The ability to identify, understand, express, manage and use emotions is known as emotional intelligence. Emotional intelligence is of utmost value in every area of a human's life. Emotional intelligence refers to a human's ability to deal with his/her feelings appropriately as well as have the capacity to find the cause of a human's vital well- being. It is concerned with one's self-concepts, social skills, creativity, and one's capacity to comprehend one's own emotions as well that of others.

Emotional intelligence is positively correlated with measures of well-being and negatively correlated with measures of deviant behaviors. Emotional intelligence have also been associated with self-reports of interpersonal sensitivity and positive relations with others as well as peer and observer ratings of social competence

Definitionsof Emotional intelligence

Ezzatabadi et al. (2012), defined emotional intelligence as the potential to feel, use, communicate, recognize, remember, describe, identify, learn from, manage, understand and explain emotions.

Walter, Humphrey and Cole (2012) use the Mayor and Salovey definition of emotional intelligence which is the ability to effectively deal with the feelings of self and others in their work connecting EI and leadership development.

Nelson and Low (2003): According to them emotional intelligence is the single most important variable in personal achievement, career success, leadership and life satisfaction. They feel that an emotionally fit person is capable to identify, understand, experience, and express human emotions in a healthy and productive ways.

Byron Stock (2007): "Emotional Intelligence (EI) is the ability to acquire and apply knowledge from your emotions and the emotions of others." You can use the information about what you're feeling to help you make effective decisions about what to say or do (or not to say or do) next.

Mayer &Salovey,(1997): Emotional intelligence is the ability to perceive emotions, to access and generate emotions so as to assist thought, to understand emotions and emotional knowledge, and to reflectively regulate emotions so as to promote emotional and intellectual growth .

Goleman (1995), Emotional Intelligence is the ability to motivate oneself and persist in the face of frustrations; to control impulse and delay gratification, to regulate one's moods and keep distress from swamping the ability to think; to empathize and hope. Emotional Intelligence consists of a learned set of competencies that determine how we interact with people.

Emotional competencies

The domain of emotional competence can be divided into two broad areas: Personal Competence and Social Competence. Personal competence is based on an individual's recognition of his/ her own emotions, ability to appropriately express emotions and the ability to maintain emotional control and adapt. Social competence refers to an individual's ability to appropriately recognize emotions in others and respond in an appropriate manner. The components that fall in the area of social competence are: (1) Social awareness and empathy, and (2) Social skills

Personal competence: Personal competence determines how one manages himself/herself. Personal competence is the foundation of all Emotional Intelligence competencies. Awareness of one's emotions and his ability to control it is the key to personal competence. In other words, personal competence in Emotional Intelligence enables an individual to recognize and accurately label his emotions, control the emotions appropriately, choose how to react, increase confidence in the ability to act appropriately in any situations. The competencies in this category includes:

1. like knowing and managing one's internal states,

2. impulses and resources,

3. managing and harnessing one's own emotions,

4. knowing one's strengths and limits,

5. having a strong sense of one's worth and capabilities,

6. maintaining standards of honesty and integrity,

7. taking responsibility for personal performance,

8. being flexible and comfortable in handling novel ideas and new information,

9. striving to meet a standard of excellence,

10. developing readiness to act on opportunities and

11. showing persistence in pursuing goals despite obstacles and setbacks, etc.

Social Competence: Empathy – Awareness of others' feelings, needs and concerns. The competencies in this category include:

- Understanding Others – Sensing others' feelings and perspectives

- Developing Others – Sensing others' development needs and bolstering their abilities

- Service Orientation – Anticipating, recognizing and meeting customers' needs

- Leveraging Diversity – Cultivating opportunities through different kinds of people

- Political Awareness – Reading a group's emotional currents and power relationships

Goleman's Model of Emotional Intelligence

Goleman (1995) has identified five characteristics of persons with high EI. They are: (i) Self-Awareness, (ii) Self-Regulation (iii) Motivation, (iv) Empathy and (v) Social Skills.

1. **Self-Awareness(SA):** The ability to "recognize a feeling as it happens. One has to be aware of his own and others' feelings

and emotions in order to have accurate data and information about the world around him. An individual's ability to monitor feelings from moment to moment is crucial for his/her psychological insight and self-understanding. Being aware of others' emotions is essential for building a successful workplace environment and quality interpersonal relationships. One can respond appropriately to a situation only if he can read his emotions in that situation. The skill comes into play in most jobs particularly those that involve dealing with people. People who are unable to know their feelings are at a tremendous disadvantage. In a sense, they are emotional illiterates.

2. **Self-Regulation(SR):** Self-regulation means managing or controlling emotions oneself. This domain of Emotional Intelligence comprises of the ability to regulate moods and emotions in one and in other people. Emotionally intelligent people must be able to monitor, discriminate, and label their feelings accurately, believe that they can improve or modify these feelings, employ strategies that will alter their feelings, and assess the effectiveness of these strategies. i.e., emotionally intelligent people will be able to handle uncomfortable emotions. Teachers who are poor in this ability are constantly battling with feelings of distress, while those who excel in it can bounce back far more quickly from life's setbacks and upsets.

3. **Motivation (MO):** Motivation means motivating oneself to achieve something determined. Positive motivation is of paramount importance for achievement. To motivate oneself for any achievement requires clear goals and an optimistic 'can-do' attitude. Emotions motivate us but also can empower us if they are too strong and if we allow them to overwhelm us. People who have this skill tend to be more highly productive and effective in whatever task they undertake.

4. **Empathy(EM).** Empathy means recognizing emotions of others and feeling with them. The capacity to know how another person feels is important in any job. This means one

can feel with someone rather than feeling about themselves. Understanding emotions includes knowledge of the emotional lexicon, including simple and complex emotional terms, and the ways in which emotions combine (anger and disgust form contempt), progress (annoyance to anger to rage), and transition to one another, the capacity to analyze emotions and their causes and the ability to predict how people will feel and react in different situations. Empathy skills are most important in managing relationships. When a person is empathetic, she has the ability to have strong bonds with other people, can communicate more clearly, can understand others' viewpoint, have compassion and can forgive others for their transgression. Goleman has explained empathy as 'social radar'. He explains empathy as being able to pick up other's feeling without having a word uttered by them.

5. **Social Skills (SS):** This is a skill in managing emotions in others and handling relationship with others. Understanding of others' emotions gives us the ability to motivate them, to be effective leaders and to work in successful teams. People who excel in these skills do well at anything that relies in interacting smoothly with others. Briefly, Emotional Intelligence is a kind of social intelligence, which involves the capacity for recognizing and controlling one's own feelings and those of others, Emotional Intelligence includes awareness and management of one's self as well as her/his societal relationships.

Models of Emotional Intelligence:

Currently, there are three main models of EI:

1. **Ability Emotional Intelligence model:** The ability-based model views emotions as useful sources of information that help one to make sense of and navigate the social environment. The model proposes that individuals vary in their ability to process information of an emotional nature and in their ability to relate emotional processing to a wider cognition. This ability is seen to manifest itself in certain adaptive behaviours. The

model claims that Emotional Intelligence includes four types of abilities:

1. **Perceiving emotions** – the ability to detect emotions in faces, pictures, voices, and cultural artifacts—including the ability to identify one's own emotions. Perceiving emotions represents a basic aspect of emotional intelligence, as it makes all other processing of emotional information possible.

2. **Using emotions** – the ability to harness emotions to facilitate various cognitive activities, such as thinking and problem solving. The emotionally intelligent person can capitalize fully upon his or her changing moods in order to best fit the task at hand.

3. **Understanding emotions** – the ability to comprehend emotion language and to appreciate complicated relationships among emotions.

4. **Managing emotions** – the ability to regulate emotions in both ourselves and in others. Therefore, the emotionally intelligent person can harness emotions, even negative ones, and manage them to achieve intended goals.

2. **Mixed models of Emotional Intelligence**: The model introduced by Daniel Goleman focuses on Emotional Intelligence as a wide array of competencies and skills that drive leadership performance. Goleman's model outlines four main constructs:

1. **Self-awareness** – the ability to read one's emotions and recognize their impact while using gut feelings to guide decisions.

2. **Self-management** – involves controlling one's emotions and impulses and adapting to changing circumstances.

3. **Social awareness** – the ability to sense, understand, and react to others' emotions while comprehending social networks.

4. **Relationship management** – the ability to inspire,

influence, and develop others while managing conflict.

3. **Trait Emotional Intelligence model**: Trait Emotional Intelligence refers to an individual's self-perceptions of their emotional abilities. This definition of Emotional Intelligence encompasses behavioral dispositions and self-perceived abilities and is measured by self-report, as opposed to the ability based model which refers to actual abilities, which have proven highly resistant to scientific measurement. Trait Emotional Intelligence should be investigated within a personality framework. An alternative label for the same construct is trait emotional self-efficacy.

Mayer and Salovey's ability model of Emotional Intelligence

The psychologists **Salovey** and **Mayer** originally coined the term 'emotional intelligence in 1990. However, Daniel Goldman popularized it in 1995 in the title of his book – "Emotional Intelligence". According to Goldman the critical period to acquire EI is probably during early to late adolescence. The young person, often a male, may experience social anxiety, discomfort and rejection while attempting to interact with and influence others.

Mayer and **Salovey's** conception of emotional intelligence is based within a model of intelligence and their theory of emotional intelligence integrates key ideas from the fields of intelligence and emotion. They propose that emotional intelligence is comprised of two areas:

1. **Experiential**: Ability to perceive, respond, and manipulate emotional information without necessarily understanding it

2. **Strategic:** Ability to understand and manage emotions without necessarily perceiving feelings well or fully experiencing them

Each area is further divided into two branches that range from basic psychological processes to more complex processes integrating emotion and cognition as under:

1. **Emotional perception**: It is the ability to be self-aware of emotions and to express emotions and emotional needs accurately to others. Emotional perception also includes the

ability to distinguish between honest and dishonest expressions of emotion.

2. **Emotional assimilation**: It is the ability to distinguish among the different emotions one is feeling and to identify those that are influencing their thought processes.

3. **Emotional understanding**: It is the ability to understand complex emotions (such as feeling two emotions at once) and the ability to recognize transitions from one to the other.

4. **Emotion management**: It is the ability to connect or disconnect from an emotion depending on its usefulness in a given situation.

The advantages of emotional intelligence are as under:

♦ improves relationships with human beings;

♦ improves communication with people;

♦ makes better empathy skills;

♦ acting with integrity;

♦ helps you to get respect from others;

♦ to improve career prospects;

♦ managing change more confidently;

♦ enjoy the work wholeheartedly;

♦ feeling confident and positive in attitude;

♦ to reduce stress levels;

♦ to increase creativity;

♦ to learn from mistakes.

Impact of Emotional Intelligence:

The impact of emotional intelligence on a person can be positive as well as negative:

By developing emotional intelligence individuals can become more productive and successful at what they do, and help others become more productive and successful too. The process and outcomes of emotional intelligence development also contain many elements known to reduce stress for individuals and therefore organizations by moderating conflict.

1. **Personal Productivity**: Emotional intelligence expertise permits an individual to think more appropriately under stressful situations, deleting time wasted by feelings of rage, anxiety and fright.

2. **Developing Leaders**: Emotional intelligence is more than 85% of what makes star performers to develop into great leaders.

3. **Career Success**: Emotional intelligence is indicative of good performance and is twice as beneficial as technical and cognitive ability together.

4. **Team Performance**: Emotionally intelligent people get along better and don't let worry and frustrations to get in the route of efficiently solving problems.

5. **Motivation /Empowerment**: Improving emotional intelligence enhances the understanding between people which decreases hours wasted in argument and defending turf.

6. **Difficult Clients /Teams**: Emotionally intelligent people expertise positively to influences every individual they contact. They are the role models of excellent performance.

7. **Customer Satisfaction**: Excellent client service is based on honest care. Emotionally intelligent people take care of themselves and spread sincere services or care to others.

8. **Creativity and Innovation**: Emotionally intelligent people calms and clear their minds rapidly and in simple manner, disclosing the route for insight, intuitive and creative ideas.

9. **Time Management**: Emotionally intelligent people don't waste time worrying, arguing and guessing themselves repeatedly. They usually go for constructive behaviours.

10. **Talent Retention**: Emotionally intelligent leaders have been with the best, most effective leaders, the type of people that

talented person wants to work for.

11. **Work/Life Balance**: If personal productivity and performance is improved, it states that people can confidently leave work at a reasonable time.

12. **Stress Reduction**: Emotionally intelligent people easily manage emotions of frighten, frustration and anxiety that may lead to stress in recent world of work

Importance of Emotional Intelligence:

In the present time, the need of emotional intelligence or its importance is increasing as the rules of workplace are changing rapidly.

1. Emotional intelligence helps you build stronger relationships, succeed at school and work, and achieve your career and personal goals. It can also help you to connect with your feelings, turn intention into action.

2. Emotional intelligence has a significantly positive role in many important aspects of human functioning such as: sensitivity for others and one's own emotions, emotional self-concept, coping with stress, maintaining positive mood, and openness.

3. Emotional intelligence training can provide solution to various problems in personal relations, work and educational process.

4. Emotional intelligence occupies a very pivotal role in our emotional, social and personal life. It includes one's ability to handle stressful environment and resolve daily hassles.

Both positive emotions and emotional intelligence are likely to play a central role in successful experiential learning for several reasons. First, as the foregoing literature has shown, both emotion variables are associated with adaptive intrapersonal and interpersonal functioning, which are likely to facilitate the experiential learning process. Second, positive emotions and emotional intelligence are both likely to serve as valuable psychological and social resources for coping with the various challenges associated with each of the developmental stages of the internship experience.

Finally, positive emotions and emotional intelligence may also contribute to successful experiential learning by fostering reflection. But sometimes, positive emotions and emotional intelligence may reciprocally influence one another.Another possibility is that high levels of emotional intelligence may serve as a protective factor against low levels of positive emotions or those conversely high levels of emotional intelligence would serve as a protective factor against low levels of positive emotions.

Positive Thinking

Positive thinking is about looking at things from a positive point of view. Positive thinking has been shown to help people live healthier, happier lives. When they have a positive outlook, they are more likely to engage in healthy behaviors such as exercising, eating healthy, and getting plenty of rest. Positive thinking just means that you approach unpleasantness in a more positive and productive way. You think the best is going to happen, not the worst.Positive thinking often starts with self-talk. Self-talk is the endless stream of unspoken thoughts that run through your head.

Benefits of Positive Thinking

The positive and optimistic people tend to live healthier lifestyles they get more physical activity, follow a healthier diet, and don't smoke or drink alcohol in excess.

The effects of positive thinking on health

- Increased life span
- Lower rates of depression
- Lower levels of distress and pain
- Greater resistance to illnesses
- Better psychological and physical well-being
- Better cardiovascular health and reduced risk of death from cardiovascular disease and stroke
- Reduced risk of death from cancer
- Reduced risk of death from respiratory conditions

- Reduced risk of death from infections
- Better coping skills during hardships and times of stress

Resilience, Self-efficacy

Resilience

There was a time when Psychology was limited to intelligence and talents among people for success in life. Today, time has changed and Psychology comes out with detailed concept of mental processes and higher level of cognitions. Human beings constantly try to adapt to both internal and external changes in their environment. The various internal and external changes demand modification of behavior that enable the individual to adapt and achieve, and this individual capacity is termed as Resilience. Resilience has originally emerged from the Latin word "resalire", which means to bounce back. The concept of Resilience emerged in 1970 from the studies conducted in the fields of psychopathology, traumatic stress, and poverty while researchers studied the effects of "risk factors" upon children's development. It may also be defined as a substance of elastic qualities. Resilience refers to successful adaptation despite risk and adversity. Circumstances demanding Resilience may include biological abnormalities and environmental obstacles which may be chronic, consistent, severe and infrequent. To be resilient, an individual must draw biological, psychological, and environmental resources to thrive, mature, and increase competence to overcome adversities. According to Masten and Obradovic (2008), Resilience acts as an umbrella and is regarded as the positive pattern of adaptation in facing adversity. Resilience is the ability of an individual to bounce back from or withstand major or multiple stresses in life. It is the capacity of an individual to thrive despite adversity, and to overcome the odds. Adversity and stress can come in the form of family or relationship problems, health problems, workplace and financial worries etc. Resilience is one of the important areas of higher level cognitions and it is the awareness and understanding of one's own thought processes which play an important role in individual's life. It helps people to understand self-cognition, personal knowledge and also helps in self-monitoring which boosts self confidence in individuals. Resilience in positive psychology refers to the ability to cope with whatever challenges in life.A resilient person works through challenges by using personal resources, strengths, and other positive capacities like hope, optimism, and self-efficacy. This capacity of resilience develops in childhood. Relationships play a vital role in building the resilience of an individual. This starts at a young age when we are heavily influenced by our guardians and parents.The type of relationship as well as the type of person in the relationship plays big roles in the development of resilience. When positive relationships occur, well-adjusted and rule-abiding behaviors are valued; these influence strong positive effects on resilience levels. The family domain also plays an influential part in children's positive development which leads to Resilience.People who are resilient might exhibit a positive attitude that guides them through the obstacle. They shift the label of failure of something negative to something helpful. According to Mandleco and Peery (2000), Resilience is coping skills and mechanisms which help to face and recover from common challenges in daily life. Resilience helps individual in normal development under difficult situations. Resilience is a psychological strength required to successfully navigate change in life. It is the ability of an individual to recover from distressing and challenging life events with enhanced knowledge to cope with similar adverse situations in the future. Resilience is also considered a fluid process that is in constant flux and affected by protective factors and risk factors.

Resilience, in general terms, is considered as a positive adaptation after a stressful or adverse situation. When an individual is bombarded by stress, it disturbs individual internal and external sense of balance. Resilience is the integrated adaptation of an individual with physical, mental and spiritual aspect in all set of circumstances varies from good to bad. Resilience is not only the overcoming from deeply stressful situation but also coming out of adverse situation with competent functioning. Resilience is also related to the nervous system and have neurobiological basis.

Neuropeptides and lower the stress response by reducing sympathetic nervous system activation and protecting the brain from the potentially harmful effects of increased level of cortical. Resilience is a positive bio-psychological adaptation which helps to understand the individual long-term health and well-being.

Resilience is also associated with intelligence. Individual with high intelligence have better creative, practical problem-solving and analytical abilities. Intelligent people are more knowledgeable and expected to have better self-skills and coping skills which they use effectively when faced with stress. Werner (1993) suggested that resilient people are not gifted but they adapt such skills from environment and surroundings. Resilient skills are also associated with interpersonal relationship where social intelligence plays a vital role towards social positive orientation and social skills.

According to Hu, Zhang and Wang (2015), Resilience is negatively correlated with personality traits (neuroticism and negative emotionality) which help in facing adverse situations and engaged individual in confronting the world with confidence in self-directed behavior.

McCrae (1992) has suggested that neuroticism is negatively associated with Resilience. Individuals with high Resilience have positive orientation toward others and usually make a positive impression of themselves with good social skills. They are more extroverts. As extroversion, scalability fits well with Resilience as a positive social orientation (Werner & Smith, 2001). Competitiveness is considered as positive because high levels of energy and drive are found to enhance coping capacity called Resilience.

Resilience is important for two reasons. First, to regain and maintain the mental health of an individual and second, it may help in the selection of personnel who will manage tough jobs. Resilience brings positivity and gives energy to face adversities boldly and in a confident manner. Resilience strengthens individual cognitive and psychological process to deal effectively with stressful environment and make environment and oneself strong to compensate with all difficulties and challenges.Resilience throws light into how people when experience adversity overcome those and become successful through challenges and grow competent.

Definitions of Resilience

Masten, (2014): Resilience is the capacity to adapt successfully to disturbances that threaten system function, viability, or development and can involve multi-faceted processes of thriving in the face of adversity, or vulnerability.

Lee, Cheung, & Kwong, (2012): The resilience research in the last few decades has taken a turn from considering resilience as an individual trait to a complex construct that involves the interplay of multiple factors.

Ungar and Liebenberg (2011): They provide a more culturally integrated view of resilience, which is used in this study "In the face of significant adversity, resilience refers to an individual's ability to navigate through psychological, social, cultural, and physical resources that preserve their well-being, as well as their capacity to negotiate for these resources to be provided in culturally meaningful ways.

Ungar, (2012): It has been identified that resilience processes make it easier for people who face adversity to navigate and negotiate for resources they experience as helpful while responding with sensitivity to the specific risks that individuals face. According to him an adolescent could utilize the opportunities as the interaction with environment promotes resilience.

Murphey, Barry, & Vaughn, (2013): Resilience is considered as one of the dimensions of positive youth development, a resilient adolescent is likely to enter adulthood with a good probability of coping well— even if he or she has experienced difficult circumstances in life.

Characteristics of Resilience

1. Cognitive skills,
2. Personality
3. Differences,

4. Problem-solving ability,
5. <u>Self-regulation</u>, and
6. Adaptability to stress
7. Positive outlook
8. Talents that are valued by self and community
9. General acceptance by others

Factors which effect Resilience

Following environments enable individuals to develop a positive self-image, believe in their strength, and develop resilience

1. Public safety,
2. Availability to health care,
3. Access to green space
4. Educational institutions
5. Social care
6. Holistic environments,
7. Pro-social organizations such as sports teams or clubs

Patterns of Resilience

Polk (1997) suggested four patterns of Resilience. These patterns reflect that all experiences of life have some positivity and provide strength to individual with more resilient thought and make life purposeful.

1. **Dispositional pattern:** Dispositional pattern concerns with physical and psychosocial attributes which promote Resilience and also consist of selfreliant, self-worth with good physical health and good physical appearance.

2. **Relational pattern:** Relational pattern relates to an individual's role in society and relationships with others.

3. **Situational pattern**: Situational pattern refers to those aspects which makes a close link between individual and stressful situations and individual response to the situation.

4   **Philosophical pattern:** Philosophical pattern addresses an individual's view about world and its parameters.

Enhancement of Resilience

Resilience can be enhanced in individual which help to manage strong impulses and feelings by

1. Boosting confidence,

2. Communication and problem solving skills

3. **Social support:** Supportive social systems, which can include immediate or extended family, community, friends, and organizations, foster one's resilience in times of crisis or trauma and support resilience in the individual.

4. **Self-esteem:** A positive sense of self and confidence in one's strengths can stave off feelings of helplessness in the face of adversity.

5. **Coping skills:** Coping and problem-solving skills help empower a person who has to work through adversity and overcome hardship. Positive coping skills (like optimism and sharing) can help bolster resilience more than nonproductive coping skills.

6. **Communication skills:** Being able to communicate clearly and effectively helps people seek support, mobilize resources, and take action. Those who are able to interact with, show empathy toward trust in others tend to be more resilient.

7. **Emotional regulation:** The capacity to manage potentially overwhelming emotions helps people maintain focus when overcoming a challenge, and has been linked to improved resilience.

Importance of Resilience

Resilience is important because it's needed to process and overcome hardship. Resilient people tap into their strengths and support systems to overcome challenges and work through problems.

Principles of Resilience

- Gratitude
- Compassion
- Acceptance
- Meaning
- Forgiveness

Types of Resilience

1. **Physical Resilience:** Physical resilience refers to how the body deals with change and recovers from physical demands, illnesses, and injuries. Research suggests that this type of resilience plays an important role in health. It affects how people age as well as how they respond and recover from physical stress and medical issues.

2. **Mental Resilience:** Mental resilience refers to a person's ability to adapt to change and uncertainty. People who possess this type of resilience are flexible and calm during times of crisis. They use mental strength to solve problems and remain hopeful even when they are facing setbacks.

3. **Emotional Resilience:** Emotional resilience involves being able to regulate emotions during times of stress. Resilient people are aware of their emotional reactions and tend to be in touch with their inner life. Because of this, they are also able to calm their mind and manage their emotions when they are dealing with negative experiences. This type of resilience also helps people maintain a sense of optimism when times are tough.

4. **Social Resilience:** Social resilience, which may also be called community resilience, involves the ability of groups to recover from difficult situations. It involves people connecting with others and workings together to solve problems that affect people both individually and collectively. Social resilience include coming together after disasters, supporting each other socially. Such responses can be important during challenges such as natural disasters.

Theories of Resilience

People face all kinds of adversity in life. There are personal crises, such as illness, loss of a loved one, abuse, bullying, job loss, and financial instability. There is the shared reality of tragic events in the news, such as terrorist attacks, mass shootings, natural disasters, a global pandemic, and war. People have to learn to cope with and work through very challenging life experiences. Resilience theory refers to the ideas surrounding how people are affected by and adapt to challenging things like adversity, change, loss, and risk. Resilience theory has been studied across different fields, including psychiatry, human development, and change management. Resilience theories are presented as set of ideas that describe the influence of adverse events that exert on individuals, and thereby impact families and environment. The theories throw light into how people when experience adversity overcome those and become successful through challenges and grow competent. Majority of the theories stress the importance of individual factors that help them thrive. Along with individual factors influence of family and environment are also discussed by few theorist as under:

Garmezy's theory of resilience: Garmezy's theory of resilience proposes that protective factors at the individual, familial and environmental levels influence resilience. To substantiate this aspect, he used three models which are compensatory, protective and challenge models and described the relation of resilience. This model of resilience gained popularity as it was effective in identifying with the process of resilience.

Werner's theory (1989) is not different from that of Garmezy's model as it dealt with protective factors which endorsed resilience in the three levels of individual, family and community. These levels were composed of attributes of individual traits, close relationships with families, and external support agents. The more stress one experience, the more protective processes are needed. The protective factors operate both directly and indirectly.

Brook, Whiteman, Gordon, and Cohen (1989): In the protective model he proposed protective factors have the effect of protecting another protective factor which is productive. Carver (1998) developed a more complex model of different trajectory for understanding functional and dysfunctional responses to adverse events, including resilience. This model assumes four different trajectories following an adverse event. The trajectories include succumbing, survival with impairment, resilience, and thriving.

Luthar in (1991): This is Protective stabilizing, protective enhancing and protective but reactive model. In protective stabilizing model there is stability to competence in spite of high risk whereas protective enhancing model states that students can involve in stressful situation and develop competence. Protective but reactive model says that there are few benefits of this but not when there is increased stress.

Bernard's theory (2004): Bernard views strength and competence as components of resilience for successful life. Social competence, problem solving abilities, autonomy and sense of purpose are seen as attributes of resilience. According to **Hopkins** theory resilience is the rapid ability to rebound from stress and strain in life. Also recovery may be followed by the application of management and rehabilitative process.

Mastan's theory: The main focus of Mastan's theory was that resilience is comprised of positive adaptation at one hand and conditions which threaten positive adaptation at another hand. Resilience is the processes or patterns of positive adaptation and development in reference to significant threats to an individual's life functions.

Signs of Resilience

Resilient people often have a number of different characteristics that help them to cope with life's challenges. Some of the signs of resilience include:

- **A survivor mentality:** When people are resilient, they view themselves as survivors. They know that even when things are difficult, they can keep going until they make it through.

- **Effective emotional regulation:** Resilience is marked by an ability to manage emotions. This doesn't mean that resilient people don't experience strong emotions such as anger, sadness, or fear. It means that they recognize those feelings are temporary and can be managed until they pass.

- **Feeling in control**: Resilient people tend to have a strong internal locus of control and feel that their actions can play a part in determining the outcome of events.

- **Problem-solving skills**: When problems arise, resilient people look at the situation rationally and try to come up with solutions that will make a difference.

- **Self-compassion**: Resilient people treat themselves with kindness, especially when things are hard.

- **Social support**: Having a solid network of supportive people is another sign of resilience. Resilient people recognize the importance of support and knowing when they need to ask for help.

Key Factors in Resilience

1. **Risk Factors**: Risk factors are difficult to life situations, they might lead to physical health problems, mental health issues, or reducing the quality of life. The following are the major setbacks that require skills of resilience to deal with:

    Childhood issues: Childhood involves many crises like the death of loved ones, chronic illness, abuse, and much more. Since they have faced such traumatic events in the earlier stages of life, learning resilience will create a promising future.

    Daily issues: Resilience is a coping skill that will help handle and demanding relationships, work overload, and fluctuating emotions. If the individual is not appropriately equipped, they will face severe losses.

    Adverse life situations: Adverse situations in life like loss of loved ones, financial breakdown, serious illness, a victim of abuse, or caught in extreme disasters like natural calamities, war, terrorism, pandemic diseases require resilience to regain the lost balance.

Meaning and purpose in life: When an individual is bombarded with stressful situations, not only the external quality of life but the internal quality of conscience is also being tested. To bring peace, the individual has to abandon the comfort zones and lead to exposure and create greater meaning and purpose in life. To develop a new philosophy of life, resilience is an effective tool.

2. **Protective Factors**: Protective factors reduce the risk of long-term consequences because of lifethreatening situations and help the individual to regain control over life. Resource utilization is required to gain back control over life. The resource may be internal or external.

Social support: The individuals can gain moral support and encouragement from family, friends, neighbors, colleagues, friends from the workplace, religious community, and more. Some individuals might experience abuse in the family, but they will handle the situation effectively if they gain warmth and support from friends. These individuals show resilience brightly. Resilient people possess good social skills to gain support. They actively seek help from others during adverse life situations, and they maintain trustworthy relationships throughout their lifetime.

The following are the benefits of having healthy relationships in life:

- They will gain positive role models to look upon and follow in life.
- They will experience warmth, care, and support, leading to trust in relationships.
- They will feel free and confidential to disclose their problems and gain guidance to move with
- They will enjoy motivation and reassurance from these healthy relationships.

Self-esteem: Self-esteem or self-worth is the way one regard and aware of one's own personal strength and weakness. It is more protective and creates space for the individual to hold on during stress. Self-confidence is the belief in self to handle adverse life situation. It is the willingness to accept hard feelings like anxiety, stress to protect personal values. Problem-solving ability is the ability to make decisions and bringing out those plans into action. This ability helps the individual to protect them self, others, and the environment. This coping strategy protects the individual from harm and improves life quality

Resilience Building Approaches

1. **Cognitive Behavioral Therapy**: Cognitive behavioral therapy handles human beings' problems by changing their thoughts, feelings, and actions based on their specific scenario. This approach helps to build resilience, and it serves as a base for other methods. It uses evidence-based techniques to handle anxiety and depression and adapt them to improve challenging issues.

2. **Problem Solving Training**: Problem solving training is a simple tool gained from cognitive behavioral therapy. It has statistically proven methods to handle adverse life situations, specifically depression.

3. **Progressive and Applied Relaxation**: Progressive muscular relaxation is an effective old technique used to relax an individual by gradually appearing pressure and releasing muscle throughout the body. Relaxation is an effective method to improve Resilience.

4. **Social Skills Training**: Social skills training involve the improvement of communication and interpersonal relationships. Assertiveness training is specific training to identify, understand, and apply the knowledge of their communication style to better their quality of life. Both these training will increase the resilience level of the individual.

Difference between Resilience and Positive Psychology

There are some substantive differences between Positive Psychology and Resilience

1. Resilience pre-supposes exposure to extreme adversity, whereas positive psychology concerns all individuals.

2. Resilience research concerns not only during childhood and adolescence, but also across adulthood but Positive psychology has been focused largely on adults

3. Resilience research works firmly in the discipline of developmental psychopathology, adhere to a core, defining feature of this field and studies of normal development of our understanding of atypical processes and normative development. But in positive psychology, the tendency has been to "use the normal as a base from which to understand the abnormal.

4. Resilience researchers have considered both the presence of competent, healthy adjustment, as well as the evasion of psychopathology whereas, positive psychology was concerned only with positive aspects of adjustment and health promotion.

5. When studying children, resilience researchers have, traditionally, emphasized over behavioral success as judged by proximal others like adaptive behaviors as rated by teachers, friends, parents, or others. In positive psychology, by contrast, there do not seem to be efforts to ascertain others' opinions on whether the individual is doing well as a good spouse or parent.

Similarities between Resilience and Positive Psychology

Despite these areas of difference, it should be emphasized that Resilience research has many similarities to Positive Psychology as under:

1. Both disciplines have matured; there have been ongoing critical appraisals of the scientific integrity of the corpus of work,

examining issues of operational definitions, methodological approaches and veridicality of conclusions.

2. Both fields have witnessed an emphasis on ensuring that research grounded in a set of strong organizing theory, with specific suggestions proffered in this regard.

3. Both disciplines entail concerted attention to interlinked, mutually beneficial salutary constructs

Both fields have faced the complexities of defining "doing well," given that meaningful variations exist across domains of adjustment.

Self-efficacy

Behaviorism was well known domain of psychology during 19th century. Skinner was developed the theory of behaviorism. Skinner said that behaviorism of people and animal should be determined only by observation and not taken place in their mind which was unobserved. Baum, was also in the same path and believed that behavior could be described scientifically without involving only thought and beliefs. But Bandura (1986) had a little different opinion and believed that predominant theory of behaviorismthat denies the thoughts can regulate actions does not lend itself readily to the explanation of complex human behavior.Therefore, it can be said that human behavior is affected by the beliefs and individuals hold about their own capabilities. Looking above concept Bandura (1997)introduced the concept of a self-system that enables individuals to exercise a measure of control over their thoughts, feelings, motivations and actions.He further added and believed that human behavior is the result of the interplay between self-system and external sources of influence. This concept became the formulation of the concept of self-efficacy beliefs.Robbins and Judge, (2007) hence believed that in different situations, people with low self-efficacy put in less effort and in high levels of self-efficacy exert more effort and tend to persevere. Self-Efficacy begins to form in early childhood as children deal with a variety of experiences, tasks and situations. However, a growth of self-efficacy does not end during adolescence but continues to evolve throughout life as people acquire new skills, experiences, and understanding.Moreover, self-efficacy beliefs have its roots in early contingency experiences and it can be used in degrees of freedom, and in the experience of success and failure. This is most basic psychological approach.Again, we can say that self-efficacy has overall belief in our ability to succeed but self-efficacy is related to value as human being, sense of self-worth.

Self-efficacy is defined as an individual's belief in his or her abilities (Bandura, 1997). Self-efficacy plays a significant role in the way people feel, think, behave, and motivate themselves. People with low self-efficacy are inclined to doubt their capabilities and often avoid circumstances where they think they will fail.Self-efficacy reflects on a person's belief in their ability to regulate their motivation, behavior, and social environment. Self-efficacy has gained increasing recognition as a predictor of health behavior change and maintenance. Higher self-efficacy means the person is more effective in performing the tasks assigned. Self-efficacy is a persons' belief about his or her chances of success.

Definition of Self-efficacy

Bandura (1997) defined self-efficacy as follows: "beliefs in one's capabilities to organize and execute the courses of action required to produce given attainments." One way in which self-efficacy can influence performance in sport, is through its potential role in regulating emotional states.

Bezjak and Lee, (1990): 'Self-efficacy' refers to an individual's personal judgements of his or her capability or skill to perform (efficacy expectations) and judgements about the outcome of performance (outcome expectations.

Vealey, (1986): Self-efficacy is more specific than sport confidence, as earlier proposed (

Pajares and Schunk (2001)agreed and added the element of competence on self-system and advised that self-efficacy is how an individual perceives his or her competency and this perception influences an individual's ability to set their goals to complete a task.

Jerusalem (2009) defined self-efficacy as "beliefs in their capabilities to organize and execute the courses of action required producing given attainments".Self-efficacy affects every area of human endeavor. By determining the beliefs a person holds regarding his or her power to affect situations, it strongly influences both the power a person actually has to face challenges competently and the choices a person is most likely to make. These effects are particularly apparent and compelling with regard to behaviors affecting health.

Characteristics of Self-efficacy

According to theory of behaviour change given by Bandura's (1997)self-efficacy determines the length of sustained in the face of obstacles and failures. Self-efficacy determines the the thinking of people, feeling and acting. Moreover, self-efficacy is associated with depression, anxiety and helplessness.Low self-efficacyand having low esteem of any individual can think only permissible thoughts about their personal development. While in the other hand, Schwarzer and Hallum, (2008) suggest that thinking is cognitive processes and performance in a variety of settings, including quality of decision-making and academic achievement

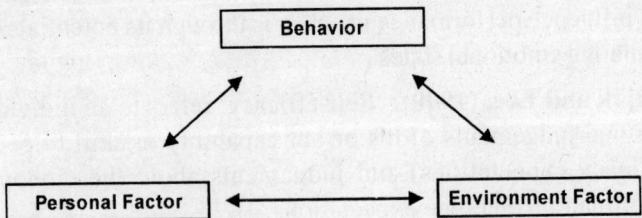

Bandura's Triadic Model

But it is true that individual either with low levels of self-efficacy or individuals with a high self-efficacy often choose to perform more challenging tasks. Their goal is always higher and sticks to them. Their actions are based on their thought, and highly self-efficacious individuals invest more effort and persist longer time to perform than low in self-efficacy persons. Even in odd circumstances highly self-efficacious individuals recover more quickly and remain committed to their goals. Person with high self-efficacy allows selecting challenging settings or creating new ones.People who trust they are capable of achieving their goals are more likely to seek out ways to overcome obstacles, whereas those who doubt their abilities are more likely to believe that more effort is futile. Self-efficacy theory also suggests that individuals who are currently struggling may not have been provided with opportunities to obtain mastery experiences or modeling necessary to develop high levels of self-efficacy.

There is adequate research evidence indicating that timely and strategic cultivation of self-efficacy in early adolescence is important and possible, for instance, it is observed that self-efficacy is associated with key motivational constructs such as causal attributions, self-concept, optimism, achievement goal orientation, academic helpseeking, anxiety, and value . Self-efficacy is also connected to self-regulate learning.

Self-efficacy is another factor that is associated with symptom management. Self-efficacy has been positively related to medication adherence and negatively correlated with psychological distress. Self-efficacy is also associated with better disease outcomes and a decrease in distress over time.

Sources of Self-efficacy

Bandura (1997) identified four sources of information that lead to the development of self-efficacy. But these sources provide only raw data, individual must cognitively process and integrate this information to develop self-efficacy. These four sources of information are as follows:

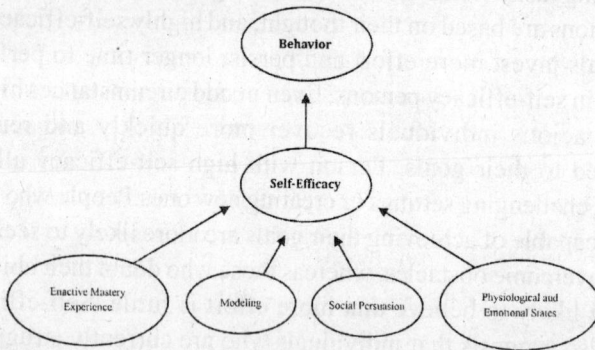

Bandura's Four Major Sources of Self-efficacy

1. **Enactive Mastery Experience**: Enactive mastery experience is an utmost important and influential source of self-efficacy, leading to stronger self-efficacy as compared to rest of the other three sources of self-efficacy. Enactive mastery experience refers to knowledge and skill gained through previous experiences. An individual's past successes and failures have a strong effect on self-efficacy for the particular task that one is facing at any given moment. Generally, previous successful performance experiences raise self-efficacy. For instance, if, an employee has experienced success in a project, similar to that which he is currently facing, he is likely to experience high level of self-efficacy. Therefore, if he has experienced failure, he is likely to experience low level of self-efficacy.

2. **Modeling**: It is another source of information that affect to the development of self-efficacy. This has also been termed as vicarious experiences or observational learning- that is learning by observing others experiences and by observing role model's attainment. Modeling includes process of comparison between oneself to another. That is "if they can do it, I can do it as well." When an individual observes a person similar to him achieve success, individual's self-efficacy goes up; but it will go down if they observe the person failing.

The similarity between observer and his model may be in terms of their ability, situations, circumstances, characteristics, age, ethnicity and educational and socio-economic level etc. Those, who have high similarity often serve as the most effective models and are more likely to increase the observer's feeling of self-efficacy. Modeling is an important source of information to develop self-efficacy for those who have limited past experiences.

3. **Social Persuasion**: It has also been termed as verbal persuasion. It is not as powerful source of information as others previous two in influencing self-efficacy. Social Persuasion is related to encouragement or discouragement. While positive persuasion increases individual's self-efficacy, negative persuasion decrease individual's self-efficacy. For instance, an employee, who receives negative feedback (negative persuasion) from his supervisor, will be more likely to report lower self-efficacy than those who randomly receives either negative or neutral feedback. Positive persuasion convinces a person about his ability of performing a particular task, helps in overcoming his self-doubt.

4. **Physiological and Emotional States**: People's perception of their physiological and emotional states can also influence their self-efficacy. In unusual or stressful situations, people commonly exhibit physiological arousals (like sweating, tremors, shakes, aches, pains and fatigue etc.) and emotional arousals (like fear, anxiety and depression etc.). If, person perceives these physiological and emotional responses as a sign of his own inability, his self-efficacy will be more likely to decrease. If, person perceives these physiological and emotional responses as normal and unrelated to his actual ability, his self-efficacy will be more likely to increase. Thus, development of self-efficacy depends on how one interprets or perceives one's physiological and emotional states.

Above mentioned these four sources of information play an important role in the development of self-efficacy. The most powerful information source of self-efficacy among them is enactive mastery experience. In the organization, management can change and enhance employees level of self-efficacy by providing them proper training targeted at these four sources of self-efficacy.

Types of Self-Efficacy:

Self-efficacy has been highlighted in different form by various researchers such as entrepreneurial self-efficacy, adolescent's self-efficacy, internal self-efficacy, occupational self-efficacy, leadership self-efficacy, mathematical self-efficacy, student self-efficacy, vocational self-efficacy, career self-efficacy, teacher self-efficacy, managerial self-efficacy and employee's self-efficacy. But specially attention of researchers has been diverted and focus has been given on the part of only three, such as:

1. **Social Self-Efficacy**: Social self-efficacy is "an individual's confidence in her/his ability to engage in the social interactional tasks necessary to initiate and maintain interpersonal relationships. As a construct social self-efficacy has been variably defined, described and measured in the scientific literature as researchers began to generalize Bandura's theory for specific applications. For example, Smith and Betz measured social self-efficacy using an instrument they developed and tested called the scale of perceived social self-efficacy, which they described as a measure of self-efficacy expectations with respect to a range of social behaviours. This instrument measured six domains: (1) making friends, (2) pursuing romantic relationships, (3) social assertiveness, (4) performance in public situations, (5) groups or parties and (6) giving or receiving help.

2. **Academic Self-Efficacy**: Academic self-efficacy refers to a student's belief that he or she can successfully engage in and complete course-specific academic tasks, such as accomplishing course outcomes, demonstrating competency skills used in the course, satisfactorily completing assignments, passing the course and meeting the requirements to continue on in his or her major.

3. **Group Efficacy or Collective Self-Efficacy**: Bandura (1997) defined collective efficacy as "a group's shared belief in its conjoint capabilities to organize and execute the courses of action required producing given levels of attainment". This was particularly important when the group faced complex tasks that required the efforts of every group member. Group performance may be better realized through promoting high group efficacy more so than by attaining high group goal commitment which in turn, will influence organizational outcomes. Efficacy beliefs play an important role in both individual and group motivation since people have to rely on others to accomplish their tasks.

Dimensions of Self-efficacy

Bandura, (1997) suggests that Self-efficacy expectancies three dimensions: magnitude generality and strength.

1. **Magnitude or Level**: Magnitude or level of self-efficacy meansa number of steps of difficulty that a person feels is capable of performing. Bandura (1997) further explains that the perceived personal efficacy may consist of performing simple tasks, extend to moderately difficult tasks or include very hard tasks. The perceived capability is measured against magnitudes of task demands that represent different degrees of challenge to successful performance. For example, urdu learners may say that they can hold basic conversations with other learners of similar proficiency level.

2. **Generality of Self-efficacy**: Generality of self-efficacy means the success or failure experiences influence self-efficacy expectancies in similar situations or contexts. For example, Urdu learners who to interact in class using their Urdu language that efficacy to other contexts in which they haven't been successful and such as initiating conversations with speakers. They may also share their feelings of self-efficacy to other domains such as reading a certain amount of literature, making telephone calls or visiting public places where Urdu is spoken. It can vary according to the degree of similarity of activities,

the features of the situations and the personal characteristics of the person who is judging his efficacy.

3. **Strength**: According to Maddux, (1995) strength of self-efficacy means the resoluteness of a people's convictions that they can perform the behavior in question.For example, two playersof basic learners may believe themselves capable of ordering play kit in a play ground where the second player is used, but one of them may believe in his ability with more conviction and confidence than the other. Strength of efficacy beliefs is given to persistence in the face of challenges, frustrations, and pain. People with strong beliefs will persevere in their efforts despite difficulties, frustrating circumstances or other obstacles but weak efficacy beliefs obstacles worsen.

Principle of Pleasure

Freud's theory of the pleasure principle is also known as the pleasure-pain principle and it is considered as the driving forces of the id. The id is considered to be the primitive, animalistic, and instinctual elements of the mind, and it is the deepest level of the unconscious. The id is one of the strongest motivating forces, but it is the part of the personality that also tends to be buried at the deepest, unconscious level. The id is the most basic and animalistic part of the personality. It is also the only part of the personality that Freud believed was present from birth. It consists of all of our most basic urges and desires. According to Freud, during childhood, the id controls our behavior and pushes us to satisfy our desires for immediate pleasure and gratification. Freud noticed how children often seek immediate gratification of their desires in order to keep their biological drives for pleasure - such as hunger, thirst, physical stimulation, and even sexual stimulation subdued. The development of another important part of the personality "the ego" we are able to keep the id's demands in check.As children mature, the ego develops to help control the urges of the id. The ego is concerned with reality. It helps ensure that the id's needs are met, but in ways that are acceptable in the real world.Freud asserted that children, whose behaviors are almost entirely controlled by their ids, seek to satisfy their powerful desires for pleasure through either direct means - such as eating and drinking anything they can get their hands on - or through ha'lucination and fantasy. Young children are not able to easily distinguish between reality and fantasy and often resort to fantasies to satisfy their urges for pleasure. The pleasure principle serves the practical purpose of unconsciously driving infants and children to attain their basic needs for survival.During early childhood, the id controls the majority of behavior. Children act on their urges for food, water, and various forms of pleasure. The pleasure principle guides the id to fulfill these basic needs to help ensure survival.

Example: Imagine that a very young child is thirsty. They might simply grab a glass of water out of another person's hands and begin to drink. The pleasure principle satisfies this behaviour but due to reality principle the ego has developed, and will push the id to realistic and acceptable ways to fill these needsinstead of simply grabbing someone else's water.

Pleasure Principle vs. Reality Principle

The reality principle is the counterpart to the pleasure principle. According to Freud, the reality principle refers to the awareness of the 'real environment' or 'reality' by a person and the need to accommodate choices and actions in order to live within society. Freud contended that during the course of normal human development, the primitive, pleasure-seeking operations of the pleasure principle gradually transform into the reality principle. As a child matures, it begins to follow the directions of the ego, which is the cluster of cognitive processes that includes problem-solving, as well as the mental mechanisms that serve to keep the id in check. During the course of normal human development, the reality principle is acquired and strengthened, and serves to halt the urges of the primitive and unrealistic pleasure principle. The reality principle does not serve to lead people away from the attainment of pleasure, but rather it leads people toward attaining pleasures which are assured and socially acceptable.Some needs cannot be met in the moment because that is not appropriate for the given moment of time. While the pleasure principle plays an essential role in motivating actions, the reality principles help ensure that our needs are met in ways that are safe and socially acceptable.

In nut shell, the id is ruled by the pleasure principle; the idea that impulses need to be fulfilled immediately butthe ego, on the other hand, is the component of personality that deals with the demands of reality.

Bandura's Theory of Self-Efficacy

Bandura (1997) defined self-efficacy as "beliefs in one's capabilities to organize and execute the courses of action required to produce given attainments". Self-efficacy is the critical component of what Bandura refers to as social cognitive theory. Other important components of social cognitive theory are agency and personal control. In order for self-efficacy to develop, the individual must believe that she is in control and that acts she performed were performed intentionally. If an athlete perceives or believes that he/she can influence for good the outcome of a contest, he/she will eagerly enter into the competition.

1. **Successful Performance**: The person must experience success in order for self-efficacy to develop. With a difficult task, this is an unrealistic expectation, so the teacher must ensure success by initially reducing the difficulty of the task.

2. **Vicarious Experience**: This is also referred to as observational learning. In learning a new skill, the learner needs a template or model to copy. This can be provided by the instructor, a skilled teammate, or a film or video of a skilled performer. An important component of Bandura's theory is the concept of participatory modeling. In participatory modeling, the learner first observes a model perform a task. The strategy and performance development functions of observational learning are both facilitated by decreased age and increased skill level.

3. **Verbal Persuasion**: Verbal persuasion usually comes in the form of encouragement from the parents, or peers. Helpful

verbal statements that suggest that the lerner is competent and can succeed are most desirable. Negative comments should always be avoided. Verbal persuasion can also take the form of self-persuasion.

4. **Emotional Arousal**: Emotional and physiological arousal are factors that can influence readiness for learning. It is important to understand that we must be emotionally ready and optimally aroused in order to be attentive. Proper attention is important in helping the lerner to master a particular skill and develop a feeling of efficacy.

Albert Bandura - there are four sources of efficacy beliefs.

Four main sources of influence can help in developing People's beliefs about their efficacy.

1. **Mastery Experiences**: The most effective way of creating a strong sense of efficacy is Mastery experiences. Having a direct experience in mastering a task or controlling an environment, will build self-belief in that area whereas a failure will undermine that efficacy belief. Without mastering experiences if people get easy success they start expecting quick results and easy success and may easily get disappointed by failure. A strong sense of efficacy requires experience in overcoming obstacles through constant, effort.

2. **Verbal Persuasion**: Self efficacy beliefs are created and develop as a result of the verbal persuasions individuals receives from influential people in their lives such as parents, teachers, managers or coaches. These persuasions involve exposure to the verbal judgments that others provide persuaders play an important part in cultivating people's beliefs in their capabilities. Positive persuasions can work to encourage and empower, negative persuasions can work to defeat and weaken self-beliefs.

3. **Emotional & Physiological States**: Some people rely on their somatic and emotional states in judging their capabilities. Mood can also affect people's judgments of one's personal

efficacy. People with high sense of efficacy are likely to view their state of affective arousal as an energizing facilitator of performance. This way of modifying self-beliefs of efficacy is to reduce people's stress reactions and alter their negative emotional tendency and misunderstanding of their physical states. Positive mood enhances perceived self-efficacy, down mood reduces it.

4. **Self Esteem**: Self Esteem can be broadly defined as the overall judgment of oneself in either positive or negative way. It shows that at what extent an individual believes himself or herself to be competent and worthy of living. Self Esteem is the evaluation of validity, approval, acceptance and self-worthiness that a person feels about him. Self-esteem is a very important aspect of personality. It is generally considered a personality trait that reflects a person's overall sense of value and self-worth. Self-esteem involves how a person generally feel about oneself, one's abilities, appearance, emotions, attributes and behaviors. It helps to accomplish identity and to adapt to society.

Questions

1. What is Well-being? Describe the indications of Subjective Well-being.

2. Describe the development of Subjective Well-being.

3. Define Subjective Well-being. What are the components?

4. Discuss the different theories of Subjective Well-being in short.

5. Discuss the factors affecting Subjective Well-being.

6. Define Subjective Well-being. Describe its types.

7. What are the causes of Subjective Well-being? Describe.

8. Describe the characteristics of Subjective Well-being.

9. Discuss the impact of Subjective Well-being.

10. What is Subjective Well-being? How will you measure Subjective Well-being?

11. How do you improve Subjective Well-being? Describe.

12. Discuss the well-being theory.

Life Satisfaction

13. What is life satisfaction? Discuss the importance of life satisfaction.

14. Define life satisfactions. Why life satisfaction is necessary? Discuss.

15. Differentiate between Happiness and life satisfaction.

16. Disuses the life satisfaction theory.

17. Define life satisfaction. How do you measure the life satisfaction?

18. What are the factors that affect life satisfaction? Discuss

19. How do you improve life satisfaction? Explain.

Peace and Happiness

20. What do you mean by Peace and Happiness? Explain.

21. What is Indian Perspective on Happiness? Discuss

22. Discuss the theory of Happiness.

23. Describe the causes of Happiness.

24. Differentiate between Happiness and Well-being.

25. Discuss the Carroll Ryff model of Positive Psychology.

26. What is Happiness? How is it associated with Positive Psychology? Discuss.

27. Define Happiness. Discuss the components.

28. What are strategies to enhance Happiness? Discuss.

29. What is Happiness? What are the keys to Happiness? Discuss.

Positive Emotion and Emotional Intelligence

30. What is Positive Emotion? Discuss

31. Define Positive Emotion. Describe the management of Emotion.

32. Describe the factors enhancing Positive Emotion.

33. What is Emotional Intelligence? Discuss.

34. Define Emotional Intelligence. What is emotional competency? Explain.

35. Discuss the different models of Intelligence.

36. What is Goleman's model of Emotional Intelligence? Explain.

37. Describe the Mayer and Salovey's ability model of Emotional Intelligence in short.

38. Describe the advantages of Emotional Intelligence.

39. Define Emotional Intelligence. Discuss the impact of Emotional Intelligence.

40. What do you mean by Positive Thinking? Discuss its benefits.

Resilience, Self-efficacy

41. Define Resilience. Discuss the characteristics of Resilience.

42. What is Resilience? What are the factors affecting Resilience? Discuss.

43. What do you mean by Resilience? Discuss the patterns of Resilience.

44. Discuss the factors responsible for enhancement of Resilience.

45. Define Resilience. Discuss the importance of Resilience.

46. Discuss the theories of Resilience.

47. Differentiate between Resilience and Positive Psychology.

48. What are the similarities between Resilience and Positive Psychology?

49. What are the signs of Resilience? Discuss the key factors in Resilience.

50. Discuss the types of Self-efficacy.

51. Discuss the Dimension of Self-efficacies.

52. What is Self-efficacy? Describe its characteristics.

53. Define Self-efficacy. Describe the types of Self-efficacy.

54. Discuss the Bandura's theory of Self-efficacy.

55. What are the sources of Self-efficacy? Discuss the Dimensions of Self-efficacy.

❑

19. What are the similarities developed by the key factors in Resilience.
20. Describe the types of Self-Esteem.

Chapter-III

Positive Cognitive States and Processes

Introduction

In today's world, society is facing extremely tough challenges in the form of global warming, natural disasters, economic recession, homelessness, terrorism and unwanted war. With all this sadness and horror, we need a science which helps to develop happiness, wellbeing, personal growth and the good life. Psychology after World War II became a science largely devoted to healing and concentrated on repairing damage using a disease model of human functioning. They have neglected the concept of building strength in human being. During the period, negative emotions were largely discussed while positive emotional states were relatively ignored although it is the fact that negative emotions have an obvious survival value. Positive psychology focuses on wellbeing, happiness, flow, personal strengths, wisdom, creativity, imagination and characteristics of positive groups and institutions. Moreover, the focus is not just on how to make individuals happy but to develop happiness and flourishing at a group level as well. Positive affect reflects a person is active, excited, strong and enthusiastic, whereas low positive affect fatigue. Positive affect has a favourable impact on learning, creativity, problem solving and interpersonal relationship whereas, negative emotions in contrast represent a person feels upset or unpleasant, distressed, nervous, guilty or anxious etc.

Cognitive States

In Psychology, there are two states of cognitive, one is Positive affectivity and second one is Negative affectivity. Positive affectivity is associated with regular physical activity: adequate sleep; regular socializing with close friends; and striving for valued goals. Individuals high on positive affectivity are usually cheerful, enthusiastic, and experience frequent episodes of pleasurable mood. In contrast, persons low in positive affectivity report low levels of happiness, excitement, and confidence. Happy people usually experience high positive affectivity and low negative affectivity. Negative affectivity is strongly related to Neuroticism. Positive Affect is strongly linked with Extraversion. Negative affect works on withdrawal-oriented behavioral, whereas positive affect works on approach-oriented behavioral facilitation system. This system is adaptive since it helps in obtaining resources thereby facilitating survival. Happy people usually experience high positive affectivity and low negative affectivity.

Various demographic variables such as age, gender, marital status, and socio-economic status are related to individual differences in happiness, and affectivity. But these demographic factors are not very good predictors of happiness and positive affectivity. Men and women report almost identical levels of happiness and positive affectivity. There are two variables which are consistent predictors of positive affectivity:

1. Positive affectivity is moderately correlated with various indicators of social behaviour

2. Positive affectivity is moderately correlated with Spiritual or religious activities

Low levels of positive affectivity have been found to be associated with a number of clinical syndromes such as social phobia, posttraumatic stress disorder, schizophrenia, substance disorders and mood disorders but high in positive affectivity report greater satisfaction with important aspects of their lives such as job and marriage. This could be due to the fact that individuals high in positive affectivity feel good about themselves and other things around them. Positive affectivity leads to so many positive outcomes; it becomes an important goal to achieve.

Enhancing Positive affectivity

Positive affectivity can be enhanced or improved by having high levels of positive mood and this can be achieved most likely when a person is actively engaged with pleasurable activities. Two of such activities are interpersonal like behavior and physical activity.

Determinants of Positive Psychology

There are many determinants of positive psychology such as flow, optimism, hope, happiness, quality of life and psychological well-being.

Optimism, Hope, Faith, Wisdom and Courage

The field of positive psychology at the subjective level is about positive subjective experience: well-being and satisfaction (past); flow, joy, the sensual pleasures, and happiness (present); and constructive cognitions about the future—optimism, hope, faith, wisdom and courage.

Optimism

Optimism has been shown to be beneficial in a variety of different domains. It has a positive relationship with subjective well-being, positive emotions and moods, success, and health. In the domain of health, there is relationship between optimism and psychological well being. More broadly, there is a positive correlation between level of optimism and coping on a task. When participants with low expectancies of success on a task were confronted with failure, they were found to feel worse about themselves than those who were more optimistic about their performance. Optimism is the belief that future events will have positive results. Optimism can influence one's ability to deal with stress and depressions. Seligman (1998) also observed that optimistic individual feel less mood fluctuation and enjoy the social interaction maximum. It results because one's intention to suppose favorable future results expected on favorable background. This is because of their ability to suppose positive future outcomes based on positive past experiences. It has been found a positive relationship among optimism, hope and health. Optimism is a mental mind set or worldwide approach, which conditions and circumstances being good. The word arises from Latin word "optimum" which means "best". The ordinary meaning of the word optimistic means expectations of best results from any worst condition. Optimism is a mindset of a person that gives people a generalized felling that they will succeed in their efforts. As a result of expectation of success, individual put in extra efforts 58 to meet their objective; this in turn increases the chances of success of a person with optimistic approach. On the other side if an individual, if he expect failure then he will make less effort to achieve the goal and the chances to loss as and when as soon as an obstacle appears. Optimistic people are capable of facing problem and overcoming them. One more important quality found in optimistic individual is that they always take positives form all the outcome, and they take lesion form the failure. Optimism is a perspective towards life which prevent individual from getting pathetic, or quitting a hope. They believe that thinks can be improved if efforts are made to improve them. Optimistic individual are healthier and happier. Their immune system work well. They cope better with stress using more effective coping strategies just as reappraisal and problem solving, 59 active for avoiding stressful life events form better social support networks around themselves, and have healthier lifestyles.

Definitions of Optimism

Scheier and Carver, (1985): Optimism is the belief that good things will happen and this belief is stable across time and situations.

Nicholas M. Butler: Optimism is essential to achievement and it is also the foundation of courage and true progress.

Arthur Schopenhauer: Optimism is not only a false but also a pernicious doctrine, for it presents life as a desirable state and man's happiness as its aim and object. Starting from this, everyone then believes he has the most legitimate claim to happiness and enjoyment. If, as usually happens, these do not fall to his lot, he believes that he suffers an injustice, in fact that he misses the whole point of his existence.

Martin Seligman: Positive thinking is the notion that if you think good thoughts, things will work out well. Optimism is the feeling of thinking things will be well and be hopeful.

Optimism and Pessimism

The concepts of optimism and pessimism concern people's expectations for the future and these influence people's behavior and emotions. Optimism and pessimism refer to the positive and negative predictions that people make regarding their future. Some people look usually on the bright side of events, while others look on the dark side. Therefore, it can be said that optimists expect good things to happen to them while pessimists expect bad things to happen to them. Optimism has been linked to psychological and physical well-being. There are several other constructs that are similar to optimism. Two of these concepts are hope and self-efficacy. People with high self-efficacy expectancies their personal efforts determine the outcome of events. Whereas self-efficacy looks at self as a causal agent, optimism takes a broader view of the potential causes at work. Hope reflects the will and the ways. The hope is similar to optimism however there is more emphasis on personal agency. Pessimism has been found to resemble the construct of neuroticism. Neuroticism involves a tendency to worry, and experience unpleasant emotions. Therefore, it can be said that a sense of pessimism is a part of neuroticism. Optimism and pessimism relate to people's expectations for the future. Due to this they are linked to the expectancy-value theories of motivation. During challenge, optimists are more confident whereas pessimists remain doubtful. It has been observed that person with optimistic approach will always find opportunities than an individual with pessimistic approach.

Types of Optimism

There are two types of optimists: (1) Realistic and (2) Unrealistic. A realistic optimist is defined as someone that has a good grip on reality, and an unrealistic optimist as someone that engages in self-delusion.

Realistic optimism: "Realistic optimism allows us to experience the best until we have to deal with the worst which often never comes". It refers "tendency to maintain a positive outlook within the constraints of the available measurable phenomena situated in the physical and social world". It describes a relation between accessible and reasonable information, apprehension and acquaintance of any given situation, probable possibilities & selected reflection. Realism is coined from "Real" which means things you observe in "everyday life". Realists likely to believe that whatever we believe now is just an estimation of reality and that each new examination brings people nearer to knowledge reality. In its Kantian sense, realism is differentiated with idealism

Walt Disney: I always like to look on the optimistic side of life, but I am realistic enough to know that life is a complex matter"

Seligman (1998) and (Schneider, 2001) have also highlighted the importance of realistic optimism, which does not take an extreme in internalizing good events and externalizing negative ones.

Schneider (2001) has outlined three forms of "realistic optimism". These are: (1) Leniency for the past, or the benefit of the doubt principle, (2) Appreciation for the present, or the "appreciate the moment" principle and (3) Opportunity-seeking for the future, or the windows of opportunity principle (an assignment or project is viewed as a challenge.

Theories of Optimism

Human beings are ambitious and goal-oriented creatures. Many, for example, aim at stable and fulfilling careers, good health, and happy families. Some also pursue broader aims, such as social justice, technological progress, or scientific discovery. But with such ambition comes adversity. When our central aims come under threat, as they inevitably do, we often find ourselves pessimistic or fearful. The concepts of optimism and pessimism concern people's expectations for the future. These concepts have ties to a class of psychological theories of motivation, called expectancy-value theories. Such theories suggest a logical basis for some of the ways in which optimism and pessimism influence people's behavior and emotions.

Expectancy-value models: It begins with the idea that behavior is aimed at attaining desired goals. Goals are actions or values when people feel goals are either desirable or undesirable. People try to fit their behavior when they see goals are desirable. They try to stay away from undesirable goal. The other core concept is expectancies which is a sense of confidence or doubt about attaining the goal. If a person lacks confidence, again there is no action. Only if they have enough confidence do people engage or remain engaged in goal-directed effort. These ideas apply to specific values to optimism and pessimism. These principles of Expectancy-value models give many predictions about optimists and pessimists. When confronting a challenge, optimists should be confident and persistent should be more doubtful and hesitant. Optimists believe it can be handled successfully, pessimists expect disaster. This can lead to differences in such domains as actions relating to health risks, taking precautions in risky circumstances, and persistence in trying to overcome health threats. The balance among such feelings differs between optimists and pessimists because optimists expect good outcomes, they are likely to experience a more positive mix of feelings but pessimists expect bad outcomes, they should experience more negative feelings like anxiety, sadness, and despair.

Unrealistic Optimism:

Unrealistic optimism is a positive difference involving the risks or dangers estimates and the danger estimate by way of an appropriate goal standard. It also includes comparing oneself to others in an unduly favorable manner. Many people tend to be unrealistic optimistic by maximize their chance for positive outcomes while reducing their risk for negative outcomes. Unrealistic optimism is also known as comparative optimism, illusion of invulnerability, and illusion of unique invulnerability, optimistic bias and personal fable. Unrealistic Optimism has been shown across a wide selection of good and bad events, with many health issues such as for example lung cancer, HIV infection and alcoholism. Unrealistic optimism may temporarily serve a protective function, when the threat is terrifying or unsolvable, but such defense mechanism becomes problematic when it prevents one from facing the reality and making the necessary adjustments. Unrealistic optimism is only a cognitive bias, which creates an individual's thinking that they're not vulnerable to knowledge and encountering an adverse event in comparison to others.

Definitions of Unrealistic Optimism

Freud (1928) viewed "unrealistic positive thinking (unrealistic optimism) as a defense mechanism against harsh reality or an illusionary religious belief, which only served to prolong human misery".

Cramer (1991) reported that "defense mechanisms, such as denial and fantasies and served as a protective mechanism, when people felt threatened and powerless, but unrealistic optimism might prove to be problematic in the long run. According to this trend of thoughts, the hallmark of mental health is being rooted in reality.

Types of Unrealistic optimism

Unrealistic optimism can be distinguished between two broad types. One is unrealistic absolute optimism and another is unrealistic comparative optimism. Both types can be expressed at either the individual level or the group level.

1. **Unrealistic absolute optimism**: It identifies to the incorrect belief that particular bad outcomes. Many outcomes (such as having a heart attack or dying from lung cancer) may not occur until the distant future and cannot be assessed within a reasonable time frame. Unrealistic absolute optimism is of 2 types in individual level; unrealistic absolute optimism does incurs whenever person's estimate of their personal risk is too low relative to some individual level standard. The individual level standard might be particular outcomes which really occur at a later date or personal risk as calculated form and

empirically validated of risk. It can assert that a person is displaying unrealistic absolute optimism of their prediction is longer compared to the prediction produced by most effective available "risk algorithm". Unrealistic absolute optimism occurs when "the average of the risk estimates given by a group of people is lower than a group level objective standard, such as the base rate for this event in this group. Indeed, the most widely used standard for such determinants is the base rate".

2. **Unrealistic Comparative Optimism**: - It is of two types.

   a. **In individuals type**, Unrealistic comparative optimism incurs while individual improperly judges now their risk analyzes with that of others as an example a person might declare that his risk is below that of the average man when an analytically validate individual risk evaluate algorithm indicated that his threat is more than average.

   b. In social level: "Unrealistic comparative optimism refers to situation in which people in a sample estimate that they are less likely on average to experience a negative outcome or more likely on average to experience a positive outcome than are their roars".

   It is proved that realistic or unrealistic optimism is not constant mean while it depends on individual's optimism which differs from situation to situation. To be able to realize the determinants of unrealistic optimism it's necessary to understand whether determinants are primarily motivational or cognitive.

Cognitive Mechanisms of Unrealistic Optimism

Unrealistic optimism can be classed into three cognitive mechanisms:

1. **Representativeness Heuristic**: -The probability of estimate related to the optimistic bias is derived from extent of strength of a situation matches an individual's over all concepts of particular events. The representativeness heuristic is just a reason for unrealistic optimism: - individual tend to believe in stereotypical groups as opposed to about their genuine

objectives when coming up with comparisons. People compare themselves with bad aspects that they think of, instead of precise evaluation among them and others.

2. **Singular Target Focus**: Drawback of the unrealistic optimism is that individuals have knowledge about himself as a single individual on the other hand they have generalized group perception about others, which leads to illusion estimates and in capabilities to develop understanding of others objectives or comparative groups, same situation occurs, while making judgments comparison about threats in comparison of, persons usually ignore the average, but primarily emphasis by themselves emotions and experiences.

3. **Interpersonal Distance**:- Higher the estimated range among the individual and target goal, greater the estimated difference in risk, When the individual have a object target nearer to the person, threats estimate looks closer together, rather than if the object goals to some extent comparison goal is at distance to the participant. There's estimated social distance support is a deciding factor of unrealistic optimism. Individuals show more unrealistic optimistic when coming up with evaluations when others a obscure individual, but biases are decreased when others is a known person such as friend or member of family.

Group of Unrealistic Optimism

Unrealistic optimism may be categorized into four different groups:

1. **Self-Enhancement:** - Self-enhancement implies that "optimistic predictions are gratifying and so it thinks good to believe that good events may happen. Persons may control their anxiety, nervousness and other bad feelings when they think they're greater off than others. They tend to concentrate on obtaining information that help what they would like to see occur as opposed to what'll occur to them. In terms of the unrealistic optimism, people may understand activities more positively because that what they'd like the results to be. It

can also be implies that individuals may decrease their dangers in comparison to the others to produce themselves look much better than average they're less at an increased risk than the others and therefore better."

2. **Self-Presentation**:-Individuals attempt to determine and keep a desired particular picture in social situations. Individuals are inspired to present themselves toward the others in a good light and some experts claim that the optimistic bias is just a representative of self-presentational process: persons want to look better off than others. But, this isn't through conscious effort. In a study wherever individuals thought their driving skills could be either tested in real-life or driving simulations.Pessimistic and more negative light are usually less acknowledged by the others of society. This may subscribe to excessively optimistic attitudes."

3. **Personal Control**: -"People are generally more unrealistic optimistic if they think they've more control over events than others. As an example individuals are more prone to believe that they may not be injured in a car accident if they're driving the car. The higher perceived control someone has, the higher their unrealistic optimism." The "relationship between unrealistic optimism and perceived control are moderators contribute to this relationship. Student also showed larger levels of the optimistic bias than non-students. Unrealistic optimism is strongest in situations where an individual needs to rely heavily on direct action and responsibility of situations.

4. **Self-versus target information**- Individuals have much more knowledge in comparison to the knowledge they have about others. It is because information about others is available randomly, collection of information about himself and others makes a person to identify findings about danger of others, ultimately causing larger, gaps in unrealistic optimism.

Optimism brings about positive outcomes in relationships by promoting favorable expectancies, which in turn cause individuals to pursue their relationship goals more flexibly. This core principle helps explain why other individual differences that correlate only modestly with optimism, such as a secure attachment style or low fear of negative evaluation.

Benefits of Optimism

Stephen Smagula has suggested following benefits of optimism:

1. **Optimism's Motivational Benefits**: Optimism appears to support goal achievement (motivation) like educational achievement, and one study found that optimistic students are less likely to drop out of college than their pessimistic peers. This indicates that optimists are better at pursuing what is an important monetary goal for their study. Optimistic people are better at avoiding inherent conflicts. It is found that optimistic students were better able to identify and pursue important goals, while their pessimistic peers found themselves pursuing important and unimportant goals in equal measure. Optimistic people do appear to face resource conflicts at a higher rate but despite often facing resource conflicts, optimistic people tend to be happier. This indicates that resource conflicts may be less distressing than inherent conflicts.

2. **Optimism's Benefits for Relationships:** Optimism comes with substantial social benefits. Optimism also appears to enhance existing relationships in predictable ways. For example, married couples who score higher in optimism are more likely to stay married. They also tend to work together better to solve problems than do more pessimistic couples. This is optimism's motivational benefits appear to intersect with its social benefits hence relationships high in optimism tend to be more stable and fulfilling.

3. **Optimism's Health Benefits: There is** potential benefits of optimism for physical health. Numerous studies indicate that when it comes to cardiovascular disease optimism is helpful. Optimists were more likely to know about the risk factors for a heart attack. This may be because optimism supports conscientiousness. Optimism predicts healthy *behaviors*. Optimism supports a range of healthy lifestyle

habits. For one, optimists tend to eat more fruits and vegetables and consume alcohol in moderation. Optimists are also less likely to smoke. Avoiding alcohol and increased physical activity were associated with higher rates of survival.

4. **Optimism's Emotional Benefits:** Optimistic people tend to experience greater emotional well-being. Maintaining optimism through difficult times can ward against the anxiety, sadness, and despair that pessimists often experience. Optimistic people tend to have a more positive emotional outlook in stressful situations.

Drawback of Optimism

Despite optimism's benefits, there are some potential drawbacks.

1. **The Drawback of Optimism:** A natural concern about optimism is that it is risky, leaving people open to crushing disappointment. The world is full of heartbreak and tragedy. By contrast, a person that is pessimistic, or at least less optimistic, may be more insulated from the emotional damage of failure and tragedy.

2. **The Drawback of Positive Illusions:** Positive illusions are intrinsically defective. Positive illusions can make it difficult for people to respond well to constructive feedback that runs counter to their optimism. Moreover, positive illusions do make us prone to disappointment. The dangers of positive illusions are especially significant in the context of education. Students with irrational beliefs about their abilities tend at first to experience greater emotional well-being. However, conflicts quickly arise between their perceived abilities and their academic results.

Hope

According to Snyder et al. (1991) hope is a human strength manifested in our perceived capacities to clearly conceptualize goals and develop strategies to reach those goals and initiate and sustain the motivation for using those strategies. Hope is positively associated with life satisfaction and serves as a buffer against the impact of negative and stressful life events. Low levels of hope, and feelings of hopelessness, is associated with, school problems, delinquency, violence, depression, substance abuse, and unsafe sexual behavior among adolescents Hope is *dynamic* cognitive *motivational system*. Hope leads to pursuit of *learning goals* and learning goals are positively related to success. Hope is something we can hold on to even when we've lost confidence. For example, a person may *hope* for justice even when they expect that it is not forthcoming and thus they aren't optimistic. We often call this "hoping against hope. " Hope has a negative correlation with depression, anxiety and is frequently applied for managing hopelessness. Hope is also identified as a mediator of resilience, well-being and in general population health, being hopeful contributes to reductions in mortality. The effects of hope on individual's behavior can have long-lasting aftermaths for well-being. Goal-directed thinking increases self-esteem and reduces emotions related to depression. People who have hope for the future and make plans for achieving future goals are less likely to participate in activities in the present that put them at risk of illness or death in the future. Moreover, Carver and Scheier (2001) concur that goals are central to life and provide structure and imbue life with meaning. However, distress results from continued commitment to an unattainable goal and emptiness results when commitment disappears. Positive psychologists focus on hope for its beneficial positive aspect of shaping human life. For example, high hope has been associated with greater wellbeing, coping, and the regulation of emotional distress. At the individual level, high hope individuals are more optimistic about the future and have a greater perceived purpose in life. High hope peoples are more likely to select more difficult goals and able to conceptualize their goals clearly. In addition to academic success, high hope levels are beneficial in the areas of health too. Seligman (1991) found that positive states of mind had associated with coping while depression, despair, and hopelessness have been linked to capitulation, illness, and even death.

Definitions of Hope

Dufault and Martocchio, (1985) defined hope as a multidimensional dynamic life force that is characterized by a confident yet uncertain expectation of achieving good, which is realistically possible and personally significant.

Lynch, (1974): Hope is a belief that the present situation can be modified and that there is a way out of difficult situations or the belief that better days or moments will come.

Rustoen, 1995): It is not completely clear whether hope is a result of successful coping or is a coping strategy.

Chi, 2007; Mclement&Chochinov, (2008): Hope is an important resource that influences an individual's ability to cope with stressful, life-threatening situations.

Importance of Hope

1. *Academic achievement:* Hope is significantly related to academic achievement. Hopeful students are more confident of finding various pathways to reach desired goals, and the motivations to pursue those goals. Hence, low-hope students can benefit by interventions to raise their hopeful thinking. High-hope students are more optimistic, and perceive themselves as being capable of solving problems. Hope is' related to positively with self-worth, life satisfaction and wellbeing.

2. *Health:* Hope predicts physical and mental health, subjective wellbeing, effective coping and healthy behaviors. People with higher levels of hope engage in more preventative behaviors like healthy diet and physical exercise. Higher hope is also related to benefits in dealing with injuries and disabilities.

3. *Athletics:* Higher hope has been positively related to superior athletic performances. Sports psychologists and coaches can use hope theory to enhance the performance of athletes.

4. *Psychological Adjustment:* Hope is related positively with positive affect and thoughts and negatively with negative affect

and thoughts. High-hope individuals also are less likely to use avoidance coping style. When people with high hope face an obstacle in reaching a goal, they try to find alternative goals. Higher levels of hope are related to more perceived social support, and more social competence.

5. *Psychotherapy:* Hope theory provides a framework for understanding the shared processes for helping people in psychotherapy. Hope before and after they had received psychological treatment in a residential setting. It was found that significantly higher levels of hope were developed during that period. Hope theory has been used to develop successful individual and group interventions especially in depression.

Types of Hope

There are different four types of hope as under:

1. **Realistic Hope:** Realistic hope is hope for an outcome that is reasonable or probable. For example, an individual suffering from chronic pain might hope for a small reduction in pain, knowing that complete eradication is unrealistic.

2. **Utopian Hope:** The utopian hoper critically negates the present and is driven by hope to affirm a better alternative. Hoping is a collectively oriented hope that collaborative action can lead to a better future for all.

3. **Chosen Hope:** Chosen hope is critical to the management of despair and its accompanying paralysis of action. Hope not only helps us to live with a difficult situation but also with an uncertain future. In addition to physical suffering, a diagnosis of a serious or terminal illness is a major contributor to distress.

4. **Transcendent Hope:** Transcendent hope describes a stance of general hopefulness not tied to a specific outcome or goal; put simply, it is the hope that something good can happen. Transcendent hope encompasses three types of hope, namely:

   1. Patient Hope – a hope that everything will work out well in the end.

2. Generalized Hope – hope not directed toward a specific outcome.

3. Universal Hope – a general belief in the future and a defense against despair in the face of challenges.

Benefits of Hope

1. Hope is significantly correlated with superior academic and athletic performance, greater physical and psychological well-being, improved self-esteem, and enhanced interpersonal relationships.

2. Hope has the potential to enhance wellbeing over time. It is found that individuals who are more hopeful and expect to be successful in achieving goals are more likely to experience a state of wellbeing.

3. Individuals with high hope are more likely to view stressful situations as challenging rather than threatening, thereby reducing the intensity and hindering the stress.

4. Hope can be perceived as a protective factor against the development of chronic anxiety.

5. Hope is a motivational factor that helps initiate and sustain action toward long-term goals, including the flexible management of obstacles that get in the way of goal attainment.

6. Hope is positively related to overall life satisfaction.

7. Hope motivates individuals to maintain their positive involvement in life regardless of any limitations imposed upon them.

Theory of Hope

Hope is a construct which closely relates to optimism, although the two are not identical. Hope represents the ability to conceptualize goals, find pathways to these goals despite obstacles and have the motivation to use those pathways. Hope helps us remain committed to our goals and motivated to take action towards achieving. Hope gives people a reason to continue fighting and believing that their current circumstances will improve, despite the unpredictable nature of human existence. Snyder (2000) suggests that hope develops over the course of infancy, childhood and adolescence. Snyder proposes that there are no hereditary contributions to hope and it is a learned cognitive set. The basic cause and effect thinking contained in pathways thinking is acquired from parents and others. Snyder also proposes that strong attachment to caregivers is crucial for the development of hope.

According to Snyder hopefulness is a life-sustaining human strength comprised of three distinct but related components:

1. Goals Thinking – the clear conceptualization of valuable goals.

2. Pathways Thinking – the capacity to develop specific strategies to reach those goals.

3. Agency Thinking – the ability to initiate and sustain the motivation for using those strategies.

Snyder Hope theory cognitions that hope are built on goal-directed thought. Hope as goal-directed thinking in which the person utilizes pathways thinking; the capacity to find routes to desired goals and agency thinking; the requisite motivations to use those routes. Only those goals with considerable value to the individual are considered applicable to hope. Also, the goals can vary temporally-from those that will be reached in the next few minutes (short-term) to those that will take months or even years to reach (long-term).

Hope theory has the following major components: goals, pathway thoughts, agency thoughts and barriers.

1. *Goals:* Goals are the targets of mental action sequences and are the cognitive component in hope theory. Goals provide direction for hopeful thinking. All purposeful human behaviour is goal-driven. The goals of people are central to their lives, and their sense of wellbeing. Hope is not relevant in the case of trivial or minor goals, such as the goal to brush one's teeth in the morning. Nor is it relevant when the goal is impossible to attain. In short, hope theory "is concerned with goals that

are at least of moderate importance and intermediate in their probability of attainment. High hope approaches their goals with positive emotions with a chance of success and a sense of challenge, while low hope approaches their goals with negative emotions a change of failure. High hope persons are more likely to set realistic, well-defined goals while low hope persons are more likely to set goals that are too large or too difficult to attain.

2. *Pathways Thinking:* Pathway thoughts refer to the routes we take to achieve our goals and the perceived ability to produce these routes. A person's sense of hope is determined in part by their perception of the available routes by which they might reach a given goal. When a person perceives that there are few such routes, or when the available routes are ineffective or become obstructed, then their hope is diminished. Pathways refer to the process by which a person generates pathways by which they could achieve their goals. In other words, those higher in pathways thinking are better able to perceive or construct effective routes to their goals. They can also think of a greater number of workable routes, and are more able to generate alternative routes when the original ones become unexpectedly obstructed.

3. *Agency Thinking:* This is the motivational component in hope theory. Agency thinking reflects the self-referential thoughts regarding moving along a pathway as well as continuing to progress along that pathway. In order to reach a goal, a person must not only have access to workable pathways leading to the goal; they must also believe in their own capacity to actually follow these pathways. They must possess a sense of agency sufficient to motivate them along the path to goal attainment; they must perceive themselves to be effective, capable agents. Agency thinking refers to the self-referential beliefs and thoughts held by a person regarding their own ability to pursue their goals. Those higher in agentic thinking make more positive appraisals of their own abilities, and are more motivated to attain the goals.

4. ***Barriers:*** Barriers block the attainment of our goals. The individual then has to make a choice to either give up or use pathway thoughts to create new routes. We have all been plagued by negative thinking. Some people feel the goal is not achievable and not going to be able to achieve your dreams, this is barrier of goal. Some of the most common obstacles include: Low motivation, Laziness, Forgetfulness, Fear of change, Feeling overwhelmed or intimidated, Not believing in your potential, Fear of failure, and Fear of success.

Hope Therapy

Hope therapy is derived from Snyder's hope theory and ideas drawn from cognitive-behavior therapy and narrative therapy. It aims to help the people to formulate clear goals and produce various pathways to attain these goals. It also aims to enable people to motivate themselves to pursue their goals and consider obstacles as challenges. Hope therapy helps individuals or groups to develop optimism and hope-driven problem-solving strategies.

Enhancement of Hope

Hope can be enhanced as under:

1. **Growth mindset**: It is developing flexible and positive attitudes about handling adverse situations. As we know that the brain structures are flexible and adaptive. While struggling to master an adverse situation, the brain also develops as muscles accordingly. The brain is ready to develop neuron connections with one another and strengthen neural networking. Thus, creating a growth mindset will make the individual more hopeful.

2. **Optimistic Self-Talk**: Optimistic self-talk is more about seeing the problem as temporary, identifying the specific cause of the problem, and motivating oneself to overcome it. Intrinsic motivation favours this method. During some severe issues, intrinsic motivation might fail, and slowly the person might drift towards pessimism. During those negative times, gaining help from others to improve goal-oriented behaviours is

essential. The individual can gain professional support. To master optimistic self-talk, resilience training and cognitive behavioral therapy is highly recommendable for enhancement of hope..

Wisdom

Humanity faces a number of challenges, including the need for sustainable development, the unequal distribution of wealth, ethnic conflict and the lack of ethically informed planning. Modern popular culture also suffers from a variety of negative trends which are frequently reflected and reinforced in the world of education. These trends include the increasing speed and frenzy of life. Wisdom is refer to the ability of an individual to make sound decisions, to find the right or at least good answers to difficult and important life questions, and to give advice about the complex problems of everyday life and interpersonal relationships. The role of knowledge and life experience and the importance of applying knowledge toward a common good through balancing one's own, others', and institutional interests are two perspectives that have received significant psychological study. Wisdom refers to the ability to take life in broad terms. It is the coordination of information about different aspects of life to improve well-being. It also allows one to listen to others, to evaluate what they say, and offer good advice. Wisdom involves exceptional personal and interpersonal competence like listening, giving advice and is used for the well-being of self and others.

Definitions of Wisdom

Sternberg (2019a) groups various definitions of wisdom into four types: (a) a personal psychological excellence, (b) a property of the situation, (c) an interaction between person and situation, and (d) a property of action.

Grossmann (2017a), wisdom is a property characteristic of individuals in situations rather than a personal excellence—whether or not a person is wise depends on the situation, and there is no general wisdom factor.

Properties of Wisdom

Baltes has identified seven properties of wisdom:

1. Superior level of knowledge, judgment, and advice
2. Addresses important questions and strategies about the meaning of life
3. Includes knowledge about the limits of knowledge and uncertainties
4. Constitutes knowledge with extraordinary scope, depth, measure, and balance
5. Involves a perfect synergy of mind and character, and of knowledge and virtues
6. Represents knowledge used for the well-being of oneself and of others
7. Easily recognized when manifested.

Meeks and Jeste (2009) identified six sub-components of wisdom:

1. Pro-social attitudes/behaviors: promotion of common good, empathy, social cooperation, and altruism
2. Social decision making/pragmatic knowledge of life: understanding others' emotions and motivations and using the information to make "wise" social decisions
3. Emotional homeostasis: self-control and impulse control; ability to manage oneself in challenging situations
4. Reflection/self-understanding: Self-knowledge
5. Value relativism/tolerance: perspective-taking behavior
6. Acknowledgment of and dealing effectively with uncertainty/ ambiguity: navigating uncertainty and acknowledging/accepting the limits of what one knows.

Theories of Wisdom

Sternberg, (2000): Sternberg suggested implicit and explicit theories of wisdom. According to Implicit theoretical approaches the wisdom discuss the folk conceptions regarding the nature of wisdom whereas, in theory of explicit, wisdom have theoretical approaches in which behavior is relatively rare.

1. **Implicit Theories:** Implicit theories refer to the beliefs or mental representations of people regarding wisdom as well as the characteristics of wise people. In studies on implicit beliefs about wisdom, one finds quite a high degree of overlap in the core aspects of wisdom. The conceptions include cognitive, social- emotional, motivational components. The cognitive components usually include strong intellectual abilities, rich knowledge and experience in matters of the human condition, and an ability to apply one's theoretical knowledge practically. A second basic component refers to reflective judgment that is based on knowledge about the world and the self, openness for new experiences, and the ability to learn from mistakes. Socioemotional components generally include good social skills, such as sensitivity and concern for others and the ability to give good advice. The motivational component refers to the good intentions which are associated with wisdom. That is, wisdom aims at solutions that optimize the benefit of others and oneself.

2. **Explicit Theories:** The second cluster of wisdom theories represents explicit psychological theories. These theories of wisdom focus on cognitive and behavioral expressions of wisdom and the processes involved in the interplay of cognition and behavior. One main objective of such theories is to develop theoretical models of wisdom that allow for empirical inquiry by means of quantitative of wisdom-related thought and behavior as well as for the derivation of hypotheses that can be tested empirically. Work on explicit psychological conceptions of wisdom can be divided roughly into three groups:

   • Wisdom as a personal characteristic or a personality disposition.

   • Conceptualization of wisdom in the neo-Piagetian tradition of post formal and dialectical thinking.

- Conceptualization of wisdom as an expert system

According to Explicit theories of wisdom is

1. **A stage of personality development:** According to Erik Erikson wisdom is considered to be the final stage of personality development within the context of his lifecycle model of personality. In the later adulthood, they are likely to face some sort of crisis and if the crisis is resolved in favour of integrity it leads to wisdom. People are more likely to develop wisdom if they have developed virtues of hope, will, purpose, competence, love and care in resolving psychosocial dilemmas at earlier stages of the lifecycle.

2. **A stage of cognitive development**: Riegel has suggested that in late state of adolescence, they enter the stage of dialectical and during this period they solve complex human problems by dialectical thinking.

3. **A high level of skill development / as expert knowledge**: Wisdom involves both personality and cognitive processes. It can be defined that wisdom relates mind and virtue as an expert knowledge system. This includes knowledge and judgments about the meaning of life and how to pursue excellence, and well-being of oneself and others.

4. **A Scientific Discourse about the Good Life**: Wisdom has been studied in philosophy and religion for thousands of years and now one can say that wisdom is becoming a center of trans-disciplinary discourse. Baltes and Staudinger have developed five criteria to evaluate the quality of a wise judgment or behavior:

   - Wisdom entails a rich store of declarative knowledge, i.e. knowing facts about development, and the contextual nature of the human condition.

   - Wisdom involves a rich store of procedural knowledge, i.e knowledge about how to perform certain skills and routines.

   - Wisdom involves an appreciation of the many themes and contexts of life such as the self, family, peer group etc.

- Wisdom entails a relativism of values and life priorities, tolerance for differences in values held by individuals and society in the service of the common good.

- Wisdom entails a recognition and management of uncertainty and a tolerance for ambiguity.

Sternberg's Balance Theory of Wisdom: The balance theory defines wisdom as the use of one's intelligence, creativity, common sense, and knowledge and as mediated by positive ethical values toward the achievement of a common good. He defines wisdom as "using one's intelligence, creativity, common sense, and knowledge" to balance three life domains. They are interpersonal, intra-personal, and extra-personal interests. People do this over the short and long-term. The goal is to achieve balance among:

- adaptation to current environments,
- shaping of those environments, and
- choosing a new environment

Components of Wisdom

There is some common components of wisdom. Wisdom is multidimensional and holistic. While any one of these components might be considered an essential element of wisdom, none are sufficient on their own The components of wisdom are discussed as under.

Knowledge

Knowledge is considered as a component of wisdom as per the theories of wisdom either old or new. But opinions vary on the exact *type* of knowledge someone possess to be considered wise.

But merely having extensive factual knowledge is not enough to be considered wise. There are many highly knowledgeable people who would not be considered wise. Wise people able to identify the important things for them, and they are able to transfer their knowledge to make their live well, cope with problems, and avoid life's more serious pitfalls. There is a strong connection between knowledge and truth in the lives of wise people. Their knowledge tends to be accurate, and their beliefs are justified and rational.

It may also be said that wisdom reflects a person's rationality more accurately than it does their knowledge, but good judgment often relies on a significant storehouse of theoretical and practical knowledge.

Experience

Generally, wisdom is associated with age, but we must have come across to some old fools also. We may really associate wisdom with experience, which tends to accrue naturally with age, but this may lead us to blur the distinction between age and experience..

When we say that someone is "wise beyond their years," we imply that they have accumulated – and learned something from – experience that would usually take much longer to obtain.

Sometimes we find some young sages and old fools. It appears that the *type* of experience gained is more important than the amount of experience as with the knowledge.

Everyone accumulates experience, yet many remain unenlightened. Wisdom tends to come from experiences that are difficult, morally challenging, and require the application of knowledge and insight

It is thought that wisdom is a positive outcome of aging, because our experiences over time enable us to develop a broader, deeper, and richer understanding of our world. We all experience disappointment, frustration, loss, stress, and sometimes even trauma. Yet, some people acquire wisdom while some don't.

It is worthy how we cope with them, what we learn from them, and how we are changed by the experiences and not likely to challenge the experiences themselves.

Reflection

Why do some people learn and grow more than others, even from very similar experiences?

The answer is reflection.

While some people simply roll along with the tide of life, others deeply contemplate the context, implications, and meaning of any given action or experience.

When we reflect on our experiences, we assimilate new approaches, concepts, knowledge, skills, and values into our existing knowledge structures. This assimilation leads to cognitive, emotional, moral, personal, and psychological growth.

Confucius said that reflection is the noblest method by which we acquire wisdom. He believed that while we can acquire knowledge by passively learning and memorizing information, we develop wisdom by actively contemplating and reflecting on this new knowledge.

Many modern wisdom theories acknowledge the reflective component of wisdom. We are transformed not by our experiences, but by reflecting on them.

Some people are probably more naturally reflective than others, but there are techniques we can use to train ourselves to be better reflective thinkers.

In the 1980s, Graham Gibbs developed a "structured debriefing" framework that can be used to support experiential learning and reflective thinking. The Gibbs debriefing process can be used as part of a continuous improvement cycle for repeated experiences, or it can be used to reflect on a single experience.

Progressing through the following steps can help you think reflectively about an experience: [11]

- Description. Describe the details of the experience, such as what happened, when it happened, who was involved, what actions were taken, and what the outcome was. Don't pass judgment or draw conclusions yet.

- Feelings. How did you react at the time? How were you feeling? What were you thinking? How do you think others were feeling? What might they have been thinking? Just record these thoughts and feelings. Don't analyze them yet.

- Evaluation. What was good about the experience? What was bad? What went well? What didn't? Did your actions positively or negatively influence the experience? What about other people's actions? You can make value judgments here.

- Analysis. Sort things out and try to make sense of the outcome. Why did things go well or poorly? Could you have responded differently? Could others have? What could have been done to achieve a better outcome? Did different participants have a different view of the outcome?

- Conclusions. What have you learned? Did you acquire any new skills? Can you transfer what you learned from this experience to future circumstances? Do you see what you could have done differently?

- Action plan. Will you do things differently in the future? What steps can you take now to build on what you learned from this experience? Do you see opportunities to apply what you learned in other places or other ways?

The Gibbs process could be done formally or informally. You could engage in reflective writing, or you could just mentally walk yourself through the steps.

Introspection

Introspection is also a reflective component of wisdom. Introspection may be considered self-reflection. We use reflection to consider, contemplate, and understand the intricacies of an experience. We use introspection to thoroughly examine our own mental and emotional processes as they relate to the experience.

The mental process can be similar. The Gibbs framework, for example, encompasses both reflection and introspection.

Self-reflection builds self-awareness. It's difficult to develop wisdom if we don't even understand our own motives and desires.

Introspection allows us to transcend our own subjectivity and projections, making us less self-centered. This gives us deeper insight into our own and others' motives and behavior, and enables us to interact with others more compassionately and constructively.

Objectivity

Wise people are able to evaluate information and circumstances without letting their own biases, emotions, or interpretations distort reality and cloud the truth.

Without objectivity, it is very difficult to exercise sound judgment. So, objectivity is integral to the kind of good judgment that many think of as a hallmark of the wise.

Unfortunately, we are all vulnerable to cognitive biases that can negatively impact our thinking and decision making. Wise people are aware of these biases, and take steps to challenge them and mitigate their effects.

Prudence

Exercising prudence means governing ourselves using reason, demonstrating sagacity when managing our lives, and showing good judgment. It is prudence that allows wise people to choose the appropriate course of action in the given circumstance.

Prudence is not merely an intellectual virtue, however. It is connected to action.

According to Thomas Aquinas, prudence involves three primary elements:

- Good counsel. We should take counsel from ourselves and others. This involves inquiry, deliberation, and discovery. We must establish the reality of the situation, and we must acknowledge and challenge our own biases.

- Good judgment. Here we consider the facts and the evidence, separate the pertinent from the extraneous, and make an informed and reasoned decision.

- Good command. This is where we apply our judgment and take positive action. We have not really exercised prudence if we fail to do what we have determined to be the right thing to do.

Prudence allows us to restrain our emotions and passions enough to exercise good judgment and act wisely.

Equanimity

Equanimity is a state of mental calmness and emotional equilibrium. Equanimous people are able to maintain their balance and composure, even in challenging situations.

In the scientific literature, equanimity may be referred to as emotional homeostasis, emotional regulation, affect control, or impulse control.

Constructively managing our emotions is essential to good judgment and effective problem resolution. Wise people tend to be attuned to the full range of their emotions, and are aware of the ways that their emotions can influence their thinking.

Wise people are also open to both positive and negative emotions, and can distinguish among subtle and mixed emotions.

Equanimity allows wise people to reframe negative emotional experiences, resolve internal conflicts, and channel negative emotions into positive thought and action.

Humility

Understanding and appreciating the limits of our own knowledge is an essential component of wisdom. Basing our beliefs and actions on things we claim to know – but really don't – leads to foolish and even dangerous behaviors. Wise people are well aware of the limits of their knowledge. Actually doorsteps to the wisdom is a knowledge of our own ignorance.

Examples of epistemic arrogance abound during a pandemic.

COVID-19 has resulted in far too many pundits and policy makers – with little to no training or expertise in epidemiology, immunology, or public health – insisting that they somehow know the best course of action. They don't, and many people have died unnecessarily due to harmful misinformation disseminated by arrogant and overconfident leaders and influencers.

We aren't always aware of exactly *what* we don't know. But wise people are at least aware that there are things *that* they don't know – or at least that they don't know *yet*.

We can't always avoid the need to make decisions with incomplete or imperfect information, but we can think and act with respect for the limits of our knowledge.

Empathy

Wisdom requires empathy, that is, a genuine understanding of other people and their emotions. Maybe someone can have empathy and still lack compassion.

Broadly, there are two dimensions of empathy:

- Cognitive empathy is our ability to understand the other person's perspective.
- Emotional empathy is our capacity to respond to the other person's state with an appropriate emotional reaction.

Wise people are usually skilled at interpersonal relations, chiefly due to their ability to understand how other people might be thinking and feeling in any given situation.

It is possible to understand how another person feels without responding appropriately. Hopefully, though, most wise people have grown to transcend mere cognitive empathy and can demonstrate genuine compassion.

Receptivity

Receptivity refers to our tendency to be open and responsive to new ideas, information, perspectives, and experiences.

Receptive people embrace novelty and opportunity, are intellectually curious, and demonstrate high levels of awareness and creativity. They also tend to make many valuable personal and **Professional Connections**.

Wise people are always exploring possibilities. They are open to different views and opinions, and to novel approaches to solving problems and overcoming obstacles.

Receptivity is strongly related to openness to experience, one of the traits described by the five-factor model of human personality.

There are several techniques can be used to cultivate

respectability, including challenging our biases, relaxing our boundaries, suspending judgment, abandoning expectations, asking open-ended questions, and becoming an active listener.

Adaptability

Wise people are able to adjust to changing conditions and environments. They acknowledge, accept, and skillfully manage ambiguity and uncertainty.

According to Sternberg's balance theory, wisdom often involves striking a balance between adapting to existing environments, shaping existing environments, and selecting new environments. When adaptation is the best course of action, wise people are adept at finding ways to conform to their existing environment.

Wise people not only acknowledge ambiguity and uncertainty, they maintain an ability to make important decisions despite the unpredictability of life.

We can manage change by adapting ourselves to the situation, or by adapting the situation to better suit us.

Wise people don't resist change when it frustrates their progress. They expect it, and they have contingencies for the obstacles, problems, disappointment, and stress that change is likely to bring.

Wisdom is Multidimensional and Integrative

It is generally accepted that wisdom is not a discrete state or trait, but rather an integration of various characteristics.

So, while most agree that wisdom has components, there is no widely accepted set of specific components that makes someone wise.

How, when, or where wisdom is applied likely determines what particular cognitive, reflective, or affective attributes someone applies to make a "wise choice."

Some people naturally become wiser than others, but we all

have the capacity for personal development and growth. Identifying and isolating some of wisdom's individual components at least gives us a foundation for building a wiser future.

There are some sub-components of wisdom also as narrated below :

The 6 Sub-Components of Wisdom:

(1) Pro-social attitudes/behaviors: Working towards a common good

(2) Social decision making pragmatic knowledge of life: Practical knowledge, judgment, life skills etc.

(3) Emotional homeostasis: Managing one's emotions amidst challenging circumstances

(4) Reflection/self-understanding: Self-knowledge

(5) Value relativism/tolerance: Able to adopt multiple perspectives

(6) Acknowledgment of and dealing effectively with uncertainty/ambiguity: Effectively navigating uncertainty and the limits of knowledge.

Creativity

Creativity can be defined as the ability to bring something original and valuable into the world. It can occur in almost any field like art, music, mathematics, engineering, science, business, education. Anywhere there are problems to be solved creativity can be found. Creativity involves the ability to develop new ideas or utilize objects or information in novel ways. It can involve large-scale ideas that have the potential to change the world, such as inventing tools that impact how people live, or smaller acts of creation such as figuring out a new way to accomplish a task in your daily life. Creativity is the tendency to solve problems or create new things in novel ways. It is the ability to create products that are original and adaptive. Creativity is a mental and social process involving the generation of new ideas or concepts.

Components of Creativity

1. **Originality:** The idea should be something new that is not simply an extension of something else that already exists.
2. **Functionality:** The idea needs to actually work or possess some degree of usefulness.

Types of Creativity

There are four different types of creativity as under:

1. **"Mini-c" creativity** involves meaningful ideas and insights that are known only to the self.
2. **"Little-c" creativity** involves mostly everyday thinking and problem-solving. This type of creativity helps people solve everyday problems they face and adapt to changing environments.
3. **"Pro-C" creativity** takes place among professionals who are skilled and creative in their respective fields. These individuals are creative in their vocation or profession but do not achieve eminence for their works.
4. **"Big-C" creativity** involves creating works and ideas that are considered great in a particular field. This type of creativity leads to eminence and often leads to world-changing creations such as medical innovations, technological advances, and artistic achievements.

Traits of Creativity

- **Energy:** Creative people tend to possess a great deal of both physical and mental energy. However, they also tend to spend a great deal of time quietly thinking and reflecting.
- **Intelligence:** Psychologists have long believed that intelligence plays a critical role in creativity. In Terman's famous longitudinal study of gifted children, found that while high IQ was necessary for great creativity, not all people with high IQs are creative.

- **Discipline:** Creative people do not just sit around waiting for inspiration to strike. They are playful, yet they are also disciplined in the pursuit of their work and passions.

How to Increase Creativity

Some strategies that can be helpful for improving creativity asunder:

- **Being open to new ideas**: Openness to experience is the personality trait that is most closely correlated with creativity. Focus on being willing to try new things and explore new ideas.

- **Be persistent**: Creativity is not just about sitting around waiting for inspiration to strike. Creative people spend time working to produce new things. Their efforts don't always work out, but continued practice builds skills that contribute to creativity.

- **Make time for creativity**: In addition to being persistent, you also need to devote time specifically toward creative efforts. This might mean setting aside a little time each day or each week specifically to brainstorm, practice, learn, or create.

Characteristics of the Creative Personality:

Creativity has been associated with a wide range of behavioral and mental characteristics; some of these are given below:

1. Creative individuals have a great deal of energy.

2. Creative individuals tend to be smart.

3. Creative individuals have a combination of playfulness and discipline.

4. Creative individuals alternate between imagination and fantasy.

5. Creative people seem to harbor opposite tendencies on the continuum between extroversion and introversion.

6. Creative individuals are also remarkable humble and proud at the same time.

7. Creative individuals to a certain extent escape rigid gender role stereotyping.

8. Generally, creative people are thought to be rebellious and independent.

9. Most creative persons are very passionate about their work

10. The openness and sensitivity of creative individuals often exposes them to suffering pain.

Courage

Psychological courage is the strength to confront and work through the problems. Such courage involves facing our deep-seated fear of psychological instability. Courage is a desirable universal value across cultures and nations. Courage needs fearlessness, awareness and active coping. Courage is usually inculcated through inspirational messages and stories. It is a value that provides an individual with great respect and admiration. Woodard and Pury found individual differences in courage based on a combination of the context and the goal of action. There are four contexts which include: work courage, belief-based courage, social courage, and family courage. The virtue of courage exhibits different forms in human life.

Definitions of Courage

Shelp (1984) defined it as, "courage is the disposition to voluntarily act, perhaps fearfully, in dangerous circumstances, where the relevant risks are reasonably appraised, in an effort to obtain or preserve some perceived good for one self others recognizing that the desired perceived good may not be realized"

Houser, (2002) which sees courage as (1) magnificence, the planning and execution of great and expansive projects by putting forth ample and splendid effort of mind; (2) confidence, that through which , on great and honourable projects, the mind self-confidently collects itself with sure hope; (3) patience, the voluntary and lengthy endurance of arduous and difficult things, whether the case be honourable or useful, and (4) perseverance, ongoing persistence in a well-considered plan. **Woodard (2004)** defined courage as "the ability to act for a meaningful (noble, good or practical) cause, despite experiencing the fear associated with perceived threat exceeding the available resources."

Snyder (2005): Courage is defined as "responding to extraordinary times with behaviours that seem natural and called for in those circumstances. It is only later, when removedfrom courage- eliciting events, that the protagonist and others view the behaviours as particularly worthy of the label courageous. This view of courage obviously gives greater weight to situational than to personal factors and suggests that most people are capable of courage iffaced with the appropriate circumstances."

Types of Courage

Types of courage can be broadly differentiated in terms of the fear which must be faced and the goal to be attained. Lopez and Peterson (2000) elaborated three types of courage as physical, moral and vital.

1. **Physical Courage:** Physical courage is characterized by overcoming a fear of death or physical harm. The goals to be achieved by its exercise are traditionally defined by society or by the requirements of survival. Example would be bravely defending self and family against a threat from nature such as a flood or dangerous carnivore.Physical Courage usually involves taking risk taking. It allows us to risk discomfort, injury and pain. An example would be the courage that a fire-fighter has or the courage to take on with your enemy.

2. **Moral courage:** In moral courage the major fear is loss of ethical integrity or authenticity. Moral courage is the expression of standing up for moral good against all odds. It involves doing the right thing even if it involves high amount of inconvenience or discomfort. Choosing between alternatives and making good decisions that are moral courage. Examples of some people who showed immense moral courage and chose to do things in the right way are Mahatma Gandhi, Mother Teresa and Martin Luther King. Moral courage involves actions towards preservation of common good. Moral courage also can be shown when we act with sensitivities

towards people that are underprivileged economically, socially or physically.

3. **Vital courage**: Vital courage was coined by Finagled. It is the capacity to be able to withstand and be resilient in the face of physical illnesses. Vital courage is only shown when one is faced with disabilities and diseases, especially chronic diseases that are there to stay. How an individual fights and takes these debilitating conditions as a part of life and learn to be optimistic represents vital courage. Vital courage is also shown by family, friends and hospital care providers like nurses and doctors who are treating patients with illnesses.

Character Strengths and Virtues

Psychology is not just the study of weakness and damage; it is also the study of strength and virtue. Virtues can be defined as, the form of excellence that allows an individual to pursue worthwhile ends in everyday activities and the pursuit of what is good. Virtues are personal strengths of people which provide momentum of adjustment and meaning in their relationship. These two things make a relationship pleasurable and enjoyable in life.

Character strengths are a family of positive traits expressed through a person's thoughts, feelings, and behaviors that are recognized for the strength that they create in individuals and communities. Unlike our height, weight, or skin color, character strengths aren't something that can't be seen with the naked eye. This is the ability which will enhance self-awareness, self-confidence, understanding and interpersonal relationships which will positively influence every individually across their lifespan. Character is the intersection of our thoughts, our feelings, and our behaviors. Character is not fixed; it can be grown. Some people think their abilities are fixed and that any failure is a confirmation of their limits while other people believe that they can grow their abilities and that failure is just a stepping stone to improvement.

Values are beliefs held by individuals and shared by groups about desirable ends. They guide how we select actions and evaluate others and ourselves. Virtues are core aspects of human excellence that allow us to survive and thrive. There are six core virtues which every person should possess for a healthy and thriving life. These attributes have to be cultivated if one wants to live meaningfully life. They are:

1. **Wisdom and knowledge**: Wisdom and knowledge consists of **cognitive strengths** that entail the acquisition and use of knowledge. Strengths of wisdom and knowledge are cognitive strengths related to the acquisition and use of information. Strengths comprised in this virtue are creativity, curiosity, open-mindedness, love of learning, and perspective.

2. **Humanity:** Humanity includes **interpersonal strengths** that involve tending and befriending others. Strengths of humanity involve caring interpersonal relationships with others, particularly in one-to-one relationships. Strengths comprised in this virtue are love, kindness, and social intelligence.

3. **Justice:** Justice consists of **civic strengths** that underlie healthy community life. Strengths of justice refer to the optimal relationship between the individual and the group or community, rather than the more one-to-one relationships in the humanity virtue. Strengths comprised in this virtue are *teamwork, fairness, and leadership.*

4. **Courage**: Courage consists of **emotional strengths** that involve the exercise of will to accomplish goals in the face of opposition, external or internal. Strengths of courage involve applying will and fortitude in overcoming internal or external resistance to accomplish goals. Strengths comprised in this virtue are bravery, perseverance, integrity, and enthusiasm.

5. **Temperance:** Temperance involves strengths that **protect against excess**. Strengths of temperance protect us from excess. Strengths comprised in this virtue are forgiveness, humility, prudence, and self-control.

6. **Transcendence**: Transcendence consists of strengths that **forge connections to the universe and provide**

meaning. Strengths of transcendence allow people to rise above their troubles and find meaning in the larger universe. Strengths of transcendence are appreciation of beauty and excellence, purpose, gratitude, optimism, and humor.

Each category of 'Virtue' further contains a set of 'Character Strengths' – these are psychological ingredients, processes or mechanisms that define the virtue. In this way there are six virtues and twenty four character strengths.

Measurement of Character Strengths

Character Strengths can be measured by

- Structured interviews
- Questionnaires
- Informant Reports
- Behavioral Experiments
- Observations

Characteristics of Character strength

Peterson and Seligman (2004) were created following characteristics of Character Strength:

1. It has to contribute to fulfillments that constitute the "good life" for oneself or for others.

2. It is morally valued in its own right, even without being attached to positive outcomes.

3. The display of a strength by one person does not diminish those surrounding him or her.

4. It does not have an obvious negative "opposite" to it (e.g., flexibility's opposite can be good, like steadfastness, or bad, like inflexibility, meaning it can easily be viewed on a spectrum from "good" to "bad").

5. It must manifest in a way that can be assessed, and it must be at least somewhat stable across time and situations.

6. It is distinct from other positive traits within the classification system and cannot be subsumed by strength.

7. It can be embodied in "paragons," people who have the strength to a remarkable degree.

8. A person can (probably) be a "prodigy" in it, meaning they have an instinct towards it.

9. On the other hand, a person might display a complete lack of it.

10. There are "institutions and associated rituals" for cultivating it, meaning that it is considered a positive and encouraged in at least some areas of mainstream society.

Development of character strength

Character strengths have been a pillar of positive psychology since it was founded. The character strengths is described as the capacities which may enable for helping, fulfill the human promise of surviving, thriving, and successfully creating a next-generation so that individuals and the society flourish and living in harmonious balance with other species. This requires that individuals survive, grow, but produce a successful next generation without substantially diminishing others rights from doing the same. Character strengths enable individual flourishing while at the same time allowing for others to do the same. They also contribute to resilience in the face of challenges and difficulties. Therefore, character strengths can contribute to successfully establishing a next generation.

Five Ways to Build Your Character

1. **Be Humble:** Humility is the beginning of wisdom in order to build your character,

2. **Live out your principles and values**: Living by your principles will make decision making easier and your character more steadfast

3. **Be intentional**: Integrity does not happen by accident. We are all products of our thoughts and habits. Be intentional about

filling your mind with good thoughts. Create a habit of this internalizes principles and breeds high character.

4. **Practice self-discipline**: Being of high character, takes the ability to do what is right over the issues.

5. **Be accountable**: Be responsible for yourself first. Lose the pride. Open yourself up to accountability. Let others push you to high character.

Flow and Spirituality

Flow is a state of concentration and absolute absorption in an activity. Everyone experiences flow from time to time and feel strong, alert, in effortless control, unconscious, and at the peak of their abilities to do work. At that period sense of time and emotional problems seem to disappear, and there is an exhilarating feeling beyond physical needs and realities. When we are in a state of flow, we are fully engaged with the task and experiencing feeling of joy. If we spend time in a state of flow then we will be fully focused, energized, and will probably be experiencing a sense of joy and satisfaction in our work. We would also be completing our work in less time, giving us extra time for our practices and other activities. The state of flow describes a feeling where, under the right conditions, you become fully immersed in whatever you are doing. State of flow is frequently credited as one of the keys to living our happiest and most meaningful lives. It is associated with the simultaneous feelings of joy, clarity, and awareness. A state flow not only feels good, but has a direct positive correlation with happiness, productivity, creativity and health.

Example of Flow: Watching Cricket became intrigued by their single-minded, unique focus, and persistence to continue in spite of any discomfort, tiredness, or hunger.

Characteristics of Flow

During the experiences of flow following characteristics are observed:

1. The individual believes that the task is worth doing

2. There is a good fit between the challenges of the task and the skills of the individual

3. Full attention is given to the task and no attention is available for anxieties about job performance or security

4. The task has clear goals and feedback that provide a structure and a basis for knowing whether one has succeeded in performing the task

5. The sense of time can be altered

6. The person experiences a sense of joy and becomes absorbed in the task

The Universal Factors of Flow

According to Csikszentmihalyi, following are the main factors of Flow:

1. Challenge-skill balance;

2. Action-awareness merging;

3. Clear goals;

4. Unambiguous feedback;

5. Concentration on the task at hand;

6. A sense of control;

7. Loss of self-consciousness;

8. Transformation of time; and

9. Autotelic experience.

How to enter in Flow stage?

Flow triggers are conditions that facilitate entry into a Flow state. There are four Flow State triggers through which we can enter into Flow stage:

A. Psychological triggers

The following four strategies are internally driven, and they work by focusing our attention on the present. They include:

1. **Intense concertration:** When we focus with undivided attention on a certain task. We aren't engaging in activities with others.

2. **Goal clarity:** The goal must be unambiguous. The task at hand needs to be clearly delineated so our minds can stay focused on the present moment and action rather than wondering the next step.

3. **Immediate feedback:** Instant feedback provides our awareness and attention.

4. **Challenge to skills ratio:** Too-challenging tasks can make us feel overwhelmed, unequipped to face them, and anxious. A task that's too simple, on the other hand, can induce boredom. To trigger flow, a goal should be halfway between these two extremes.

B. Environmental triggers

Environmental triggers are aspects of our surroundings that help us get further into a flow state:

1. **High consequences:** Our concentration and focus are instinctively heightened when we detect a sense of danger in our environments. This is a subjective and perceived threat. It could be speaking publicly or approaching another person.

2. **Rich environments:** When we're in new or unpredictable environments, our focus and attention are enhanced. With regard to environmental complexity, our attention on to the different information should be aware carefully.

3. **Deep embodiment:** Here, referring to total physical awareness, this may make more sense. It relates in one way to our sense of control over our physical performance, and the link between this perceived control and goal achievement.

C. Social triggers

Social triggers have great importance in group flow. Some practical applications would include as under.

1. **Serious concentration**: We aren't solo for this type of Flow, rather we need to focus as a team on the present, to the exclusion of outside distractions.

2. **Clear, shared goals**: Clear goal as a psychological trigger, this has implications for how we communicate in groups.

3. **Good communication**: This provides paying attention to and building on what others contribute to group discussions.

4. **Familiarity**: This relates to a collective language within the group, andit is easy to see how this can be linked closely to organizational culture.

5. **Equal participation and skill level:** This means different participants should have an equal part to play in the execution of a project. It's connected to the idea that a certain challenge-skill ratio will be ideally suited to group members who are similarly equipped to handle the task.

6. **Risk**: 'Rich Environments' trigger for individuals and this is very nicely to the idea that innovation and risk go hand-in-hand.

7. **Sense of control:** There's no spark of intrinsic motivation without being able to link our group actions to the collective goalandnor will we feel adequately equipped for tasks that are perceived to be too difficult.

8. **Close listening**: Listening is very important to aware of what is happening in the moment.

9. **Always say yes**: Interactions should be additive more than argumentative.

D. Creative triggers

Creativity: Flow triggers creativity, which triggers flow, and so forth in a domino effect.

Stages of Flow

Flow is a positive emotional state that occurs when a person is fully immersed and absorbed in an activity. Flow is composed of nine dimensions divided into three interconnected stages:

1. **Antecedents**: The antecedents are composed of a clear goal that involves a challenge that is in balance with the individual's abilities, and that provides direct feedback.

2. **Experiences**: The experiences that follow are the concentration on the task, the merging of action and awareness, and the consequent sense of control over the activity that is taking place.

3. **Effects**: The effects are a loss of self-consciousness, the distortion of time and the auto telic experience

Flow is one of life's highly enjoyable states and helping us tomore creative, productive, and happy. It gives significant role in positivity, and its implications is for both individuals and groups.

Spirituality

Flow is a concept that's gained traction in western culture over the past few decades. Psychologist Mihaly Csikszentmihalyi coined the term flow in the 1970's but the experience of flow has been alive for centuries. Spiritual Cognition has been studied extensively over ages by our great philosophers, thinkers and psychologists. It is not a new term to know. There is so much in the ancient scriptures which we can utilize for the benefit of today's world. Spiritual traditions around the world teach ways of being in the flow, and describe it in such as connecting to oneness, plugging into universal life force, "letting god," achieving nirvana or enlightenment, and many others. Spirituality involves the recognition of a feeling or sense or belief that there is something greater than myself, something more to being human than sensory experience. Spirituality involves exploring certain universal themes like love, compassion, altruism, life after death, wisdom and truth.

Samkhya tradition of Ancient India and established the fact that Indian scriptures contain rich empirical theories of psychology which are amalgamated with religious and philosophical concept. Not only Hindu and Buddhist tradition rather the philosophy of Socrates, Plato, Aristotle, Confucius etc. also laid emphasis on the development of cognitive functions. The Vedic philosophy has related cognition with knowledge, learning, memorization, creativity, purity of heart and mind. Nowadays, spirituality and religion becomes a burning discussions for almost all aspects of human life. Religions are mostly treated as pathways to either head for spirituality or connect with God Himself. In some of them, the final destination is God which means someone is expected to be totally connected with Him. Traditionally, spirituality referred to a religious process of re-formation which aims to recover the original shape of man which is oriented at the image of God. Spirituality is the place within yourselves where your soul can find a sense of peace. It stands for something greater in life than the physical or material world.

Types of Spirituality

There are various paths for a person to achieve peace of mind through spirituality but most common ones are as under:

1. **Mystical Spirituality:** This type of spirituality is focused on the intuitional part of the soul. People who have mystical spirituality believe that there's a greater unity to every experience in life. Every experience goes beyond the material or physical world, and everything can be brought into one greater unity. For example, people with this type of spirituality may support the idea that everything happens for a reason.

2. **Authoritarian Spirituality:** This type of spirituality believes in a hierarchical structure of things or in authority and *associated with religious beliefs.* There are cases when not following the spiritual rules of religion may cause conflicts. People with authoritarian spirituality can develop a form of fundamentalist religion. Fundamentalists believe that their religion is the most truthful one. They tend to exclude every other religion which, unfortunately, can be the cause for radical religious terrorism.

3. **Intellectual Spirituality:** The core belief behind this type of spirituality is knowledge. Intellectually spiritual people are prone to gaining knowledge of spiritual theories and analyzing the information they get. However, this type of spirituality is not solely related to studying religion. Any knowledge that

helps people *toimprove their spirituality* is a form of intellectual spirituality.

4. **Service Spirituality:** This is one of the most common types of spirituality. It's because people experience spiritual peace when they serve others. There are many ways to achieve this spirituality, but the core of it is helping others without expecting nothing in return. Doing something that will benefit someone without getting something back is a common way for people to get in touch with their spiritual selves.

5. **Social Spirituality:** Experiencing spiritual awakening when you are surrounded by other people and developing spirituality in contact of others.

Ways of Spiritual Practices

There are five spiritual practices through which anyone can achieve a true spiritual self:

1. **Path of Knowledge:** The main idea behind this practice is the power knowledge gives to people. This practice revolves around the idea that ultimate liberation can happen with acquiring knowledge. This is not only about learning new things about the world but most importantly, knowledge about you. Self- reflection, which you are, why you do the things the way you do are the main principles of this spiritual practice. To achieve this, people use methods like studying, meditation and contemplation. Some of the most famous approaches are Buddhism and Yoga.

2. **Path of Devotion:** This spiritual practice has *liberation from your ego as its core element.* This is partly because many people who consider themselves religious will use some of these methods to express their spirituality. However, it's not always connected with religion. People also devote themselves to a higher power source or their consciousness to experience spiritual freedom. Some of those methods are *chanting, praying, mantras, and belief* to become more spiritually aware.

3. **Path of Meditation:** Meditation is one of the most common methods people are using to get better in touch with their true spirit. *Meditations are breathing techniques and teacher relationship.* The basis of this spiritual practice is calmness. People believe that whatever they accumulate through their life can be channeled through these methods. This removes negative thoughts and help to reduce the challenges of day to day life.*Raja Yoga, Nada Yoga, and Buddhism* are some examples of this spiritual practice.

4. **Path of Service:** This spiritual practice is about active selflessness. The ultimate peace of mind is that when helping and expecting nothing in return. These people are believed to rely only on giving rather than receiving. *Volunteering, helping in Red Cross, and helping those in need, working with people or children with disabilities* – any type of selfless act falls under this category.

5. **Path of Energy:** This practice is basically the idea of purification of body and mind. There are all kinds of methods, such as meditation, breathing, somatic techniques, and teacher relationship. Some people use ritual behavior or activity to achieve this, others may concentrate solely on improving their physical health. Whatever the action, the goal is to achieve purified both body and mind, liberated from the toxic elements you encounter in everyday lives.

Spirituality in India

In context of Indian culture, spirituality has been deeply rooted phenomenon and in earlier times, it used to be important goals of one's life. For centuries, India has been a mystical land of meditation and enlightenment where spiritual traditions flourished and still continuing to inspire millions. Being the birthplace of many dharma-based saints, India also has had the privilege of being the fertile land for many enlightened masters and spiritual Gurus. India as a hospitable and flourishing home not only for Hinduism but also for other traditions including Sikhism, Jainism, Sufism, Buddhism and Christianity with its deep rooted belief in universal humanism and spiritual ideals. According to Bhawuk (2011), "Spirituality has been valued in the Indian culture and it is no surprise that many innovations in the field of spirituality originated in India.Spirituality is rooted in the very way of life of masses in India and hence cannot be rigidly defined with specific terminology. India continues to be known as the land of spiritual wisdom offering invaluable insight into the higher states of human consciousness and various paths to attainment of pure bliss.

Difference between Religion and Spirituality

Religion is a specific set of organized beliefs and practices, usually shared by a community or group whereas; Spirituality is an individual practice and has to do with having a sense of peace and purpose. It also relates to the process of developing beliefs around the meaning of life and connection with others. Religious does not automatically make anybody spiritual or at the same time spirituality does not make religious.

To understand the relationship between spirituality and religion - imagine a game of football. The rules of game, role of referees, players, and field markings provide guide to play the game in a similar way religion might guide to find spirituality.

Reason of Practice Spirituality

Spirituality is a great way of seeking peace of mind in the life. It can often be practiced yoga, which ultimately focuses on stress relief and release of emotion. Spirituality is also used as a way of gaining perspective, recognizing the role in life which has a greater value than just what we do every day. It can separate a person from dependence on material things and establish a greater purpose. Moreover, spirituality is a way of coping with change or uncertainty.

Savoring

Bryant and Veroff define savoring as attending, appreciating, and enhancing positive experiences that occur in one's life. Savoring can be associated with an internal or external event, which might not necessarily be tangible. Savoring is more about becoming aware of the experience of pleasure and appreciating the positive emotions derived from that experience. To savor an experience, one must possess and apply a certain degree of mindfulness and meta-awareness.

Types of savoring

1. Savoring the past, also known as *reminiscence*. For example, remembering funny moments from school with a friend.

2. Savoring the present or *savoring the moment*. For instance, enjoying a new meal by drawing your attention to the flavors and smells.

3. Savoring the future also referred to as *anticipation*. For example, visualizing the trip you have planned with your partner for this upcoming weekend.

Levels of savoring

1. **Savoring experiences:** It refers to the overall experience while intentionally focusing attention on appreciating positive events. It includes sensations, emotions, perceptions, thoughts, and behaviors that are linked to the particular..

2. **Savoring processes:** These processes connect a positive event to positive emotions by modulating different positive states. For example, the process of appreciating a kind action from a stranger regarded as beneficial regulates gratitude as a positive emotional state.

3. **Savoring responses:** These are the specific behaviors or thoughts emerging as a response to a positive event. These responses regulate the influence of such positive events on positive affect by either amplifying or dampening the intensity and duration of positive emotions.

Benefits of Savoring

The benefits of savoring derive from the process and personal experience rather than from the positive nature of the event. Some documented benefits of developing and using an increased savoring ability include the following:

1. Counterbalances the experience of unpleasant emotions during stressful events

2. Boosts happiness in people experiencing fewer daily positive events

3. Predicts greater levels of positive affect and self-esteem

4. Predicts higher levels of life satisfaction, happiness, and perceived

5. Predicts decreased depressive symptoms in older adults

6. Predicts reduced levels of depression and anxiety

7. Predicts decreased levels of obsessive-compulsive disorder and social phobia

8. Positively relates to higher levels of positive affect and life satisfaction

9. Positively influences satisfaction in long-distance romantic relationships

10. Relational savoring, such as explicit disclosure of positive events to a partner, increases the quality of the relationship and levels of self-esteem

11. Helps people balance family and career responsibilities more effectively

12. Promotes positive relationships when experiencing a wholehearted response to a narrated positive event by other people

Mindfulness

Mindfulness is the practice of purposely focusing your attention on the present moment and accepting it without judgment. Mindfulness is examined scientifically and has been found to be a key element in stress reduction and overall happiness. We train in this moment to moment awareness through meditation, allowing us to build the skill of mindfulness so that we can then apply it to everyday life. Mindfulness is a skill that can be taught, learned, practiced, and developed. When we practice mindfulness, we intentionally focus our attention on our sensory experience by moment to moment. This is done with an attitude of openness, curiosity, and compassion toward what is arising in the present, whether pleasant or unpleasant. Mindfulness is a powerful tool to regulate stress and other emotional challenges. Of course, stress reduction is not the only benefit. Mindfulness can help to pay more attention in work and improve their ability to concentrate and focus. It can also help to develop more empathy and compassion for their peers, enabling them to resolve conflicts more constructively. The word "mindfulness" is translated from the Pali word, "sati", which can be interpreted "awareness, attention, and remembering "Mindfulness originated as a movement to peace and non-violence in the world. Gradually, its impact have expanded to a vast number of areas such as medical practice, psychology and research, personal well-being and awareness, improving and enhancing relationships at home and the workplace. The concept of mindfulness is mostly aimed to inculcate a sense of self and the capability to create positivity. Mindfulness, deep-rooted in the realms of Buddhism, is being given its due regard since its resurgence in the recent times. The topic is not confined only to the spiritual and academic exploration but also has become part of popular imagination. Mindfulness is gift of Indian Buddhist tradition and the *Pali* language espoused by them. Mindfulness is the intentional, accepting and non-judgmental focus of one's attention on the emotions, thoughts and sensations occurring in the present moment. M*indfulness* is living in the present moment without being preoccupied by thoughts of the past or the future. Mindlessness is a state of mind, in which the individual is neither mindful nor aware. It is a kind of component of Buddhist practices of meditation, including *vipassana* (insight into reality), *anapanasati* (mindfulness of breathing) and *satipatthana* (foundation for mindfulness).

Concepts of Mindfulness

Mindfulness has certain concepts, which are as under:

1. *Awareness:* It is the ability to be conscious of the events, objects, surroundings or a particular situation. Awareness can be either internal or external. Duval &Wicklund (1972) postulated a theory of self-awareness which is based on motivational properties deriving from social feedback. It is of utmost importance to be aware about one's choices, goals, values and beliefs. During meditating awareness means accepting life as it comes.

2. *Wakefulness:* Wakefulness can be best described as a state of awareness, in every waking moment. Wakefulness enhances our subjective well-being and heightens our contentment with our inner selves and the world.

3. *Positive Evaluations:* Positive evaluations of oneself, or self-acceptance could lead to emotional difficulties. If an individual is engaging more in self--evaluation than self-acceptance, s/he is more likely to compensate for the deficits perceived in self.

Definitions of Mindfulness

Mindfulness is a term that is used in a variety of ways. Different people working in the area of 'mindfulness' assign different meanings to this term so as to fit their own perceptions regarding what they do.

According to the American Psychological Association (2012), Mindfulness is moment-to-moment awareness of one's experience without judgment. In this sense, mindfulness is a state and not a trait. While it might be promoted by certain practices or activities, such as meditation, it is not equivalent to or synonymous with them.

Jon Kabat Zinn (2015): The awareness that arises from paying attention, on purpose, in the present moment and non-judgmentally.

Brown et al., (2007) stated that,"Mindfulness is characterized by pre-conceptual awareness, purposeful control of attention, non-judgmentally acceptance of experience and present-focused orientation."

Dane (2011) defined mindfulness as, "a state of consciousness in which attention is focused on present-moment phenomena occurring both externally and internally."

Daniel J. Siegel: Mindfulness in its most general sense is about waking up from a life on automatic, and being sensitive to novelty in our everyday experiences. . . . Instead of being on automatic and mindless, mindfulness helps us awaken, and by reflecting on the mind we are enabled to make choices and thus change becomes possible".

Sharon Salzberg: Mindfulness isn't just about knowing that you're hearing something, seeing something, or even observing that you're having a particular feeling. It's about doing so in a certain way—with balance and equanimity, and without judgment. Mindfulness is the practice of paying attention in a way that creates space for insight.

Achieving Mindfulness

According to Jon Kabat-Zinn (2012) Mindfulness can be achieved by following five ways:

1. *Entering:* The beginning of mindfulness starts with inculcating awareness about one's thoughts, deeds and reactions. Meditation is necessary to aware of our own breathingin Mindfulness. Buddha's teachings find awareness of breath as an important phenomenon. Mindfulness meditation shouldn't be considered 'seriously', as it is supposed to be an effortless element of our lives. It should be pursued with authentic integrity. Preoccupation with thoughts of past or future disrupts the process of meditation, but practice helps in this case.

2. *Sustaining:* The phase of *sustaining* is applying in the entering phase in our daily routine. This phase integrates all sensory systems of an individual and the individual feels connected to his inner self.

3. *Deepening:* In the deepening process, the practitioner employs an attitude of nonviolence and experiences empathy for others. He teaches himself to conserve the energy that would usually

drain out during meditation in his beginning phase. The practitioner spreads his knowledge of mindfulness to others who would need this knowledge.

4. *Ripening:* This phase is the all-round attitudinal change of the practitioner. By reaching this phase, he has mastered how to lead his life with the 'right attitude at the right time'.

5. *Practicing:* After an individual has mastered mindfulness meditation, he practices it 'moment by moment'. He becomes mindful of his eating habits, breathing, body, mind and emotions.

Advantage of Mindfulness

Mindfulness has several advantages in field of psychological, emotional and physical well-being. Practicing mindfulness can bring improvements in both physical and psychological symptoms as well as positive changes in health, attitudes, and behaviors. Some of these benefits are mentioned below:

1. *Inter-connectivity of the Mind and the Body:* Mindfulness activates the connection of mind and the body. It develops the inter-connectedness of all systems, organs and cells. This integration makes more consciously aware of inner selves. The connection with our inner selves helps us be more socially connected with others as well.

2. *Healing:* Mindfulness not only enables us to achieve physical relaxation but also the ability to get rid of our fears. This belief enables one to realize that these are the physical conditions that make us suffer, and we are capable of coming to terms with the situation and transforming suffering into well-being.

3. *Attunement of the Mind:* Practicing mindfulness and complete awareness stimulates emotional circuits in the brain, to increase levels of well-being, happiness, resilience and a great improvement in cardiac functions.

4. *Relaxation:* Though relaxation is not an objective of mindfulness, but it is surely one of its many positive outcomes. Through relaxation individuals suffering from high amounts of stress and burnout can relieve oneself of stress and other

negative experiences. Such relaxation based mindfulness helps in being calm and relaxed.

5. *Improving Productivity Levels:* Occupational and organizational stress directly affects an individual's productivity levels. By practicing mindfulness, the employee would be able to manage his stress levels, making him/her a healthier person and easier to manage work stress. The technique of mindfulness, when applied by the employers of an organization, will improve their relations with the employees and will prove to be beneficial to the organization as well.

6. *A Compassionate Mind:* Mindfulness meditation can train the practitioner's mind to inculcate reactions to most events with positivity. The alterations in emotional circuits of the brain after practicing mindfulness increase in happiness, compassion and optimism.

7. *Better Relationships:* Intrapersonal relationships improve by practicing mindfulness. Inadequate and inefficient communication in relationships is bound to increase emotional pain between couples. Suppressing one's feeling and emotions toward his/her partner doesn't help. Mindfulness training for couples is the most appropriate solution for cases of conflicts, anger outbursts or even divorce.

8. *Better Societies:* The prime objective of the mindfulness movement is to create better societies. Mindfulness when applied effectively and efficiently by all would create a society with positivity and compassion in bold letters.

Benefits of Mindfulness

1. **Mindfulness improves well-being.** Mindfulness supports to increase capacity of attitudes that contribute to a satisfied life. Mindfulness makes easier to savor the pleasures in life, helps to become fully engaged in activities, and creates a greater capacity to deal with adverse events.

2. **Mindfulness improves physical health:** Scientists have discovered that mindfulness techniques improve physical health

in a number of ways. Mindfulness can help relieve stress, treat heart disease, lower blood pressure, reduce chronic pain, ,and improve sleep.

3. **Mindfulness improves mental health:** Mindfulness meditation is an important element in the treatment of a number of problems, including: depression, substance abuse, eating disorders, couples' conflicts, and anxiety disorders.

4. **Decreased Depression:** Reduced depression is one of the important benefits of mindfulness. It can help relieve symptoms of depression and may help prevent these symptoms from returning in the future.

5. **Increased Emotional Regulation:** Another potential benefit of mindfulness is that the practice may help you identify and manage your feelings. Emotional regulation refers to your ability to exert control over your own emotions. This means being able to both enhance emotions depending on the situation and need.

6. **Reduced Anxiety and Stress:** Chronic stress is a significant problem for many adults that can contribute to a variety of health problems, including an increased risk of depression and anxiety. According to the American Psychological Association, mindfulness can be helpful for soothing feelings of anxiety and stress.

7. **Better Memory:** Mindfulness may also have potential as a way to boost your memory. Many of these moments of forgetfulness are caused by something known as proactive interference, where older memories interfere with your ability to access newer ones.

Applications of Mindfulness

The mindfulness meditation is applicable in various areas. Some of the major areas are given below:

1. *Healing our own Self:* Mindfulness has been used successfully to heal people in emotional and physical pain. It is a transformative way of healing that is easily applicable end effective.

2. *Mindfulness in Relationships:* Couples who practice mindfulness together tend to alleviate their emotional pain and difficulties in the relationship. It is an effective way to avoid conflicts at home, and makes one better at dealing with relationships, romantic.

3. *Mindfulness in Schools:* Successful attempts have been made to apply mindfulness in school children. The Mindfulness showed statistically significant improvements in behavior as compared to the control group with only 4 hours or mindfulness instructions given to the students.

4. *Mindfulness at Work:* Introducing mindfulness at work could help strengthen the foundations of an organization.

Mindfulness Techniques

There is more than one way to practice mindfulness, but the goal of any mindfulness technique is to achieve a state of alert, focused relaxation by attention to thoughts and sensations without judgment. This allows the mind to refocus on the present moment. All mindfulness techniques are a form of meditation.

1. **Basic mindfulness meditation:** Sit quietly and focus on your natural breathing or on a word or "mantra" that you repeat silently. Allow thoughts to come and go without judgment and return to your focus on breath or mantra.

2. **Body sensations**: Notice body sensations such as an itch or tingling without judgment and let them pass. Notice each part of your body in succession from head to toe.

3. **Sensory:** Notice sights, sounds, smells, tastes, and touchesandwithout judgment and let them go.

4. **Emotions:** Allow emotions to be present without judgment. Practice a steady and relaxed naming of emotions: "joy," "anger," "frustration." Accept the presence of the emotions without judgment and let them go.

5. **Urge surfing**: Notice how your body feels as the craving enters. Replace the wish for the craving to go away with the certain knowledge that it will subside.

Psychological Theories and Principles of Mindfulness

Psychological theories and principles that shape the structure of 'mindfulness' can be summarized under four levels of analysis such as:

1. **Networks of Attention:** There are three components of attention networks such as alerting, orienting, and executive attention.

   i. **Alerting**: Alerting is a kind of vigilance which is regulated largely by noradrenalin.

   ii. **Orienting:** The function 'orienting' is controlled by brain areas to mainly involves the selection of specific information from sensory inputs.

   iii. **Executive attention:** The executive attention component involves the anterior cingulated cortex, the anterior insula, the prefrontal cortex and basal ganglia. The executive attention network is the most manipulated domain.

2. **Perception and Awareness:** Mindfulness can also be explained in terms of 'processing mode' which refers to the style of thinking while processing information like many psychological disorders, especially depression, and the style of thinking. There are three components of perception - 'Cognitive reactivity', 'Rumination' and the 'Interactive cognitive subsystem.

3. **Motivation and self determination:** We know that mindfulness is an intentional process and a voluntarily carried out cognitive practice. According to the self determination theory, there are two types of motivation namely autonomous motivation and controlled motivation. Autonomous motivation gives rise to behavior and attitudes which last longer and go deeper. The autonomous motivation is intrinsic motivation which concerns people's engagement in an activity because they find it interesting and enjoyable. On the other hand, controlled motivation is comprised of two types of extrinsic motivation such as external regulation and internal regulation. People possessing these later forms of motivation have been

found to have lower degree of satisfaction of their basic psychological needs.

4. **Cognitive and behavioural models:** Cognitive and behavioural models is related to understanding mindfulness within the framework of learning processes and the social environmental characteristics. There are different psychotherapeutic techniques, which largely incorporate the philosophy of mindfulness, they are Mindfulness based cognitive therapy (MBCT), met cognitive therapy, acceptance and commitment therapy (ACT), dialectical behavioral therapy (DBT).

Enhancement of Mindfulness

Mindfulness practices are simple. Basic mindfulness exercise is to involve the sensory organ's experience, such as breath (nose), sound (ear), vision (eye) or physical (Skin) sensation. Initially the mind gets distracted and attention wavers away from the object. Mindfulness can be used to anybody, it doesn't require specific amount of time for teaching and it can be practiced effectively at any time and no restriction on the location.

Mindfulness is a skill that enhances from ongoing, repeated use and continuous encouragement. The Mindfulness is to be practiced to bring aware on the sensory organs and skill to be experienced and retained. The instructions and practices are very simple with commitment and it is a personal experience as individual alone can gauge the improvement.

Model of mindfulness

Bishop et al. (2006), offered two component model of mindfulnessconsisting of (1) attention and awareness and (2) acceptance, the first component of mindfulness involves the regulation of attention so that it is maintained on immediate experience, thereby allowing for increased recognition of mental events in the present moment. The second component involves adopting a particular orientation towards ones experiences in the present moment, an orientation that is characterized by curiosity, openness and acceptance.

Uses of Mindfulness

1. Mindfulness systematically regulates our attention and energy
2. It influences and transforms the quality of the experience
3. It aids in realizing the full power of humanity
4. It improves the relationship between self, others, and the environment
5. It reduces stress-related problems like anxiety, panic attacks, and depression
6. It increases the quality of life of chronic illness patients, for example – pain management in cancer patients; relaxation for cardio patients, etc
7. By regular practice, mindfulness strengthens the immune system and general health of the practitioner 8. It also improves emotional balance, attention, thinking, problem-solving

Foundations of Mindfulness

Following are main foundations of mindfulness:

1. **Sensory organs:** The external world is full of information. Sensory organs connect the external world with the internal world. Eyes, nose, ear, mouth, and skin are known as primary sensory organs. Any information from the external world can enter into the mind only through the passage of sensory organs. Neurons receive power from the secretions of bio-chemicals and aid in the transportation of this nerve impulse to reach the brain. Once the nerve impulse comes from the mind, the individual will know the information, called sensation. Sensory organs are not capable of filtering the enormous mass of data available in the external world. There is a limitation to information that a human body can handle. The brain will attend only to needed information and reject unnecessary data from the external world. The process of selection the news from

he outer world is called attention. Mindfulness can enhance attention into a way of living by adding up another skill called awareness. Attention and awareness are the two trainable skills essential for building Mindfulness. When sensation, awareness, and attention combine, a human being can visualize the object.

2. **Awareness:** Awareness can be referred to as the complete presence of one individual's consciousness to internal and external surroundings. It can also be called the mode of mind. Human beings actively include their lives with society. This society expects and pressurizes an individual to fulfill a list of tasks. On any given day, a human being can function without consciousness, and that is called the doing mode of the mind. Without bothering about the present moment, an individual can think deeply with their memories and do the current life activities in automatic mode. Awareness is a practical way of living by systematically freeing oneself from the clutches of suffering and embracing the present reality. Mindfulness will help the individual to shift from doing mode to mode of mind. Habituating awareness is an essential practice of Mindfulness. The primary hindrance of awareness is the habitual pattern of thinking. Human beings genetically possess the capacity to be aware and attend to the present moment. But it was underdeveloped.

3. **Attention**: Information enters the brain through sensation. The brain will process the data to decide - whether to attend it or not. Learners may relate the information is necessary for the person or not. Selection and focusing on one stimulus from an enormous amount of stimulus available in the environment are called attention. An individual who is trained in attention is capable of attaining mindfulness. Since the external world is full of information, getting carried away will quickly happen. The willingness and openness to bring the self back to the present moment instead of pulling other information is the critical skill. Attention is not only about the objects or knowledge of the environment. The process of engagement that an

individual is attending itself is enough to create awareness. For example, focusing on the flower's smell is attention; I smell the flowers scent is meta-cognition; understanding and experiencing the life energy of flower and self as one is mindfulness. Learners can turn attention into mindfulness by balancing the flow of thoughts and bringing a broader perspective.

4. **Emotions**: Emotions are the physical reactions for the thought process associated with the stimulus. Emotions possess both positive and negative elements in it. Primary emotions are anger, fear, happiness, sadness, disgust, and surprise. Prolonged negative emotions pave the way for psychosomatic disorders like ulcer, skin issues, breathing-related diseases, digestion problems, and in extreme cases, cancer. Practicing mindfulness will create positive emotions and pave the way for healthy living. This awareness and affectionate attention will lead to mindfulness.

Questions

1. Define Optimism and Pessimism. Discuss the theories of Optimism.
2. What is Optimism? Describe types of Optimism.
3. What is Unrealistic Optimism? Describe the types of Unrealistic Optimism.
4. Discuss the cognitive mechanisms of Unrealistic Optimism.
5. Discuss the group of Unrealistic Optimism.
6. What is Optimism? What are the benefits and drawback of Optimism?
7. Define Hope. Describe the theory of Hope.
8. What is Hope? Describe its types.
9. What is Hope? Discuss its importance.
10. What are the benefits of Hope? Describe.
11. What is Hope therapy? Discuss the enhancement of Hope.

12. Define Wisdom. Describe its theories.

13. Describe the properties of Wisdom.

14. What is Wisdom? What are the components of Wisdom?

15. Define Creativity. Describe its types.

16. What is Creativity? Describe the Traits of Creativity.

17. What are the characteristics? How do you increase Creativity?

18. What is Courage? Describe the types of Courage.

19. How do you measurement of Character Strengths? Describe the characteristics.

20. Discuss the development of Character Strengths. How do you build your Character?

21. Discuss the characteristics of Flow. What are the universal factors of Flow?

22. Describe the stages of Flow.

23. What is Spirituality? Describe the types of Spirituality.

24. Discuss the Spirituality in India. Describe its Practices.

25. What is the difference between Religion and Spirituality?

26. What is Savoring? Describe its types, level and benefits.

27. What do you mean by Mindfulness? What is the advantage of Mindfulness?

28. Define Mindfulness. How would you achieve Mindfulness? Discuss.

29. What are the benefits of Mindfulness? What are the applications of Mindfulness? Discuss.

    1. What are mindfulness techniques? Describe the theories and principles of Mindfulness.

    2. Describe the model of Mindfulness.

    3. Discuss the foundation of Mindfulness. Describe the uses of Mindfulness.

❑

Chapter-IV

Application Positive Psychology

Introduction

Application of positive psychology is to provide a theoretical basis as well as practical solutions to enable people to improve their mental well-being and to achieve better physical health. Positive psychology is to provide a theoretical basis as well as practical solutions to enable people to improve their mental well-being and to achieve better physical health and provide much application for betterment of life. This new trend focuses on scientific research into resources, strengths and happiness. According to the World Health Organization, mental depression is the main cause of disability and become the fourth health problem throughout the world. World Health Organization's expert estimates that depression will have become the second largest health problem in the world. Moreover, epidemic of depression is dangerous in view of the fact that depression increasingly affects younger people. An epidemic of depression, pessimism and lowered self-esteem in the young generation constitutes not only one of the major threats to mental health, but also becomes a serious social and economic problem. According to Martin Seligman, education is the most important weapon in combating and preventing the above identified problems and threats because positive psychology alone is not capable of coping effectively with an epidemic of depression in the young generation. Improved mental well-being, and effective prevention of an epidemic of depression will not be possible unless the concepts of hard determinism are questioned; the hard determinism which treats the individual as a victim of his or her own biological and socio-demographic characteristics.

Positive psychology as a science is based on three pillars. The first is a positive life experience for individuals – '**exploiting positive emotions**'. The second pillar is a person's positive physical properties – '**exploiting positive personality traits**', mainly virtues and strengths, but also aptitudes. The third pillar is a positive society – '**exploiting positive social institutions**', in particular those such as democracy, a strong family, and education which promotes positive development.

Application of Positive Psychology in Education (Relationship between positive psychology and education)

It is true that a man learns throughout life, but the student life is such a phase in which the learning is at its peak and one gains so much in this phase of his life because in this age he is surrounded with so many intellectual persons. These persons include the teachers, the parents, the siblings, the classmates and so many other persons. It is the period of pure joy and happiness, because the mind of a student is free from cares and worries. Internal and external factors influence overall personality of the student. Teacher is the most important person who plays a vital role for the overall development of the student's personality and students can leads to the right path. Teachers use methodology which includes a blend of various types of psychological techniques as these help in making the adolescents succeed in academic scores without imposing much pressure. But in this race of getting academic scores, all the teachers and parents involved in the process of education whether directly or indirectly, forget the basic aim of education which is to develop the overall personality of the adolescents. Every parent and teacher want from their child to stand first and they can't accept anything less than that. But they forget that the adolescents have their own life and aspirations and they are not machines to fulfill the unfulfilled desired of their parents and teachers. This attitude of teachers and parents has led to serious mental tensions among the Adolescents. Due to the cut throat competition, the adolescents are more stressed for getting top academic scores. According to World health organization (2005), studies of mental stress among adolescents younger than 18 years conducted worldwide and found 8% to 20% reported that mental stress have led to suicidal tendencies among the adolescents. In such a situation, adolescents need to be motivated or encouraged to participate in the process of education in a constructive way and the use of positive psychology techniques can be a suitable option. Not only this but in today's increasingly modern society, have many problems arisen at the same time that requires immediate solution.

Educational psychology deals with both in its theory and practice with the development of the affective, cognitive and social competence of young people. The aim of educational psychology is to help young people find their self-esteem, the meaning of life, and to gain self-confidence. In this dimension, positive psychology converges with the assumptions and practice of educational psychology. The objective of positive psychology is to establish the good life. Hence, there is the possibility of practical implementation of positive psychology related to a wider concept of education – that of lifelong learning. According to Seligman, positive psychology has immense importance to education in the widest sense. Accordingly, Seligman says, positive psychology can be useful in education and become a reliable tool for definite increases in mental well-being. The theoretical as well as the practical solutions of educational psychology are based on the assumption that the development of a young individual is to be made due to impacts and requirements of social surroundings such as family, school setting and culture. The aim of educational psychology is to help young people find their self-esteem, the meaning of life, and to gain self-confidence. In this dimension, positive psychology converges with the assumptions and practice of educational psychology. The objective of positive psychology is to establish original theoretical models concerning the good life in general, with their practical large-scale application going beyond educational settings. Hence, there is the possibility of practical implementation of positive psychology related to a wider concept of education. Education consists of a foundation of care, trust, and respect for diversity, where school is one of the primary places where children and youth engage in identity and social development and to develop the plans and motivation to reach their goals. It is the best setting to promote positive psychology interventions that increase student wellbeing.Positive psychology provides a learning environment that focuses on giving all students a chance to build their resilience and learn to cope with and manage challenging situations.The importance of social and emotional development in young children has become a primary priority of early education. Successful developmental during this period includes the ability to form positive relationships, to establish positive self-esteem, to effectively express feelings and regulate emotions, to persevere and engage positively with challenging tasks, and to adopt a positive outlook in a dynamic environment. Therefore, the increasing psychological and mental health focus on the foundational early childhood developmental period has led to promoting socio-emotional development and personal strengths in early childhood education. This area has flourished recently in the form of Positive Education that seeks to integrate positive psychology with educational practices. This educational intervention programs helps to improve children's well-being and mental health positive through psychology constructs like character strengths, gratitude, positive emotions and engagement. Positive psychology is very well in the field of education, such as the training of optimism – the Penn Resiliency Program – or supporting positive emotions – Three Blessings – or the diagnosis and further development of strengths – Signature Strengths

Seligman suggests that the field of education, particularly as far as the younger generation is concerned, should turn to look to the future, should focus on positive emotions, social commitment, the search for meaning, for harmony in human relations; on positive achievements, as well as upon health and growth.

The contribution of Positive Psychology in Education:

1. The aim of positive education is to develop scientifically positive psychology programs in school settings that promote student and staff wellbeing.

2. Positive psychology has top priority ensuring the wellbeing of students n improving academic outcomes, school retention, and student engagement.

3. Positive education interventions aim to facilitate skills that help students achieve a high level of life satisfaction and overall wellbeing, centering on character development and proactive programs to boost mental health.

4. The focus of positive psychology revolves around subjective wellbeing of students.

5. Positive psychology increases in student wellbeing, the quality and quantity of student learning, boosts positive mood and provides attention and motivation in students.

6. Positive psychology interventions increase student wellbeing since school is one of the primary places where children and youth engage in identity and social development.

7. Positive psychology is largely centered on students to makes them happy, regardless of their age, orientation, or life status.

8. Positive psychology provides insight to form the foundation for a successful life and gives an individual further insight into their personal strengths.

9. Positive psychology in the classroom can also have practical benefits. Students who feel supported and engaged will be more focused in class, will connect better with their teachers and classmates, and will achieve better academic outcomes.

Positive classroom environment will have the following characteristics:

- a safe, welcoming atmosphere
- a sense of belonging among students
- trust between students and the teacher
- willingness in students to ask questions, participate and take risks
- clear expectations, and fair and honest feedback, from the teacher.

There are lots of tools and activities can be used to bring positive psychology into the classroom. The PERMA framework is successful tool to be used in positive psychology as under:

- **Positive emotions**: students can focus on things that make them feel good, like being recognized for quality work or having the chance to help a classmate.

- **Engagement**: students feel absorbed by their work because they find it challenging but achievable, and it explores new ideas in interesting ways.

- **Relationships**: students feel able to build strong connections with you, and with other students, through feedback and activities.

- **Meaning**: students understand the purpose of their work and why it's important for them to learn.

- **Achievement**: students receive encouraging and honest feedback on their work and feel a sense of accomplishment and success.

By focusing on each of these areas, student can build their classroom into a positive learning environment.

Positive Psychology in Ageing

The progressive ageing of the world's older population is perhaps one of the most significant demographic changes in modern times. Old age means people transition into their golden years. Positive aging is widely regarded as a multidimensional approach of maintaining high physical and cognitive functions, remaining free of debilitating disease and disability, and staying engaged in productive and socially-focused activity. Elderly or old age consists of ages nearing or surpassing the average life span of human beings. The boundary of old age cannot be defined exactly because it does not have the same meaning in all societies. According to the Maintenance and Welfare of Parents and Senior Citizens Act (2007), senior citizen means any person being a citizen of India, who has attained the age of 60 years or above. However, Aging can be a very difficult thing to accept. When we are no longer able to do the same energetic and physical things we did in our younger years, it can have a severe psychological impact. Bones break easier, vision weakens, hair turns white or falls out, and muscles lose elasticity. They are neglected by society and having feeling of being less valued to society and even to friends and family. Anxiety and depression often accompany the trials of coping with disease and relating aging challenges and also leads to poor mental health. It becomes difficult to manage typical daily activities which can inspire frustration, anger, and family infighting. Positive Psychology recognizes positive aging as "the process of maintaining a positive attitude, feeling good about yourself, keeping fit and healthy, and engaging fully in life as you age. Positive aging is about living intentionally with a mindset and lifestyle toward maintaining a vibrant and rewarding conclusion of years. Other names for this are healthy aging, productive aging, and competent aging. Older age around the world are rapidly becoming major components of our population, the number is significant because of increasing lifespan. Basically, the successful ageing model challenges the presumption of aging as a period of decreasing health and social losses. With increasing age suffering from some type of chronic disease becomes a normal experience. Despite this, the physical health and functionality are relevant factors when determining the sense of general well-being. However, older adults can experience happiness and well-being regardless of their physical problems by compensating for them through psychosocial resources.

These increases in longevity and the quality of life of older adults constitute a challenge to mental health professionals working to help the growing older population not only to live longer and healthier but also better and happier.

The Positive psychology in Ageing defines: "the process of maintaining a positive attitude, feeling good about yourself, keeping fit and healthy, and engaging fully in life as you age.

Strategies to Promote Positive Aging (Strategies to Enhance Positive Aging)

The objective of positive health psychology is to encourage

190 :: Positive Psychology

sen ors to be more cognizant of their own resources and their strong heal h points to cultivate their rich physical, cognitive, and social quali.ies. It should be so designed to encourage better health through changes in diet, cutting down on cigarettes and alcohol, getting more exercise, and learning ways to manage stress and increase relaxation. Taking these steps toward maintaining a healthier lifestyle can reduce the impact of disease. Seniors are encouraged to acquire a more positive attitude toward one's own self and the past including improving interactions with significant others. Seniors can work on their autonomy, learn to have a voice, and reinforce their capabilities to make decisions affecting their lives.

1. **Loneliness:** One of the most effective approaches to implement and maintain positive aging in your life is do not keep yourself loneliness.

2. **Conversation**: Keep frequent and genuine conversations with other people and we need connection.

3. **Friendship**: Don't pretend older age; celebrate it, go against the grain and do the opposite of what is expected, and make new friendships.

4. **Exercise**: Do exercise minimum of 30 minutes or some kind of movement every day

5. Engage in activity that challenges your mental capacities and never stop learning.

6. **Live healthy.** Eat a healthy diet, get plenty of sleep, keep your weight manageable, don't drink too much and don't smoke.

7. **Stay connected to others**. Maintain vibrant relationships with friends, family, spouse, and people you meet or know in your community.

8. **Practice positive emotion:** Be intentional about feeling good about your age.

9. **Ask for help**: You won't be able to do everything you used to and there's no shame in asking help.

Theoretical Perspectives of Ageing

Ageing is the stage in a person's life that begins at 60 and goes on till death. This period is full of struggles and challenges and is characterized by both physical and psychosocial changes and change in life style and the relationship with the family and society. Theorists have expressed different perspectives to ageing some are a few theories that elucidate the challenges, struggles and joys of the ageing process but some have positive approach and old age as a stage of innumerable possibilities.

1. **Biological approaches to ageing:** The biological theories such as the 'wear and tear' theory, decline in energy theory, cross linkage theory, genetic ageing and ageing due to a decrease in function of the immune system explain the cause of the weakening of the body, including the nervous system. But due to increase in lifespan and medical advances in such a manner that help to reduce health risks and disability in later life are easily available. Bowling and Dieppe (2005) explain that the biomedical theories define successful ageing by laying emphasis on the optimization of life expectancy and minimizing on mental and physical deterioration and disability. Their focus is in the absence of chronic disease and the risk factors associated with disease, good health, mobility, increasing levels of independent physical and cognitive functioning.

2. **Psychosocial approaches to ageing:** Eric Erikson was one of the first who developed a psychological theory that extended into old age. Successful ageing as a dynamic process and are the result of one's experiences and development through life. It is the ability to develop and learn by using one's past experiences to cope with circumstances in the present and in the process being able to maintain a realistic sense of self. They proposed that successful ageing is a result of being satisfied with one's past and present life. Satisfaction includes happiness for life, determination and resilience, self-concept, mood, morale, relationships between anticipated and achieved goals and overall wellbeing. Effective social functioning is another important domain of successful ageing in which there

will be social integration, positive relationships along with reciprocal interactions and participation in society. Some of the psychological characteristics for successful ageing suggested which include a positive outlook, self-efficacy, self-worth, autonomy and effective coping when faced with challenging situations.

Erikson's criteria of successful aging are subjective. Individuals who view their life as having been a failure or as very unproductive lead to depression, anger, and finding fault with oneself and the surrounding world.

3. **Sociological approaches to ageing**: Successful ageing in older adults can be seen from the point of view of the sociological theories of ageing, namely the disengagement theory and the activity theory. They focus on the role and status of the elderly and relationship of the older person to society. Cumming and Henry (1961), state that as people age, they voluntarily slow down by retiring and are less involved with life. They withdraw from society as it relieves them from difficult roles and responsibilities and also helps to maintain life satisfaction. In short, they disengage themselves from society. However, some amount of activity is necessary to live a fulfilling life irrespective of how old the person and keeping healthy and enhancing life satisfaction. People who are mentally, physically and socially active can adjust better life to the ageing process. According to Continuity theory some older adults in society, they do not change but maintain their personalities, behaviour, relationships and life style and continue their activities as when they were younger. However, this theory has also been criticized as it does not consider monetary aspects, illness, physical decline and disorders that are associated with old age. It also does not consider differences in gender, ethnicity, race and life style of older adults.

4. **Theory of Cognitive Appraisal:** The theory of cognitive appraisal states that stress is not a response to a stimulus in the environment but a cognitive appraisal of a particular event. Stress results when a person appraises a situation and feels

that it is taxing or exceeds his/her resources and endangers his/her well – being. The amount of stress experienced by the older adults depends on how he/ she appraises the challenges they experience especially during the death of a spouse. Stress can result from a feeling of helplessness, physical exhaustion, depression, inadequate or absence of family or social support, depletion of economic resources, emotional attachment and uncertainty about the future.

5. **Family Approaches**: Family is an integral part of the life of an individual and hence family life cycle stages and its impact on individuals within a family context need consideration. Structural family therapy is also relevant here as it believes that the family comprises of individuals who are constantly interacting and influencing each other and it gives a framework to understand and analyze these family interactions. The family in later life where the couple accepts retirement and old age. There is a shift in generational roles where the older couple begins to explore new roles in the family and society. The older couples make their contribution in terms of wisdom and experience and they in turn are cared for and supported by the younger generation. They have to cope with the death of spouse, siblings and peers and finally while they integrate and review their life, they begin to prepare for their own death.

Positive Approach to Ageing

Older adults can also enjoy a productive and positive life and therefore it is important to understand the dimensions to positive ageing and the contribution older adults make to the family and society in more detail. Often after retirement, there is a change in life style and economic status which could result in a change in personal identity. Older people have less to contribute in terms of economic resources and this often makes them feel powerless and incapable. But at the same time, they have much to share in terms of wisdom and experience. Those who age positively live longer and healthier lives, and enjoy a good quality of life. Positive psychology focuses on people's strengths and enhancing their positive functioning. Psychology generally had a threefold mission namely curing mental illness, helping people live fulfilling lives and identifying and fostering new talent.

There are four important approaches successful ageing as under:

1. Firstly, self- efficacy or confidence is the belief in one's ability that helps an individual make the necessary effort to be successful in times of challenges.

2. Secondly, hope is a way of thinking that comprises of goals, pathways and willpower. It is the positive motivational state that involves goal oriented determination and productive planning in order to achieve one's goals.

3. Thirdly optimism helps one to persevere with a hope to succeed not just in the present but in the future as well. Optimism reinforces self-efficacy and hope.

4. Lastly, resiliency is a positive way of coping with stress, conflict or change and helps one bounce back when faced with problems and adversity.

Application of Positive Psychology in Health

Many aspects of life are necessary to promote psychological health, including meaningful relationships with family and/or friends, adequate sleep and movement/exercise, strategies for stress management, recreation, and a healthy diet. Another important consideration for optimal mental, emotional, and even physical well-being is one's attitude toward healthy life. Psychological health involves the emotional, behavioral, and social health aspects of a person's life. These three facets are the foundation of mental health, determining how a person functions daily and reacts to adverse situations that may arise. Psychological health assets positive emotions, life satisfaction, optimism, life purpose, social support and associated with good health. The World Health Organization also defines health to include physical, social, and psychological factors. Habits of healthy person, according to positive psychology, include intentional gratitude, savoring, mindfulness, and acts of kindness, as well as the intentional pursuit of meaning and purpose, high-quality connections, and engagement. The field of positive health overlaps with allied approaches like disease prevention, health promotion, and wellness. The explosion of research on "positive psychology" includes multiple theoretical and research areas that share a common focus on positive human functioning, psychological health, and adaptation to illness and other forms of adversity. Positive psychology increased emphasis on positive effect, meaning, mastery, personal growth, forgiveness, gratitude, hope, optimism, and spirituality, their relation to mental and physical health, and their potential for applications to promote well-being and health. When we consider the contribution of these perspectives to health psychology, we find many ideas that may lead to interventions that promote healing and health.

Positive psychology characteristics positive health not only as a long and disease-free life but additionally in a variety of ways as under:

- Positive emotions
- Greater recuperative ability
- Rapid wound healing
- Life satisfaction
- Optimism
- Forgiveness
- Self-regulation
- Vitality and zest
- Life meaning and purpose
- Helping others and volunteering
- Good social relationships
- Spirituality and religiosity

Positive psychology is the scientific study of a healthy and flourishing life and study positive emotions, positive behaviors, and character strengths that enable individuals and communities to thrive. Positive psychological factors play a protective role against health risks. There have been extensive studies on negative psychological factors such as stress, depression, hostility, and their effects on increased risk of various health problems.

Positive psychology interventions influence some of the biological and behavioral processes implicated in good health. For example, inducing positive emotions speeds cardiovascular recovery following a stressful event. Moreover, training in mindfulness meditation can boost immune function. On the positive side, research shows that what we call positive psychological health assets (eg, positive emotions, life satisfaction, optimism, positive relationships, life purpose) are prospectively associated with good health measured in a variety of ways. Also on the positive side, interventions have been developed that increase these assets; lasting effects require a lifestyle change.

Lifestyle-related diseases, such as cardiovascular disease (CVD), stemming from the risk factors of tobacco use, physical inactivity, poor nutrition, high stress, and social isolation, are a global health concern. Additional public health crises include the epidemic, risky alcohol use, and rising suicides rates. Stress, anxiety, depression, or life dissatisfaction can lead to these unhealthy habits and conditions. Positive psychology offer the potential to improve all of these factors by promoting emotional well-being, facilitating healthy lifestyles, and leading to physiologic shifts that can address the major lifestyle-related public health crises. The physiologic improvements associated with positive psychology-based habits are broad. For example, a greater sense of meaning correlates with fewer strokes and myocardial infarctions, fewer urgent care visits, increased healthy behaviors, better preventive care, better heart rate variability. Increased mindfulness is associated with lower pain, anxiety, depression, hostility, somatic focus, and stress; and increased energy, enthusiasm, relaxation, healthy habits, immune function, cognitive capacity, self-regulation and social connection.

The field of medicine has long focused on the prevention, diagnosis, treatment, and cure of disease. But psychological health is more than the absence of disease. The emerging concept of Positive Health takes an innovative approach to health and well-being that focuses on promoting people's positive health assets like strengths that can contribute to a healthier, longer life. Positive psychology helps identify these assets, which might include biological factors, such as high heart rate variability; subjective factors, such as optimism; and functional factors, such as a stable marriage. Positive Health encompasses the understanding that people desire well-being in its own right and they desire it above and beyond the relief of their suffering. Seligman and a team of researchers are working to identify potential health assets and see if they may reveal a variety of potent, low-cost approaches to enhance well-being and help to protect against physical and mental illness. If health assets can be scientifically linked to positive health outcomes, the ultimate goal would be to design interventions that can help build and sustain these assets to help people increase their chances of living a healthier, longer life.

Mental health disorders affect the vast majority of the world population today. And the root of all these troubles lies in our brain – the key to understanding which lies in the study of neuroscience. Mental disturbances activate neural connections that provoke negative thoughts, actions, and emotions. By understanding the neuroscience behind these psychological problems positive psychology is very useful by applying motivation, positive thinking, happiness, and emotional resilience, and more on mental illness. Neuroscience makes mental health interventions more focused and evidence-based. For example, schizophrenic patients suffer a lot in terms of their cognitive functioning. Their dysfunctional thoughts prevent them from getting back to their usual lives or perform daily life activities.

Positive interventions are now an integral part of mental health treatment as under:

1. **Strength-based Therapy:** Strength-based techniques help in finding strengths and act on them with focused attention. It improved their quality of life and helped them focus on their strengths. Strength-oriented techniques involve:

   • Solution-focused therapies, including conversations, objective tests, and group sessions. The therapist and the client focus on how to accept what is wrong and outgrow his negativities for a better outcome.

- Case management that focuses on understanding the capabilities of the person.
- Family support and individual supportive counseling.
- Narrating encouraging stories of resilience and positivity that might inspire the individual and help in recuperation.

2. **Quality of Life Therapy:** The quality of life measure works on the principles of positive psychology and cognitive therapy. It helps clients discover their goals in life, motivates them to follow their dreams and look inside for finding a deeper meaning of self-satisfaction. It uses measures like the Quality of LifeInventory and the CASIO model of self-satisfaction and follows a step-by-step treatment process. The Quality of Life therapy is evidence-based, research-oriented, and caters to the needs of today's adult population.

3. **Hope Therapy:**Hope therapy operates on the theory of hope that suggests that emotions can be evaluated or changed according to fruitful goal pursuits. Hope therapy aims to promote a hopeful attitude among the clients who are undergoing a mental turmoil. It works exceptionally well for major depression and other stress disorders. The goal of the hope therapy is to enhance insight and help to reconnect with the self.

4. **Well-being Therapy:** The wellbeing therapy model roots to Carol D. Ryff's model of psychological wellbeing. Ryff's model was multidimensional, including factors like environmental mastery, personal satisfaction, a more profound sense of meaning in life, acceptance, resilience, and positive social connections. wellbeing therapy promotes happiness by letting clients identify their thought blocks. Wellbeing therapy is useful as a relapse or prevention management intervention.

Use of these techniques such as:

- Writing about significant life experiences and the emotions associated with it.

- Identifying the negative thoughts that cause trouble by active communication with the therapist or counselor.
- Challenging the negative thoughts with the help of the therapist and planning practical ways to overcome them.
- Growing a positive attitude towards the self by accepting, forgiving, and integrating.
- Encouraging positive actions such as self-expression, journaling, active communication, and an overall healthy lifestyle.

Advantage of Positive Psychology in Health

1. Positive psychology has helped to articulate the meaning of health and well-being. Positive psychology is an umbrella term for the scientific study of the various healthy and thriving lives for the self and others like - positive emotions, life meaning, engaging work, and close relationships.

2. Positive psychology plays a protective role against health risks.

3. **Optimism**—Positive psychology usually assessed with self-report surveys relates to good health and a long life. For example, in the case of optimism, biologically, it has been linked to better immune system functioning, and behaviorally, people who are optimistic engage in healthier behaviors. They eat healthy, exercise, do not smoke or drink, and seek medical care when they need. Socially. All of these are associated with health benefits.

4. **In addition,** the importance of social support and positive relationships on good health and well-being has long been documented. Supportive social relationships were associated with longevity, less cognitive decline with aging, greater resistance to infectious disease, and better management of chronic illnesses

5. **Practice:** It promotes healthy lifestyles with positive psychology interventions can effectively prevent, treat, and even reverse the majority of chronic disease burden globally.

For some people, being happy comes naturally and easily. Others need to work at it. How does one go about becoming happier? That's where positive psychology comes in. This relatively new field of research has been exploring how people and institutions can support the quest for increased satisfaction and meaningful life. There is power in positive thinking. Positive emotions are linked with better health, longer life, and greater well-being. It has uncovered several routes to happiness as under:

1. **Feeling good**: seeking pleasurable emotions and sensations

2. **Engaging fully:** pursuing goals and activities that engage you fully

3. **Doing good**: searching for meaning outside yourself

4. **Gratitude**: expressing appreciation for what you have in your life

5. **Savoring pleasure**: placing your attention on pleasure as it occurs and consciously enjoying the experience as it unfolds

6. **Being mindful**: focusing your attention on what is happening at the moment and accepting it without judgment

7. **Self-compassion**: consoling yourself as needed, taking the time to nurture yourself, and building the motivation to try again.

Factors of Positive Health and Well-being

Factors facilitating positive health and well-being are:

1. Diet:

Diet can affect health independently or may enhance or modify the effects of stress in combination with other factors:

1. How much nutrition one needs depends on one's activity level, genetic structure, climate and health history. In fact, there is no one diet, which is ideal for everyone, in all situations.

2. Stress is supposed to affect diet and weight in many ways. People, who are under stress or in negative moods, are often seen eating more. They seek 'comfort foods' or foods that make them feel better.

3. Stress may increase consumption of less healthy foods. Such people gain weight and loose stamina to fight stress.

4. Obesity and weight gain is a problem for a section of the society. A much larger section of the society, which is below the poverty line, suffers from malnutrition.

5. In the condition of poverty, women are the one who are most malnourished. Studies have shown that in India diets of female children and women are inadequate due to discriminatory practices.

2. Exercise:

1. Exercise is directly related to promoting positive health.

2. Two kinds of physical exercises essential for good health are 'stretching exercises' such as yogic asanas and 'aerobic exercises' such as jogging, swimming and cycling.

3. Stretching exercises have a calming effect.

4. Aerobic exercises increase the arousal level of the body.

5. Yogic asanas provide systematic stretching to all the muscles and joints of the body and massages the glands and other body organs.

6. Regular exercise reduces stress because it improves efficiency of vital body organs and improves immune system.

7. Positive health and well-being come through a positive attitude of the mind.

8. Positive health is the state of complete physical, mental, social and spiritual well-being. It is not merely the absence of disease.

9. Positive health comprises high quality of personal relationships, a sense of purpose in life, self-regard, mastery of life skills and resilience to stress, trauma and change.

3. Positive Attitude:

Positive health and well-being can be realized by:

1. Perceiving the reality fairly accurately.

2. Tolerating and understanding different points of view.

3. Having a sense of purpose in life

4. Having a sense of responsibility, accepting blame for failures and taking credit for success.

5. Being open to new ideas, activities, or ways of doing things.

6. Having a good sense of humor, to be able to laugh at oneself and absurdities of life helps to see things in their proper perspective.

4. Positive Thinking:

1. Positive thinking leads to a belief that adversity can be handled successfully whereas negative thinking and pessimism anticipate disaster.

2. Optimism: which is the inclination to expect favourable life outcomes is directly linked to psychological and physical well-being.

3. Optimists use more problem-focused coping and seek advice and help from others. This optimism function helps the individual to cope up stress effectively.

Application of Positive Psychology in Sports

Sports is fundamental to the early development of children and youth and sports contribute to the holistic development such as honesty, teamwork, fair play, respect for themselves and others and adherence to the rules. Physical activity is the most important factor in reaching optimal functioning. Increased activity levels have been linked with improved cognitive functioning, better mood, lower incidence of mental illness and also increased life span. Sports can be stressful with the time demands, emphasis on winning and high expectations. Maintain emotional control may be essential to the ability to cope with the various demands of sports. These elements are characteristics of *mental toughness*. Mental toughness is dependent upon situational factors such as stress, pressure, and adversity. Mentally tough people are generally high in conscientiousness, extraversion, and agreeableness and show low levels of neuroticism.Positive psychology focuses on those things in life that make life worth living and it is foundations in the science of human strengths, happiness and wellbeing. There are three pillars of happiness pleasure, engagement and meaning.. Some of the basic tenets of positive psychology include: "happiness, hope, optimism, wellbeing, resilience and flow". It is about how people can feel good and thrive applying their natural strengths so as to make the best of them. These two aspects of psychology have so converged that the frequently field is now referred to as "positive sports psychology".

A sports psychologist teaches mental skills for an enhanced performance and at times of poor emotional well-being and provides assistance as well. On the other hand, a positive psychologist works in the health model with a goal of moving from starting point into the plus scale of wellbeing. Positive Psychology has a number of positive constructs that can be implemented in healthy populations to improve well-being, i.e. from exercises focused on positive emotions to improved performance. Positive psychology in sports has been defined as the science of happiness and strength. Sports can be an integral platform for developing positive psychology constructs such as mental toughness, grit and resiliency among athletes that can increase their motivation levels which is essential to target goals.

Theories of Positive Psychology in Sports:

1. Self-Determination Theory: This theory postulated the existence of three inherent universal needs, or basic psychological nutrients. These needs enhance motivation and well-being. These needs inspire progression from extrinsic to intrinsic motivation, thus enabling individuals to feel more self-determined. Self-determination is associated with higher self-esteem, work enjoyment, and other positive outcomes. These are as under:

1. **Autonomy**: The need to choose what one is doing, being an agent of one's own life
2. **Competence**: The need to feel confident in doing what one is doing
3. **Relatedness**: The need to have human connections that are

close and secure, while still respecting autonomy and facilitating competence.

2. Mental Toughness Theory: According to this theory, when someone possesses these characteristics, are considered to be mentally tough. This theory comprising of twelve characteristics as under:

1. Unshakable self-belief in one's ability to achieve goals in competition
2. Unshakable self belief that one has qualities and abilities that are unique in a way to make one better than everyone else
3. The ability to come back from set-backs due to motivation to succeed
4. An insatiable desire and internalized motives (internal locus of control)
5. Thriving on pressure
6. Knowing that anxiety in competition is inevitable and that one has the skills to cope with it
7. Not negatively affected by another's good or poor performance
8. Doesn't let personal/life issues distract one from the task at hand
9. The ability to turn on focus for a sport, and also turn it off
10. Not distracted by task/competitive specific distractions
11. Can push aside physical or emotional pain when present and maintain proper technique and high performance and
12. Have psychological control during unexpected and uncontrollable events that occur in competition.

4. Growth Mindset Theory: This theory puts forth an important fact that growth mindset individuals don't mind failure much because they realize their performance can be improved. According to Dweck (2006), sportsmen having growth mindset are aware of where does achievement comes from and are more likely to perceive a challenge as an opportunity rather than an obstacle to overcome, and respond with constructive thoughts in the belief that they can improve, achieve and get better.

4. PERMA Model: The model is a theory of well-being which clearly has emerged as a link between positive psychology and performance. "PERMA" stands for Positive Emotions (P), certain skills and exercises can boost our experience of positive emotions. Engagement (E), it involves identifying and cultivating personal strengths, virtues and talents. Positive Relationships (R), it is key to all relationships to balance. It is not enough to surround ourselves with 'friends' - we must also listen and share, make an effort to maintain our connections, and work to make those connections strong. Meaning (M), people who belong to a community and pursue shared meaningful goals are happier than people who don't. Achievement (A) creating and working toward goals helps us anticipate and build hope for the future.

5. Performance Pyramid Model: This is latest model given by Pidgeon in 2016. This illustrates the lower order skills are placed at the bottom, with the higher order skills to the top. The General skills placed at the very bottom of the pyramid comprises of attitude and motivation of traditional sports skills. These are skills that are thought to provide a base from which growth mindset follows allowing for awareness of learning opportunities, and encourages challenge. Middle order skills are next to general skills in the performance pyramid. Self-talk from traditional sports skills are linked with positive psychology concepts of self-awareness, strengths, and positive emotions. Effective use of strengths can help to provide a sense of direction, build resilience, increase positive emotions, and help to achieve goals. Finally, moving to the top part of the traditional sports skills of the pyramid i.e. Peak performance skills that are associated with the management of emotions. It is related to the positive psychology concepts of resilience and emotional intelligence. Resilience is characterized by learning from adversity, rising above it, and performing even better. In sport, developing emotional intelligence can enhance a sportsmen's ability to control emotional impulses that may lead to poor performances and create emotions that lead to good performances. There are certain areas of sport psychology that may be matched with constructs from positive psychology, to illustrate the benefits of drawing upon both disciplines for a fuller picture. Using a performance pyramid which allows for a visual representation in which they move up through the levels.

Importance of Positive Psychology in Sports

1. Sports place tremendous pressure on the competitor's mind in competition and in training, and that pressure must be supported by robust and reliable psychological constructs

2. The abilities to maintain focus under such pressure and also control actions during extreme circumstances of uncertainty can be strengthened by the mental training and skills a sports psychologist provides.

3. Mental preparation helps ready the individual and team for competition and offers an edge over an adversary while optimizing performance.

Meeting Life Challenges

Life has full of challenges but one must have the knack of turning winds in their favour and meeting life challenges effectively. The term 'challenging' emphasizes that the behavior constitute a challenge. The problem lies in the interaction between the persons, their behavior and their social environment. Challenging behavior often result in self- injury or injury to others, causes damage to the physical environment, interferes with the acquisition of a new skill or socially isolate the learner. Life is full of challenges. Such as challenges posed by examination to students, challenges about a carrier, think of a child who loses his/her parents, a young women who loses her husband in an accident or children who are physically or mentally challenged and so on. All of us try to meet these challenges in our own way. Life challenges are not necessarily stressful. Much depends how a challenge is viewed. Stress is like electricity which provides energy but too high or too little energy, becomes hazardous. Similarly too much stress or too little stress have adverse effect for our well-being, optimum stress is healthy. Stress is a part of life.Stress is neither a stimulus nor a response but an ongoing transactional process between the individual and the environment. Stress has two levels: Eustress-that is good, healthy, positive inspiring and motivating. Distress: It is negative, unhealthy de-motivating and causes our body's wear and tear. Life poses challenges all the time. Life is a big challenge. All of us try to meet these challenges in our own way. Some of us succeed while others succumb to such life stresses. Life challenges are not necessarily stressful. Much depends on how a challenge is viewed. A number 11 batsman in a cricket team will view facing a fast bowler's delivery differently than would an opening batsman, who will look forward to such a challenge. It is said that one's best comes out when one is challenged. We will like to consider in this chapter how a life condition turns into a challenge or a cause of stress. Further, we will also see how people respond to various life challenges as well as stressful situations.

Life Challenges and adjustment:

Life is a big challenge. It presents a continuous chain of struggle for existence and survival for example if one aspires to join civil services, one works very hard but is not selected one may change one's goal and feel inclined to join lectureship in any university. By restoring to such means one protects one's self from the possible injury to ones ego, failure or frustration. It is sort of shifting to more defensive position in order to face the challenge of circumstances after getting failure in earlier attempt or attempts. This special virtue and strength of the living organism is termed as adjustment. Adjustment is a process by which living organism maintains a balance between its need and the circumstances that influence the satisfaction of these needs.

1. Different stressors may produce different patterns of stress reaction.

2. Stress is embedded in the ongoing process that involves individuals interacting with their social and cultural environment.

3. Stress is a dynamic mental/cognitive state. It is a disruption in homeostasis/imbalance that gives rise to resolution of the imbalance/ restoration of homeostasis.

4. Perception of stress is dependent on an individual's cognitive appraisal of events and the resources available to deal with them.

   Primary Appraisal: Primary appraisal refers to the perception of a new or changing environment as positive, neutral or negative in its consequences. Negative events are appraised for their possible harm, threat or challenge.

   1. Harm appraisals is the assessment of the damage that has already been done by an event.

   2. Threat appraisals are the assessment of possible future damage that may be brought about by the event.

   3. Challenge appraisals are associated with more confident expectations of the ability to cope with the stressful event, the potential to overcome and even profit from the event.

   Secondary Appraisal: Secondary appraisal refers to that assessment of one's coping abilities resources and whether they will be sufficient to meet the harm, threat or challenge of the event. These resources may be mental, physical, personal or social. If he/she thinks one has a positive attitude, health, skills and social support to deal with the crises, he/she will feel less stressed. Appraisals are very subjective and will depend on many factors:

   1. Past experience of dealing with such a stressful condition: If one has handled similar situations very successfully in the past, they would be less threatening for him/her.

   2. Whether the stressful event is perceived as controllable, i.e., whether one has mastery or control over a situation.

Stress

Positive psychology is a newer and increasingly popular branch of psychology that seeks to focus not on pathology, but on what contributes to human happiness and emotional health. It focuses on strengths, virtues, and factors that help people thrive and achieve a sense of fulfillment, as well as more effectively manage stress. Stress is derived from Latin word 'strictus' which means tight or narrow. Stress can be described as the pattern of responses an organism makes to stimulus event that disturbs the equilibrium and exceeds a person's ability to cope. All the challenges, problems, and difficult circumstances put us to stress. Stress can be defined as any type of change that causes physical, emotional, or psychological strain. Stress is the body's response to anything that requires attention or action. It gives energy, increases human arousal and affects performance. High stress can produce unpleasant effects and cause our performance to deteriorate. Stress is a situation that triggers a particular biological response. When you perceive a threat or a major challenge, chemicals and hormones surge throughout your body. Conversely, too much stress may cause one to feel somewhat listless and low on motivation which may lead us to perform slowly and less efficiently. It is important to remember that not all stress is inherently bad or destructive. This effects the constriction of the muscles and breathing problem under stress. Stress is often explained in terms of characteristics of the environment that are disruptive to the individual. Stressors are events that cause our body to give the stress response. Such events include noise, crowding, a bad relationship. Stress is not a factor that resides in the individual or the environment, instead it is embedded in an ongoing process that involves individuals transacting with their social and cultural environments, making appraisals of those encounters and attempting to cope with the issues that arise. Stress is a dynamic mental/cognitive state. It is a disruption in homeostasis or an imbalance that gives rise to a requirement for resolution of that imbalance or restoration of homeostasis. The perception of stress is dependent upon the individual's cognitive appraisal of events and the resources available to deal with them. An individual's response to a stressful situation largely depends upon the perceived events and how they are interpreted or appraised.

Behavioral Effects of Stress

1. **Physiological Effects:** When the human body is placed under physical or psychological stress, it increases the production of certain hormones such as adrenaline and cortisol. It causes:

1. Changes in heart-rate, blood-pressure levels, metabolism and physical activity.
2. Slowing down of digestive system.
3. Constriction of blood vessels.

1. **Cognitive Effects:** High levels of stress can lead to:
   1. Mental overload.
   2. Impairment in the ability to make sound decision.
   3. Poor concentration.
   4. Reduced short term memory.

2. **Emotional Effects:** Those who suffer from stress are more likely to experience:
   1. Mood swings.
   2. Erratic behaviour.
   3. Maladjustment with family and friends.
   4. Feeling of anxiety and depression.
   5. Increased physical and psychological tension.
   6. Intolerance.
   7. Impatience.

4. **Behavioural Effects:** Stress affects our behaviour in the form of:
   1. Eating less nutritional food.
   2. Increasing intake of stimulants such as caffeine or excessive consumption of cigarettes, alcohol and drugs.
   3. Disrupted sleep pattern.
   4. Reduced work performance.

Nature of stress:

The word stress has its origin in the latin word 'strictus', meaning tight or narrow and stringer, the verb meaning to tighten. These root words reflect the internal feelings of tightness and constriction of muscles and breathing, a common sign of stress.

The reaction of external stressor is called strain. Stress functions as a causes as well as effects.

Signs and symptoms of stress:

Stress is not always easy to recognize, but there are some ways to identify some signs that you might be experiencing too much pressure. There are individual differences in coping pattern of stress response and therefore the warning signals or signs also vary in its intensity. The signs of stress are very much dependent on how individual views them or its dimension. Intensity duration, predictability or complexity. The warning signs and its manifestation as symptoms of stress can be physical, emotional, cognitive and behavioral.

- **Psychological signs:** such as difficulty concentrating, worrying, anxiety, and trouble remembering
- **Emotional signs:** such as being angry, irritated, moody, or frustrated
- **Physical signs:** such as high blood pressure, changes in weight, frequent colds or infections, and changes in the menstrual cycle and libido
- **Behavioral signs:** such as poor self-care, not having time for the things you enjoy, or relying on drugs and alcohol to cope

However, following are some things you may experience if you're under stress:

- Physical reactions, such as headaches, body pains, stomach problems, and skin rashes
- insomnia and other sleep problems
- lower sex drive
- digestive problems
- eating too much or too little
- difficulty concentrating and making decisions
- fatigue

- Feelings of fear, shock, anger, sadness, worry, numbness, or frustration
- Changes in appetite, energy, desires, and interests

Types of Stress

A. **Physical and Environmental Stress: Physical and Environmental Stress** demands that change the state of our body like overexert ourselves physically, lack a nutritious diet, suffer an injury, or fail to get enough sleep. Environmental stresses are aspects of our surroundings that are often unavoidable such as air pollution, crowding, noise, heat of the summer, winter cold, and disasters.

B. **Psychological Stress:** These are stresses that we generate ourselves in our minds. These are personal and unique to the person experiencing them and are internal sources of stress. We worry about problems, feel anxiety, or become depressed.

   1. Frustration results from the blocking of needs and motives by something or someone that hinders us from achieving a desired goal (social discrimination, low grades).

   2. Conflicts may occur between two or more incompatible need or motives.

   Pressure (Expectations)

   a. Internal pressure stem from beliefs based upon expectations from inside us to ourselves

   b. Social pressure may be brought about from people who make excessive demands on us. Also, there are people with whom we face interpersonal difficulties.

C. **Social stress:** Social stress is caused due to social interaction.

   Social events like death or illness in the family, strained relationships, trouble with neighbors, rapid social change, poverty, discrimination, poor societal conditions are example of social stress

Sources of Stress

These vary widely from person to person.

1. **Life Events**: Major life events can be stressful, because they disturb our routine and cause upheaval. If several of these life events that are planned (e.g., moving into a new house) or unpredicted (e.g., break-up of a long-term relationship) occur within a short period of time, we find if difficult to cope with them and will be more prone to the symptoms of stress.

2. **Hassles:** Personal stresses we endure as individuals, due to the happenings in our daily life. These daily hassles may sometimes have devastating consequences for the individual who is often the one coping alone with them as others may not even be aware of them as outsiders.

3. **Traumatic Events**: Variety of extreme events (fire, train or road accident, robbery, earthquake, tsunami). The effects of these events may occur after some lapse of time and sometimes persist as symptoms of anxiety, flashbacks, dreams and intrusive thoughts, etc. Severe trauma can also strain relationships. Professional help will be needed to cope with them.

Effects of Stress of Psychological Functioning and Health

1. **Emotional Effects**: Experience mood swings, show erratic behaviour that may alienate them from family and friends, start a vicious circle of decreasing confidence, leading to more serious emotional problems.

2. **Physiological Effects**: Increases the production of certain hormones, such as adrenaline and cortical. These hormones produce marked changes in heart-rate, blood-pressure levels, metabolism and physical activity. Helps us function more effectively when we are under pressure for short periods of time, it can be extremely damaging to the body in the long-term effects.

3. **Cognitive Effects**: If pressures due to stress continue, one may suffer from mental overload. This suffering from high level of stress can rapidly cause individuals to lose their ability

to make sound decisions, poor concentration, and reduced short-term memory capacity.

4. **Behavioural Effects**: Disrupted sleep patterns, increased absenteeism, reduced work performance.

5. **Burn out**: State of physical, emotional and psychological exhaustion.

Stress Management Techniques:

1. **Relaxation Techniques**: Reduces symptoms of stress and decreases the incidence of illnesses such as high blood-pressure and heart diseases. Starts from the lower part of the body and progresses up to the facial muscles in such a way that the whole body is relaxed. Deep breathing is used along with muscle relaxation to calm the mind and relax the body.

2. **Meditation Procedures**: A sequence of learned techniques for re focusing of attention that brings about an altered state of consciousness. Such a thorough concentration that the mediator becomes unaware of any outside stimulation and reaches a different state of consciousness.

3. **Bio-feedback**: Monitors and reduces the physiological aspects of stress by providing feedback about current physiological activity and is often accompanied by relaxation training.

   1. Developing an awareness of the particular physiological response.

   2. Learning ways of controlling that physiological response in quiet conditions.

   3. Transferring that control into the conditions of everyday life.

4. **Creative Visualization**: Creative visualization is a subjective experience that uses imagery and imagination. Before visualizing one must set oneself a realistic goal, as it helps build confidence. It is easier to visualize if one's mind is quiet, body relaxed and eyes are closed.

5. **Cognitive Behavioural Techniques**: These techniques aim to inoculate people against stress. Stress inoculation training is one effective method developed by Meichenbaum. Replace negative and irrational thoughts with positive and rational ones, i.e., Follow through.

    i. Assessment involves discussing the nature of the problem and seeing it from the view-point of the person/client.

    ii. Stress reduction involves learning the techniques of reducing stress such as relaxation and self-instruction.

6. **Exercise**: It can provide an active outlet for the physiological arousal experienced in response to stress. Improves the efficiency of the heart, enhances the function of the lungs, maintains good circulation, lowers blood pressure, reduces fat in the blood, and improves the body's immune system. Promoting, Positive, Health and Well-being.

Causes of Stress (Assessment of Stress)

Some typical causes of acute or chronic stress include:

1. living through a natural or manmade disaster
2. living with chronic illness
3. surviving a life-threatening accident or illness
4. being the victim of a crime
5. experiencing familial stressors such as:
    o an abusive relationship
    o an unhappy marriage
    o prolonged divorce proceedings
    o child custody issues
6. care giving for a loved one with a chronic illness like dementia
7. living in poverty or being homeless
8. working in a dangerous profession
9. having little work-life balance, working long hours, or having a job you hate

10. military deployment

Causes of Stress

Stress is a highly subjective experience. Many of us are stressed by roughly the same things like jobs, money, being overscheduled, and relationship conflict. Different people may react more or less strongly to the same situation for several reasons.

There are many different causes of stress, and each one can affect you differently.

1. Financial obligations

Not being able to meet financial obligations is a big stressor for a lot of people.

Some situations that might cause financial stress include:

- The inability to pay your bills
- Long-term unemployment
- Increasing debt

2. Death of a loved one

Most of us have experienced the devastating emotional impact of the passing of a loved one. For many of us, it is not only grief that we feel. As well as the stress from a major loss, some people experience a mix of other emotions like loneliness, disappointment, and even anger.

3. Job loss

The loss of a job is not just about the loss of income. Very often, it causes our self-confidence to take a knock as well. In some cases, being stressed and unable to find work for a long period of time can lead to job search depression. Feeling hopeless about your job prospects and career path can further exacerbate stress levels.

4. Traumatic events

Traumatic events like natural disasters and car accidents are often completely out of our control. These kinds of unpredictable and unforeseen events naturally create a lot of stress and even post-traumatic stress disorder (PTSD) for those that experience them.

5. Problems at work

In today's increasingly fast-paced world, many of us feel that we constantly have to do more at work to keep our jobs. These compounds with the increase in time pressure that most of us feel from today's near-instantaneous communications. Workplace stress can be especially prevalent among working parents and women in male-dominated industries. Regardless of the reason, though, constant stressors at work can cause many employees to suffer from burnout.

6. Emotional Well-being struggles

All of us are subject to low moods and experience worry. But these emotional states can lead to chronic stress without the right emotional regulation skills.In turn, this can develop into anxiety and depression.

7. Relationship issues

While all relationships create stress, many types of stressors are relatively mild and easily dealt with. It is the larger issues within relationship, such as divorce or an unhappy marriage, that produce a lot of stress for the people involved.

Stress vs. Anxiety

Stress can sometimes be mistaken for anxiety, and experiencing a great deal of stress can contribute to feelings of anxiety. Experiencing anxiety can make it more difficult to cope with stress and may contribute to other health issues, including increased depression, susceptibility to illness, and digestive problems.

Stress and anxiety contribute to nervousness, poor sleep, high blood pressure, muscle tension, and excess worry. In most cases, stress is caused by external events, while anxiety is caused by your internal reaction to stress. Stress may go away once the threat or the situation resolves, whereas anxiety may persist even after the original stressor is gone.

Impact of Stress

Stress can have several effects on health and well-being. It can make it more challenging to deal with life's daily hassles, affect interpersonal relationships, and have detrimental effects on health. The connection between mind and body is apparent when examine stress's impact on life.

1. Feeling stressed over a relationship, money, or living situation can create physical health issues. The inverse is also true. Health problems, whether you're dealing with high blood pressure or diabetes, will also affect your stress level and mental health. When your brain experiences high degrees of stress, your body reacts accordingly.

2. Serious acute stress, like being involved in a natural disaster or getting into a verbal altercation, can trigger heart attacks, arrhythmias, and even sudden death. However, this happens mostly in individuals who already have heart disease.[6]

3. Stress also takes an emotional toll. While some stress may produce feelings of mild anxiety or frustration, prolonged stress can also lead to burnout, anxiety disorders, and depression.

4. Chronic stress can have a serious impact on your health as well. If you experience chronic stress, your autonomic nervous system will be overactive, which is likely to damage your body.

Life Skills

Life skills are abilities for adaptive and positive behaviour that enables individual to deal effectively with stressful situations. Life skills are defined as "a group of psychosocial competencies and interpersonal skills that help people make informed decisions, solve problems, think critically and creatively, communicate effectively, build healthy relationships, empathize with others, and cope with and manage their lives in a healthy and productive manner. Life skills may be directed toward personal actions or actions toward others, as well as toward actions to change the surrounding environment to make it conducive to health. The Basic Life skills provide readily available tools to deal with challenges of daily lives from managing their emotions to make an informed decision. It also helps develop personality, talents, and mental and physical abilities, and realize their true potential through learning to know one and others, and make effective decisions to live harmonically together in the society.

Few such skills are as follows (Types of Skill):

1. Assertiveness:
1. It helps to communicate, clearly and confidently, our feelings, needs, wants and thoughts.
2. It is ability of an individual to say 'no' to a request which is against his wishes.
3. If one is assertive then he or she feels confident high self-esteem and maintains his/her identity. '

2. Time: Management:
1. Learning time management determines quality of life.
2. It is setting the priorities, goals and values in life.
   Each day making list of things one wants to accomplish:
3. Arranging work schedule.
4. Changing perception of time.
5. Setting aside time in schedule for exercise and leisure activities
6. Learning to plan time.

3. Rational Thinking:
1. It is challenging the distorted thinking and irrational beliefs.
2. Deriving the anxiety provoking thoughts.
3. Making positive statements.
4. It is learning to ignore negative thoughts and images.

4. Improving Relationship: It consists following essential skills:
1. Listening to what the other person is saying.
2. Expressing what one feels and thinks.

3. Accepting the other person's opinions and feelings, even if they are different from your own.

4. Avoiding jealously and sulking behaviour.

5. Self-care: Healthy mind in healthy body.

1. Learning right pattern of breathing i.e., relaxed, slow, stomach-centered breathing from diaphragm.

2. Avoiding environmental stress like pollutions, because it affects our mood.

6. Overcoming Unhelpful Habits: Perfectionism, avoidance, procrastination and our strategies which provides short-term gain but makes the individual vulnerable to stress.

P ostponing the things like 'I will do it later' just to avoid confrontation due to the fear of failure.

Basic Life Skills

The Basic Life Skills is based in evidence-based psychosocial methodology including cognitive-behavioral therapy, mindfulness and resilience-building activities. These skills can help youth better understand themselves, get along with others, and gain tools to cope with life's inevitable difficulties.

1. **Self-awareness**: Knowing and living with oneself: This theme covers topics that foster the student's relationship and understanding of themselves including their thoughts, feelings and behaviors.

2. **Interpersonal SkillsorSocial skills:** Knowing and living with others: The lessons in this theme explore how to establish healthy, respectful relation- ships; lessons highlight the use of non-violent communication, assertiveness and dispute resolution.

3. **Thinking Skills:** Making effective decisions: The skills taught in this theme include concrete ways of thinking and executing tasks so that youth will make effective decisions, set relevant goals, and be informed consumers of information.

4. Emotional skills: This might involve being comfortable in your own skin, dealing with emotions effectively, and knowing who you are.

Importance of Life Skills

The developing life skills is key not only to being successful in life but it's key for our health and well-being. Life skills can include the ability to manage your emotions, your health, your finances, your relationships, your school performance, etc. – and your ability to master these things has a direct impact on how you feel about yourself, your emotional balance, your physical health and your independence. some basic life skills can also protect you from dealing with mental health challenges or make dealing with mental health issues more manageable. Read on for some simple skills that you can learn and use every day.

Life skills are an essential part of being able to meet the challenges handle issues and problems often encountered in daily life. The developing life skills may help to

1. Reduce drug, alcohol, and tobacco use.
2. It may also reduce aggression and violence.
3. Life skills can just make life a bit easier.
4. It can regulate our emotions effectively and develop enduring, supportive relationships, we're happier and healthier.
5. Find new ways of thinking and problem solving
6. Recognize the impact of their actions
7. Build confidence
8. Analyze options, make decisions and develops understanding
9. Develop a greater sense of self-awareness and appreciation for others They help to.
10. Life skills like decision-making skills

Examples of Life Skills

Any skill that is useful in your life can be considered a life sl ill. Tying your shoe laces, swimming, driving a car and using a co nputer are, for most people, useful life skills. Broadly speaking, the erm 'life skills' is usually used for any of the skills needed to deal well and effectively with the challenges of life. Therefore, everyone will have a different list of the skills they consider most essential in life. It can be defined as "Life skills are based on executive functions; they bring together our social, emotional and cognitive capacities to problem solve and achieve goals".

However, following are the basic life skills

- **Self-awareness**: It is conscious attention directed towards the self. When we have this life skill, we often find ourselves pondering why we do the things we do.

- **Critical thinking**: Critical thinking can be defined as reflective thinking that focuses on deciding what to believe or do. It may involve organizing facts, analyzing ideas, and evaluating arguments. Overall, having this life skill means we use disciplined thinking to make the best judgments we can and take actions that make the most sense.

- **Creative thinking**: Creativity involves the ability to understand a problem and also to redefine it, transform thoughts, reinterpret information, and ignore existing boundaries to find new solutions. This life skill may also include keeping an open mind

- **Decision making**: Decision making can be defined as identifying and choosing from alternatives. Our decision making process depends on our **values**, beliefs, **goals**, etc

- **Problem Solving**: Problem solving may be defined as a thinking process where we use our knowledge, skills, and understanding to manage an unfamiliar situation.

- **Effective communication**: Communication might be defined as the act of disclosing, or explaining something in detail. This life skill also involves achieving a goal with our communication.

- **Interpersonal relationships**: To have successful, healthy relationships, we need a variety of social skills. These life skills might include things like sensitivity to nonverbal cues, low fear of rejection, and the ability to easily adapt when moving from one social situation to the next

- **Empathy**: Empathy refers to our ability to understand and share the feelings of another.

- **Coping with stress**: Our ability to have resiliency in the face of stress is another key life skill. This might involve developing healthy coping skills, engaging in stress management strategies, and using self-care.

- **Coping with emotion**: Tolerating distress and regulating emotions is another type of life skill. This is especially important for our well-being but skills of this type also have important impacts on our relationships.

Individual Interpretation of Stress as a Response

Some people are more sensitive and reactive to stress. Differences in temperament, a collection of inborn personality traits can cause some people to be more resilient in the face of stress while others can feel more threatened and less able to cope. Thoughts, emotions, and behaviors are all linked to the response of stress and it depends upon individual to individual. Again it varies individual to individual for looking at the same situation as a "challenge" instead of a "threat" can make a potentially stressful experience feel invigorating instead of overwhelming. If stress is interpreted as the event of threat then it will lead to a different emotion and behavior. Stress and anxiety are flight-or-fight responses to threats. Feeling emotional or having difficulty sleeping and eating can all be natural reactions to stress, whether it's acute or chronic. Fear and worry can activate the physiological release of hormones that speed up our hearts, increase our breathing rates and enhance our blood flow. Long-term activation of the body's stress response can impair the immune system and increase the risk of physical and mental health problems.

There are many ways that people strive to cope with stressors when feelings of stress in their lives. The stress response is the emergency reaction system of the body. The stress response includes physical and thought responses to your perception of various situations. Stress as a response model, initially introduced by Hans Selye (1956), describes stress as a physiological response pattern and was captured within his general adaptation syndrome (GAS) model. This model describes stress as a dependent variable and includes three concepts:

1. Stress is a defensive mechanism.

2. Stress follows the three stages of alarm, resistance, and exhaustion.

3. If the stress is prolonged or severe, it could result in diseases of adaptation or even death.

Selye introduced the idea that the stress response could result in positive or negative outcomes based on cognitive interpretations of the physical symptoms or physiological experience. Stress could be experienced as *eustress* (positive) or *distress* (negative). However, Selye always considered stress to be a physiologically based construct or response. The response model of stress incorporates coping within the model itself. The idea of adaptation or coping is inherent to the GAS model at both the alarm and resistance stages. When confronted with a negative stimulus, the alarm response initiates the sympathetic nervous system to combat or avoid the stressor (i.e., increased heart rate, temperature, adrenaline, and glucose levels). The resistance response then initiates physiological systems with a *fight or flight* reaction to the stressor, returning the system to homeostasis, reducing harm, or more generally accommodating the stressor, which can lead to adaptive diseases such as sleep deprivation, mental illness, hypertension, or heart disease.

Exposure to a stressful event activates a series of autonomic system reactions within organs. The reactions found were the activation of the sympathetic nervous system (SNS). These causes hormonal secretions of adrenaline and cortical and show the behavioral "fight or flight" reaction. According to Berger et al., the "fight or flight" response is triggered by osteocalcin, a protein released by the skeleton as a hormone, which is a messenger, sent by bone to regulate crucial processes all over the body, including how we respond to danger. Stress can trigger the body's response to a perceived threat or danger, during this reaction, speeds the heart rate, slows digestion, shunts blood flow to major muscle groups, and changes various other autonomic nervous functions, giving the body a burst of energy and strength. These changes pitch your body into a fight or flight response. Stress can also lead to some unhealthy habits that have a negative impact on your health. For example, many people cope with stress by eating too much or by smoking. These unhealthy habits damage the body and create bigger problems in the long-term

Stress Management Techniques: These techniques lower stress level temporarily to compensate the biological tissues involved. Stress management techniques are more general and range from cognitive (mindfulness, cognitive therapy, meditation) to physical (yoga, art, natural medicine, deep breathing) to environmental (spa visits, music, pets, nature).

Coping with Stress (Strategies for stress) reduction)

Stress is inevitable but it can be manageable. When you understand the toll it takes on you and the steps to combat stress, you can take charge of your health and reduce the impact stress has on your life.

- **Learn to recognize the signs of burnout:** High levels of stress may place at a high risk of burnout. Burnout can leave feeling exhausted and apathetic about job.ÿþ When start to feel symptoms of emotional exhaustion, it's a sign that you need to find a way to get a handle on your stress.

- **Try to get regular exercise:** Physical activity has a big impact on your brain and your body. Whether you enjoy walking or want to begin jogging, exercise reduces stress and improves many symptoms associated with mental illness.ÿþ

- **Take care of yourself:** Incorporating regular self-care activities into daily life is essential to stress management. Take care of your body and others also. Learn how to take care of your mind and spirit and discover how to equip yourself to live your best life.

- **Practice mindfulness in your life:** Mindfulness isn't just something you practice for 10 minutes each day. It can also be a way of life. Discover how to live more mindfully throughout your day so you can become more awake and conscious throughout your life.ÿþ

- **Take breaks from watching, reading, or listening to news stories,** including those on social media. It's good to be informed but hearing about the traumatic event constantly can be upsetting. Consider limiting news to just a couple of times a day and disconnecting from phone, TV, and computer screens for a while.

- **Make time to unwind**. Try to do some other activities you enjoy.

- **Talk to others.** Talk with people you trust about your concerns and how you are feeling. Share your problems and how you are feeling and coping with a parent, friend, counselor, doctor, or pastor.

- **Connect with your community- or faith-based organizations**.

- **Connect with Supportive People:** Talking face to face with another person releases hormones that reduce stress. Lean on those good listeners in your life.

- **Deep Breathing:** It is also found that some people have other ways of coping which are not advisable. For example, lots of people use screen time like watching TV or movies and surfing the net to reduce stress. Although, screen time is effective as a stress management strategy but it is not advisable because it creates others health problems.

Similarly, some people may feel relief from stress after eating junk food or having a few drinks. These coping strategies give people temporary relief, but can cause other problems. This can cause health problems if they become habits. WE should use coping methods that are both effective and low-risk.

Application of Positive Psychology in Work (Workplace, Workforce)

One of the defining features of scarcity, which deals with how people satisfy unlimited wants and needs with limited resources. Scarcity affects the people place on services and how governments and private firms decide to manage workforce. The workplace is a critical part of hiring employees, keeping them, and meeting organizational goals with good reason. Workforce carries the most important weight in the organization. It is also importance to retain the workforce in the organization without break. A manager-employee relationship describes an organization's constant effort to engage its employees through strategies that help maintain open communication in the workplace and promote togetherness. Positive manager-employee relationships in the workplace encourage productivity and cooperation among workers. Thus, a mutual level of respect between a manager and an employee brings more willingness from both sides to offer support and perform better.Positive psychology is more than just a self-help concept but it's a powerful tool that has the power to transform workplaces. Positive psychology has been a game-changer for workplace dynamically. Positive psychology can help staff be friendlier and happier with one another and increase productivity, original thinking, conflict resolution, and performance. It also helps staff settle into an organization and stay longer, something that's critical in posts with global shortages. Positive psychology is an area of psychology focused on the strengths and behaviours that help people to build meaningful, purposeful lives. When applied in a workplace, positive psychology enables people to simply surviving in their jobs with feeling that they're flourishing meaningfully in their careers. Positive psychology in the workplace is that it boosts individual and increase organizational performance. The reason is that more satisfied employees are more productive in general and put in more discretionary effort. They're also likely to be more innovative and better at solving problems. When positive psychology applied in the workplace, it can help employees to feel happier and be more productive.

The PERMA Model

Seligman's PERMA model has been critical in developing the positive psychology field and helping many people and employees to find meaning in their lives and work. The PERMA model, which stands for positive emotion, engagement, relationships, meaning and accomplishments, is an evidence-based model that, when applied in the workplace, can help employees feel happier and be more productive.

1. **Positive emotion:** Positive emotions are keys to becoming and staying happy. When we experience positive emotions, we're more likely to feel great, get along with those around us, and set higher goals for our future and have the energy to walk towards them. At work, we experience less stress and fatigue if these positive emotions are present. One positive emotion that really impacts performance at work is gratitude.

2. **Engagement:** In the PERMA model, engagement specifically says happiness comes from employees' finding and using their strengths. By emphasizing their strengths, employees are more likely to focus on the future, including how they can better themselves, instead of thinking about what they may need to "fix." When people are focused on their strengths, they're more likely to feel fulfilled and be innovative.

3. **Relationships:** Relationships built connection in the workplace which influences our happiness greatly. When we feel connected to other people, we feel happier, and that happiness is contagious. Organizations can help encourage employees to form better relationships in many ways.

4. **Meaning:** Creating meaning at work is important.

5. **Accomplishments:** The final element in the PERMA model is accomplishment. Accomplishment is the positive feeling that comes from setting realistic goals and achieving those goals through specific actions. Feeling that they've accomplished something helps employees thrive at work and feel invested in outcomes.

Importance of Positive Psychology in Workplace

We spend, on average, half of our working hours at work so a positive, happier work environment is needed that prides itself on mental, physical and spiritual wellbeing to employees.

1. It promotes moral in the workplace to boost productivity

2. Positive psychology can impact talent retention to better employee health.

3. Positive psychology helps in hiring employees, keeping them, and meeting organizational goals

4. Positive psychology emphasizes individuals over tasks and work-related skills

5. Positive psychology can help staff be friendlier and happier with one another and increase productivity, original thinking, conflict resolution, and performance.

6. Positive emotions can broaden minds and increase creativity and focus.

7. Positive psychology improves strengths leading meaningful lives, enjoying high quality relationships and achieving our goals.

8. It also helps staff settle into an organization and stay longer

9. Mindfulness and compassion builds awareness and compassion for self and others. This leads to a kinder, supportive and considerate team

10. Positive psychology creates meaningful connections which are a key ingredient for happier employees

Questions

1. Define Positive Psychology. Describe the contribution of Positive Psychology in education.

2. What are the characteristics of Positive Psychology in education?

4. Describe the strategies to enhance Positive Ageing.

5. Discuss the Positive Psychology to Ageing. What are the Theoretical Perspectives of Ageing? Describe.

6. What are the characteristics of positive health? Describe the advantage of positive psychology in health.

7. Discuss the positive interventions of mental health treatment.

8. Describe the factors of positive health and well-being.

9. Describe the theories of positive psychology in sports.

10. What are the life challenges? What are the adjustments required to face the life challenges? Discuss.

11. Discuss the importance of positive psychology.

12. What are the behavioral effects of stress? Discuss the nature of stress.

13. Describe the signs and symptoms of stress.

14. Discuss the sources of stress. Describe the types of stress.

15. What are the causes and effects of stress?

16. What are the causes of stress? Describe the stress management techniques.

17. Differentiate between stress and Anxiety. Describe the impact of stress.

18. What is Life Skill? Describe the different types of Skill.

19. What are Basic Skills? Describe the importance of Life Skills.

20. Explain the stress as a Response. How could you cope with the stress?

21. Discuss the role of Positive Psychology in work.

22. What is PERMA model? Discuss.

23. Discuss the importance of Positive Psychology in work place.

❏

Chapter-V

Pro-social Behaviour & Positive Environments

Empathy

The term empathy was first introduced in 1909 by psychologist Edward B. Titchener as a translation of the German term *einfühlung*. Empathy is the feeling that you understand and share another person's experiences and emotions or the ability to share someone else's feelings. Feeling sorry for a person automatically generates feelings of pity, which is not helpful in situations where people are in pain. It is ability to read and respond to others' emotions. It is the ability to put oneself in the place of another person and feel what she/he does. It is about having an accurate sense of what she/he might be feeling like. Empathy is defined as it's the ability to understand another person's thoughts and feelings in a situation from their point of view, rather than your own. It differs from sympathy, where one is moved by the thoughts and feelings of another but maintains an emotional distance. Empathy is the ability to emotionally understand what other people feel, see things from their point of view, and imagine yourself in their place. Essentially, it is putting you in someone else's position and feeling what they are feeling. It permits people to understand the emotions that others are feeling.

Feeling the same emotion that another person would feel is a common understanding of empathy.

Definitions of Empathy

Merriam-Webster defines empathy, in part, as "the action of understanding, being aware of, being sensitive to, and vicariously experiencing the feelings, thoughts, and experience of another.

Signs of Empathy

Following are the sign of empathy:

- You are good at really listening to what others have to say.
- People often tell you about their problems.
- You are good at picking up on how other people are feeling.
- You often think about how other people feel.
- Other people come to you for advice.
- You often feel overwhelmed by tragic events.
- You try to help others who are suffering.
- You are good at telling when people aren't being honest.
- You sometimes feel overwhelmed in social situations.
- You care deeply about other people.
- You find it difficult to set boundaries in your relationships.

Uses for Empathy

Empathy has many beneficial uses.

- **Empathy allows you to build social connections with others**. Social connections are important for both physical and psychological well-being.By understanding what people are thinking and feeling, you are able to respond appropriately in social situations.
- **Empathizing with others helps you learn to regulate your own emotions**. Emotional regulation is important and it allows you to manage what you are feeling, even in times of great stress, without becoming overwhelmed.
- **Empathy promotes helping behaviors**. Not only are you more likely to engage in helpful behaviors when you feel empathy for other people, but other people are also more likely to help you when they experience empathy.

Impact of Empathy

Your ability to experience empathy can impact your relationships. Siblings have found closer when empathy is high and so siblings have less conflict and more warmth toward each other. In romantic relationships, having empathy increases your ability to extend forgiveness.

Types of Empathy

Daniel Goleman and Paul Ekman have identified three components of empathy: Cognitive, Emotional and Compassionate. However, there are several types of empathy that a person may experience. The sethreearemain ways we can empathize with others, understanding their emotions as our own. The differences between these forms of empathy highlight the challenges we face in responding to other people's pain. But they also make clear how the right approach can move us to compassionate action.

1. **Cognitive empathy**: It is just feeling or simply knowing how the other person feels and what they might be thinking. People try to understand another person's point of view without actualizes his or her emotions and they're not motivated to do anything to actually help that person. It is a type of people's emotions to their own advantage, without necessarily caring about those people very much. Therefore, cognitive empathy alone is not enough to help someone. In a state of emotional empathy, people sometimes lack the ability to manage their own distressing emotions. We are just feeling stressed when we detect another's fear or anxiety. It refers as our ability to identify and understand other people's emotions. The empathetic person will recognize the person's struggle without minimizing it.**Simply knowing how the other person feels and what they might be thinking.**Having only cognitive empathy keeps you at a distance from your friend.

2. **Emotional empathy**: To truly connect with your friend, you need to share their feelings. This is where emotional empathy comes in. So, you've successfully understood what your friend

is feeling, and put yourself in a similar emotional space. So, you've successfully understood what your friend is feeling, and put yourself in a similar emotional space. In a state of emotional empathy, people sometimes lack the ability to manage their own distressing emotions, which can lead to paralysis and psychological exhaustion. Medical professionals often inoculate themselves against this kind of pain by developing a sense of detachment from their patients.

3. **Compassionate empathy**: With this kind of empathy we not only understand a person's problem and feel with them, but are spontaneously moved to help, if needed. These forms of empathy highlight the challenges we face in responding to other people's pain and move to find how the right approach to compassionate action.

Altruism

Altruism refers to behavior that benefits another individual at a cost to oneself. For example, giving your lunch to other person is altruistic because it helps someone who is hungry, but at a cost of being hungry yourself. It is an act doing something to help another person with no expectation of reward. Such behaviors are often performed unselfishly and without any expectations of reward. It can be said that helping someone despite personal costs or risks. Altruism is the unselfish concern for other people doing things simply out of a desire to help, not because you feel obligated to out of duty, loyalty, or religious reasons. It involves acting out of concern for the well-being of other people. Everyday life is filled with small acts of altruism, from holding the door for strangers to giving money to people in need.

Characteristics of Altruism:

- Doing something to help another person with no expectation of reward
- Forgoing things that may bring personal benefits if they create costs for others

- Helping someone despite personal costs or risks
- Sharing resources even in the face of scarcity
- Showing concern for someone else's well-being

Types of Altruism

There are several different types of altruistic behavior. These include:

- **Genetic altruism**: As the name suggests, this type of altruism involves engaging in altruistic acts that benefit close family members. For example, parents and other family members often engage in acts of sacrifice in order to provide for the needs of family members.

- **Reciprocal altruism**: This type of altruism is based on a mutual give-and-take relationship. It involves helping another person now because they may one day be able to return the favor.

- **Group-selected altruism**: This involves engaging in altruistic acts for people based upon their group affiliation. People might direct their efforts toward helping people who are part of their social group or supporting social causes that benefit a specific group.

- **Pure altruism**: Also known as moral altruism, this form involves helping someone else, even when it is risky, without any reward. It is motivated by internalized values and morals.

Further Altruism can be classed into two categories as under:

Behavioral altruism : Behavior is normally described as altruistic when it is motivated by a desire to benefit someone other than oneself for that person's sake. This refers to helping behavior that is either very costly to the helper or conveys no self-benefit for the helper. From a biological or evolutionary perspective, altruism is a behavior that decreases the fitness or genetic contribution of one individual while increasing the fitness of another. In psychological research, altruism behavior is conceptualized as a motivational state that a person possesses with the goal of increasing the welfare of another person. According to pro-social behaviors, such as altruism, it is often contrary to our own self-interest.

Psychological altruism : This refers to a motivation to increase the welfare of another. This definition is commonly used among psychologists and philosophers. Psychological altruism is contrasted with psychological egoism, which refers to the motivation to increase one's own welfare

Impact of Altruism

Altruism has a wide range of benefits, like:

- **Better health**: Behaving altruistically can improve physical health in a variety of ways. People who volunteer have better overall health, and regularly engaging in helping behaviors is linked to a significantly lower mortality.

- **Better mental well-being**: Doing good things for other people can make you feel good about yourself. People experience increased happiness after doing good things for other people.

- **Better romantic relationships**: Being kind and compassionate can also lead to a better relationship with your partner, as kindness is one of the most important qualities that people across all cultures seek in a romantic partner.

Enhancing Altruism

Some people come by altruistic tendencies naturally, but there are ways by you can do to help enhance helpful behaviors in yourself and others. These include:

- **Find inspiration**: Look to inspirational people who engage in altruistic acts. Seeing others work to actively improve the lives of individuals and communities can inspire you to act altruistically in your own life.

- **Practice empathy**: Rather than distancing you from others, practice empathy by building connections and putting a human face on the problems you see. Consider how you would feel in that situation, and think that you can do to help make a difference.

- **Set a goal**: Find ways that you can regularly perform random acts of kindness for others. Look around you for people who may need help, or look for ways that you can volunteer in your community. Fix a meal for someone in need, help a friend, donate during a blood drive, or spend some time volunteering for a local organization.

- **Make it a habit**: Try to keep kindness in the forefront of your thoughts. For example, think about the altruistic acts you've performed, how they might have helped someone, and how you might repeat them going forward. Or, consider performing at least one act of kindness a day, and take some time to reflect on it.

Causes of Altruism

Altruism is one aspect of what is known as pro-social behavior. Pro-social behavior refers to any action that benefits other people.

1. **Evolution**: Some people are just born with a natural tendency to help others and hence theory suggests that altruism may be influenced by genetics. Kin selection is an evolutionary theory that proposes that people are more likely to help those who are blood relatives because it will increase the odds of gene transmission to future generations, thus ensuring the continuation of shared genes. The more closely the individuals are related, the more likely people are to help.

2. **Brain**-Based Rewards: Altruism activates reward centers in the brain. Neurobiologists have found that when a person behaves altruistically, the pleasure centers of their brain become more active. Engaging in compassionate actions activates the areas of the brain associated with the reward system. The positive feelings created by compassionate actions then reinforce altruistic behaviors.

3. **Environment**:Interactions and relationships with others have a major influence on altruistic behavior, and socialization may have a significant impact on altruistic actions in young children. Children who observed simple reciprocal acts of altruism were

238 :: Positive Psychology

far more likely to exhibit altruistic actions. On the other hand, friendly but non-altruistic actions did not inspire the same results.

4. **Social Norms**: Society's rules, norms, and expectations can also influence people engage in altruistic behavior. The norm of reciprocity is a social expectation in which we feel pressured to help others if they have already done something for us. For example, if your friend loaned you money in need a few weeks ago, you'll probably feel compelled to reciprocate when they ask you some help. They did something for you, now you feel obligated to do something in return.

5. **Incentives:** As we know altruism involves doing for others without reward however, it may be cognitive incentives that are not obvious. For example, we might help others to relieve our own distress or because our view of ourselves as kind people. Other cognitive explanations include:

- **Empathy**: People are more likely to engage in altruistic behavior when they feel empathy for the person in distress. Children also tend to become more altruistic as their sense of empathy develops.

- **Helping relieve negative feelings**: Altruistic acts may help alleviate the negative feelings associated with seeing someone else in distress. Essentially, seeing another person in trouble causes us to feel upset, distressed, or uncomfortable, but helping them reduces these negative feelings.

Empathy-altruism Hypothesis

The theory that explains helping behaviors as resulting from feelings of compassion empathy toward others, which arouse an altruistic motivation of improving another person's welfare. The empathy-altruism hypothesis states that feelings of empathy for another person produce an altruistic motivation to increase that person's welfare. In the empathy-altruism hypothesis, the term empathy refers to feelings of compassion, sympathy, tenderness, and the like. Altruism refers to a motivational state in which the goal is to increase another person's welfare. For centuries, humans possess the capacity for altruism. It was assumed that all human behavior, including the helping of others, is egoistically motivated. The term egoism refers to a motivational state in which the goal is to increase one's own welfare. Specifically, some have suggested that people may help because they feel empathy for another person's welfare, which may lead to altruism. Those who have argued that empathy may be a source of altruism. The empathy-altruism hypothesis predicts that those feeling high levels of empathy for a person in need will be more likely to help than will those feeling less empathy. Such people have high levels of empathy may feel more distress and, consequently, may be more likely to help because they are egoistically motivated to reduce their own distress. Another possibility is that those feeling high levels of empathy are more likely to help because they are more egoistically motivated to avoid feeling bad about themselves or looking bad in the eyes of others should they fail to help. Similarly, those feeling high levels of empathy may be more likely to help because they are more egoistically motivated to feel good about themselves or to look good in the eyes of others should they help.

Gratitude

The word 'Gratitude' is derived from the Latin term *gratia*, which means grace, gratefulness, and graciousness. It's a concept that is close to kindness. According to positive psychology gratitude is strongly and consistently associated with greater happiness. Gratitude helps people feel more positive emotions, relish good experiences, improve their health, deal with adversity, and build strong relationships. Positive psychology defines gratitude is more than feeling thankful and scientists can measure its effects. It is a deeper appreciation for someone that produces longer lasting positivity. People can use gratitude to form new social relations or to strengthen current ones. Gratitude is a selfless act. Its acts are done unconditionally; to show to people that they are appreciated. Gratitude is a foundational human emotion. There is a variety of things that can conjure positive feelings of appreciation or gratitude that may guide people towards meaning and better health. Positive psychology research has found neurological reasons why so many people can benefit from this general practice of expressing thanks for our lives, even in times of challenge and change. Gratitude is an emotion similar to appreciation. Gratitude is a positive emotion that involves being thankful and appreciative and is associated with several mental and physical health benefits.

Moreover, the concept of gratitude has been highly respected in most cultures and religions.Gratitude has been described in different ways, it has been prevalently conceptualized as a general disposition[9] or a temporary emotional state. According to the first perspective, gratitude is defined as a generalized predisposition to acknowledge and answer with appreciation to others' benevolence (person, God, luck, fate or nature).[11] In the second sense, gratitude has been depicted as a complex emotion which follows a costly, unexpected, and intentionally given benefit.

Definitions of Gratitude

According to the **Harvard Medical School**, gratitude is defined as "a thankful appreciation for what an individual receives, whether tangible or intangible. With gratitude, people acknowledge the goodness in their lives ... As a result; gratitude also helps people connect to something larger than themselves as individuals–whether to other people, nature, or a higher power"

According to **Sansone & Sansone, (2010)**,gratitude is defined as "the appreciation of what is valuable and meaningful to oneself and represents a general state of thankfulness and/or appreciation"

According to**Fox et al., (2015)**,gratitude is defined as "a social emotion that signals our recognition of the things others have done for us"

Stages of Gratitude

According to **Dr. Robert Emmons** - There are two stages of gratitude comprise the recognition of the goodness in our lives, and then how this goodness came to us externally lies. By this process, we recognize the luck of everything that makes our lives andourselves better. The feeling of gratitude involves two stages as under:

1. First, gratitude isthe acknowledgment of goodness in one's life. In a state of gratitude, we say yes to life. We affirm that all in all, life is good, and has elements that make worth living, and rich in texture. The acknowledgment that we have received something gratifies us, both by its presence and by the effort the giver put into choosing it.

2. Second, gratitude is recognizing that some of the sources of this goodness lie outside the self. One can be grateful to other people, to animals, and to the world, but not to oneself. At this stage, we recognize the goodness in our lives and who to thank for it, ie., who made sacrifices so that we could be happy.

Types of Gratitude

There are three types of gratitude as under:

1. As an affective trait: meaning that it is related to a person's general disposition. Some people naturally experience gratitude more frequently than others. As a trait, individual practices gratitude as part of their daily life and it would be considered character strength, to possess gratitude. As a trait, gratitude can be developed with practice and awareness. In this type, gratitude is defined as a generalized predisposition to acknowledge and answer with appreciation to others' benevolence.

- As a mood, which means it may fluctuate over time. People might experience periods where they feel more grateful in general, and at other times they may experience this less often.

- Trait : State : When a person experiences the rich emotion from someone expressing gratitude for them, it is referred to as state. In this type, gratitude has been depicted as a complex emotion which follows a costly, unexpected, and intentionally given benefit.

Perspectives on Gratitude

Gratitude is formed a hybrid psychological-philosophical perspective, as well as from an outright philosophical perspective.

1. **Religious and Spiritual Perspectives on Gratitude:** Historically, many religions referred to gratitude strictly regarding the need to be thankful for a higher power. More so, Christianity, Islam, and Judaism stressed gratitude as an integral step on the path to a good life. Some psychologists believe that Christianity incorporates a "gratitude to God" that binds many Christians together. For Islam, the purpose of the five daily prayers is not to ask Allah for anything, but instead, to show gratitude towards Allah. Similarly, in Judaism, followers are encouraged to start every day by being grateful for waking up again. These three religions offer a unique role of gratitude of thanks for this existence and who created it. Gratitude and the concept of karma is a driving force behind concept of Buddhism in China.

2. **Modern Psychological Perspectives on Gratitude:** Robert Emmons has expanded research on the importance of gratitude in modern psychology. Emmons has authored several papers on the psychology of gratitude, showing that being more grateful can increase levels of well-being.

There arenine recent psychological findings related to the study of gratitude:

1. **Enhanced Wellbeing:** Grateful people are more agreeable, more open, and fewer neurotics and believing that thanks can improve overall sense of wellbeing. Furthermore, gratitude is related inversely to depression, and positively to life satisfaction. Because gratitude practices need to be a part of the therapy and treatment for people who struggle with depression.

2. **Deeper Relationships:** Gratitude is also a powerful tool for strengthening interpersonal relationships. People who express their gratitude for each other tend to be more willing to forgive others and less narcissistic. Giving thanks to those who have

helped you strengthens your relationships and promotes relationship formation and maintenance, as well as relationship connection and satisfaction.

3. **Improved Optimism:** The people who focused on gratitude showed more optimism in many areas of their lives, including health and exercise. When people are optimistic about their wellbeing and health, they may be more likely to act in ways that support a healthy lifestyle.

4. **Increased Happiness**: In the pursuit of happiness and life satisfaction, gratitude offers a long-lasting effect in a positive-feedback. Thus, the more gratitude we experience and express, the more situations and people we may find to express gratitude towards.

5. **Stronger Self-Control:** Self-Control helps with discipline and focus. Long-term wellbeing can benefit from self-control, for example, resisting nicotine in cigarettes for someone who is trying to quit smoking. Self-control helps us stick to the "better choice" for our long-term health, financial future, and wellbeing.

6. **Better Physical and Mental Health:** The patients with heart failure who completed gratitude journals showed reduced inflammation, improved sleep, and better moods; this reduced their symptoms of heart failure after only 8 weeks.

7. **An Overall Better Life:** Gratitude towards a higher power, can reduce levels of stress.

8. **Stronger Athleticism:** An athlete's level of gratitude for their success can influence their levels of wellbeing. Adolescent athletes who are more grateful in life are also more satisfied and tend to have higher levels of self-esteem. Gratitude also affects sports fans and fans' levels of gratitude influence their happiness, connection, and identity with a team. In turn, stronger fan support and pride can influence the performance and pride of the team itself for representing a greater team.

9. **Stronger Neurologically-Based Morality:** The brain's response to feelings of gratitude is observed with functional magnetic resonance imaging (FMRI). This feelings of gratitude

in their participants and found that gratitude increased activity in areas of the brain that deal with morality, reward, and judgment.

The Effects of Gratitude

The effect of gratitude showed that there was a mean 23% reduction in the stress hormone cortical after the intervention period. During the use of the techniques, 80% of the participants exhibited an increased coherence in heart rate variability patterns, indicating reduced stress. In other words, these findings suggest that people with an "attitude of gratitude" experience lower levels of stress. Expressing gratitude not only helps people appreciate what they've received in life, but it also helps people feel like they have given something back to those who helped them.

Social Effects of Gratitude

Gratitude can be observed at an individual level, with its greater social level. The recipient of gratitude may not reciprocate directly back, but in turn, may lend a favour to a third party, effectively expanding a network of good. Sometimes, the recipient may give back to the initiator as well. Effectively gratitude can create social networks and help individuals work towards goals and challenges, and overall, simply have stronger coping skills for life's hardships.

Signs of Gratitude

Expressing your appreciation and thanks that can happened in a number of different ways. For example, it might entail:

- Spending a few moments thinking about the things in your life that you are grateful for
- Stopping to observe and acknowledge the beauty of wonder of something you encounter in your daily life
- Being thankful for your health
- Thanking someone for the positive influence they have in your life

- Doing something kind for another person to show that you are grateful
- Paying attention to the small things in your life that bring you joy and peace
- Meditation or prayer focused on giving thanks

Influence of Gratitude

Following acts are important to influence gratitude:

1. **Releasing emotions:** It is the process in which an individual releases strong emotions. Crying provides a means for such a strong release after a stressful or traumatic event. For example, consider the guilt associated with "failing" to meet obligations. Perhaps in this situation, you would express gratitude in an attempt to release that guilt. The acts are meant to convey the appreciation that the friends possess, despite a recent disappointment.

2. **Reciprocity:** Reciprocity, as a concept from social psychology, is about the exchanging of actions. It is a kind of exchange of positive emotion. When someone performs an act of gratitude for another person, in turn, that person may be motivated to do something gracious for the former person or continue the favor for a stranger.

How to Practice Gratitude

Developing a sense of gratitude isn't complex or challenging. It doesn't require any special tools or training. The better you will become and put yourself into a grateful state of mind. Here's how to do this:

- **Observe the moment**: Take a second to focus on your experience and how you are feeling. Realize your senses and think about what is helping you cope. Are there people who have done something for you, or are there particular things helping you manage your stress, feel good about your life, or accomplish what you need to do? You may also find the practice of mindfulness, which focuses on becoming more aware of the present moment, a helpful tool.

- **Write it down**: You might find it helpful to start a gratitude diary writing where you write a few things you are thankful for each day. Being able to look back on these observations can help when you are struggling to feel grateful.

- **Savor the moment**: Give yourself time to really enjoy the moment. Focus on the experience and allow yourself to absorb those good feelings.

- **Create gratitude rituals**: Pausing for a moment to appreciate something and giving thanks for it can help you feel a greater sense of gratitude. A meditation, prayer, or mantra are examples of rituals that can inspire a greater sense of gratitude.

- **Give thanks**: Gratitude is all about recognizing and appreciating those people, things, moments, skills, or gifts that bring joy, peace, or comfort into our lives. Show your appreciation. You might thank a person to show you are thankful for them, or you might spend a moment simply mentally appreciating what you have.

Expressing your appreciation for others is an important component that can affect your interpersonal relationships, particularly those with your partner. People who are high in gratitude experience sharp declines in marital satisfaction when their partner does not express gratitude in return.

Impact of Gratitude

The practice of gratitude can have a significant positive impact on both physical and psychological health. Some of the benefits of gratitude are listed below:

- Better sleep
- Better immunity
- Higher self-esteem
- Decreased stress
- Lower blood pressure

- Less anxiety and depression
- Stronger relationships
- Higher levels of optimism

The people who tend to be more grateful are also more likely to engage in other health-promoting behaviors, including exercising, and sticking to a healthier lifesty'e. According to psychologist Robert Emmons, gratitude can have a transformative effect on people's lives for several reasons. Because it helps people focus on the present, it plays a role in magnifying positive emotions. He also suggests that it can help improve people's self-worth. When you acknowledge that there are people in the world who care about you and are looking out for your interests, it can help you recognize your value.

Forgiveness

Forgiveness in positive psychology is most often viewed as character strength and a virtue worth pursuing for everyone who desires a greater sense of wellbeing. Positive psychology explores human strengths that help us live more satisfying and fulfilling lives and forgiveness is one such strength. Positive psychology also leads research on forgiveness, and the trends that place greater weight on the importance of forgiveness in maintaining and promoting wellbeing are growing steadily. Forgiveness is defined as a conscious, deliberate decision to release feelings of resentment toward a person or group who has harmed you, regardless of whether they actually deserve your forgiveness. Not only that but forgiveness as an emotional and cognitive process is characterized by releasing of anger, and anger elsewhere has been proven to have negative physical, emotional and cognitive consequences over time. Moreover, forgiving can be used as an emotion-focused coping strategy, and therefore could contribute to overall health. Inability to forgive was linked to anger and hostility, and those, in turn, have proven to have negative health effects, especially with regard to cardiovascular conditions. Forgiveness, on the other hand, was linked to positive emotions of empathy and compassion. It is found that forgiving people experience more life satisfaction and less depression than others. Forgiveness has been an important concept in many religious and spiritual practices for millennia but it is fairly new as an object of psychological research. Forgiveness can be initiated by different means and can be a result of changes in cognition, the offender's behavior, the victim's behavior, willful decision, emotional experience or expression, spiritual experience, or any combination of those. Forgiveness is a choice one makes over and over again. It can be a fresh perspective or a healthy distance. Some of us are more forgiving than others and forgiveness can be conceptualized as a personality trait or as an aspect of more complex enduring quality like resilience. These capacities give us hope that we can make the world a more forgiving and less vengeful place. Forgiveness can help repair a damaged relationship. It brings the forgiver peace of mind and frees him or her from corrosive anger and creates positive feelings toward the offender. The capacity for forgiveness is a part of human nature that has evolved in the process of natural selection, and it developed in the same way as our tendency toward revenge. Both forgiveness and revenge are social instincts that solved problems for ancestral humans. The process of forgiveness may take many forms and involves cultivating empathy, perspective taking, and benefit finding. Forgiveness can be understood as a situational response and a skill, it is also influenced to a large extent by an aspect of one's personality traits like agreeableness and neuroticism are most strongly related to forgiveness but not openness. Forgiving disposition can also come by nature and by nurture and forgiveness might be apparent soon after birth. Moreover, forgiveness raises self-esteem and hope of people who've been hurt and lowers their anxiety. It is true that when we are deeply hurt or betrayed by a close friends or relatives, it is easy to feel hatred and desire revenge. Forgiveness doesn't mean reconciliation. One doesn't have to return to the same relationship or accept the same harmful behaviors from an offender. But forgiveness is important for the mental health of those who have been victimized. It propels people forward rather than keeping them emotionally engaged in an injustice or trauma. Forgiveness has been shown to elevate mood, enhance optimism, and guard against anger, stress, anxiety, and depression.

Forgiveness is one of the supreme human virtues. The idea of forgiveness is integral to many religious texts, scriptures and philosophical discourses. In the Hindu religious mythology, a defining quality of all gods is the ability to forgive and punish. The idea and ability of forgiveness has been more often connected with the idea of divinity as compared to the ability to punish. In Buddhism a form of forgiveness called compassion has been considered a way of achieving Nirvana or salvation. There is an increasing need in the society for an absolute understanding of forgiveness.

Forgiveness has been defined either as a response, or as a personality characteristic, or as a characteristic of the social unit.

1. **As response:** Forgiveness can be defined as a pro-social change in thoughts, emotions and/or behaviors of a victim toward the wrongdoer. Conceptualizations of forgiveness as a response are based on one primary feature: when people forgive, their thoughts and behaviors towards the offenders become less negative and more pro-social eventually.

2. **As a personality characteristic**: Forgiveness may be explained as a tendency to forgive others in diversified circumstances. Although most people fall around the mean of the population in forgiveness-unforgiveness continuum, the disposition to forgive itself may have certain aspects. Although most people fall around the mean of the population in a forgiveness-unforgiveness continuum, the disposition to forgive itself may have certain aspects.

3. **As a characteristic of social units**: Forgiveness may be described as a virtue similar to intimacy, trust or commitment. Some social institutions like families or marriages are characterized by a higher intensity of forgiveness, whereas other institutions, which cast out members who transgress, are characterized by less forgiveness.

Benefits of Forgiveness

It would be of enormous benefit to humanity to cultivate

forgiveness as it is an antidote to our predisposition toward revenge and avoidance.

Following are the prime benefits of forgiveness:

1. reduction in negative affect and depressive symptoms
2. restoration of positive thinking
3. restoration of relationships
4. reduction in anxiety
5. strengthened spirituality
6. raised self-esteem
7. a greater sense of hope
8. greater capacity for conflict management and
9. greater ability to cope with stress and find relief.

Types of Forgiveness

There are two types of forgiveness in positive psychology as under:

1. **Positive Forgiveness**: Positive (or emotional) forgiveness is a therapeutic process of absolute forgiveness, which also involves reinstituting positive feelings and thoughts toward the offender. In pure positive forgiveness, cognitive restructuring is used to create the belief that retribution, of any kind is unnecessary. Retribution is instead a coping mechanism in situations where the hurt avoidance failed. Emotional forgiveness is not expected to improve psychological well-being but to restore well-being following the negative feelings or grudges.

2. **Negative Forgiveness**: Negative forgiveness, on the other hand, is a situation in which forgiveness is extended while brooding over the act of transgression. Negative forgiveness, also known as decisional forgiveness, involves mere overt inhibition of a retributive response, mostly in the interests of social acceptance. It involves a dissonance in the thought process of the victim; his positive well-being maybe enhanced

by the thought that he has 'forgiven' the transgressor, but the negative effect of grudge holding and anger would sustain.

Differences between Positive and Negative Forgiveness

Positive Forgiveness

1. Arrived at emotionally; through a pro-social change in thoughts or behavior
2. Reduces unforgiving emotions
3. Occurs with or without decisional forgiveness
4. Emotions and behavior toward the transgressor already consonant
5. Positive emotions toward the transgressor tend to continue.

Negative Forgiveness

1. Arrived at by logic or by will
2. Unforgiveness is sustained; chances of increase in unforgiveness levels
3. Occurs without emotional forgiveness
4. Attempts to justify behavior as in consonance with their emotion
5. Emotions of vengeance and anger maybe suppressed, resulting in frustration or magnification of negative feelings

Forgiveness as Technique of Positive Living

Many psychologists believe that forgiveness plays an important role in the well-being of individuals and societies. The common acts of forgiveness are known to indicate potential benefits, when trying to resolve social conflicts or a relationship or general health of society. Forgiveness goes a long way in creating a harmonious society. Positive emotions, thoughts and behavior are inculcated depending on the degree of genuineness. Genuine forgiveness requires the victim to be compassionate and benevolent toward the transgressor and to part with the right to revenge and resentment. Forgiveness generally leads to small but positive outcomes in psychological and physiological health and well-being. Forgiveness indicates high levels of compassion and empathy toward the wrongdoer. Forgiveness interventions have positively correlated self-report measures of psychological health and well-being. This indicated that people who had a tendency to feel forgiven were less vulnerable to psychological issues.

Models of Forgiveness:

REACH Model of Forgiveness: Worthington (2001) proposed the Pyramid Model of Forgiveness, in which the acronym REACH is used, to indicate a five-step process of Forgiveness. These steps are briefly discussed below:

1. **R: Recall the Hurt**: Recall the hurt focuses on remembering the transgression objectively. Recalling helps to do a reality check of the transgression, while controlling one's emotions and thoughts.

2. **E: Empathize with the one who hurtyou**: Empathizing involves taking the offender's perspective and to feel what s/he feels. During this phase, the transgressor seems more 'humane' and also, the victim might turn revengeful.

3. **A: Altruistic gift of forgiveness**: This process further involves three sub-processes i.e. guilt, gratitude and gift.

   Guilt: The victim contemplates own wrongdoings from his/her own past. During this, s/he may realize that s/he is also capable of inflicting such harm, or that s/he has harmed others in different ways. The emotion tried to incite in this process is guilt &not shame, which is an absolutely distinct term.

   Gratitude: The 'transgressed' individual is then questioned how s/he would feel to be forgiven for the transgression, recalled in the previous step. The experience of forgiveness in that situation is recalled and recorded. This will give him/her a sense of relief and freedom, for that s/he has for being forgiven. Gratitude, in this context, is actually, an 'empathetic projection'. **Gift:** The empathetic state of the 'victim' arouses a motivational frame of mind and then identifies with the transgressor's experience. The facilitator then makes an explicit invitation to gift forgiveness to the offender.

Steps to True Forgiveness

Jon Nigroni suggested following seven important steps to true forgiveness:

1. **Acknowledge**: Remember the person who hurt you, the context of the situation and acknowledge the hurt.

2. **Consider**: Consider how the hurt and pain has affected you. The word "consider" involves thinking before making a decision. Before you decide on whether or not you will forgive this person, consider the negative feelings you've acquired since the incident.

3. **Accept:** Accept that you cannot change the past. No matter how much you wish this pain could be reversed, it's time to admit to yourself that your anger toward the person won't redeem what they have done. It is during this step that you must thoughtfully consider whether or not you want to forgive.

4. **Determine:** Determine whether or not you will forgive. This is when the forgiveness process will either begin or end. This decision should not be made lightly, as it will determine the future of your relationship with this person.

5. **Repair:** Repair the relationship with the person who wronged you. Before any act of forgiveness or reconciliation, rebuild the connection you used to have with this person.

6. **Learn:** Learn what forgiveness means to you. Up until now, you've probably thought that forgiveness is more for *their* benefit, not yours.

7. **Forgive:** Forgive the person who wronged you. In some cases, this will be silent.

You may be compelled to verbally forgive the person, even if you do not expect a kind response, but if you have followed through on the previous steps, then their reaction won't really matter. What will matter is that *you* have found a way to let go and move on.

Applications of Forgiveness

The concept of forgiveness has been applied in many situations and disciplines. Below are listed some of the major areas of human life where forgiveness has its applications:

1. *Forgiveness & Health:* Worthington pointed out that unforgiving responses lead to poor health, especially cardiovascular activity and blood pressure. People with high blood pressures, generally are less forgiving than those who are forgiving. Researches also explain that forgiving people have better social support, are less likely to depend on alcohol or drugs, and are less prone to anxiety and depression. Acquiring the capacity to forgive can prove to be beneficial to families dealing with health issues (Friedman, 2009). Studies indicate that individuals who are forgiving have lesser risks of heart attack and experience less anger and physical pain than unforgiving individuals. Hence, forgiveness enhances your health.

2. *Forgiveness in Marriage:* Researchers studying forgiveness in interpersonal relationships are of the opinion that forgiveness is essential part of marriage and relationship dynamics. People who are capable to forgive experience greater levels of marital satisfaction and longevity, better communication, and enhanced intimacy. It also reduces the negative effect in the relationship. . It is necessary to learn to forgive your spouse. It saves one from repression of emotions of sadness or anger toward the spouse, which could instead result in more negativity and frustration. It is not necessary that all marriages benefit from forgiveness interventions and hence, it is necessary to highlight the need for intensive research on appropriate targets for such interventions.

3. *Forgiveness as a Healing Process:* Forgiveness can help alleviate psychological problems like anxiety, stress, depression, etc. Also, forgiveness has an impact on psychological well-being of an individual. It can be used to recover from psychological issues and to boost one's self-esteem and

hopefulness. It is important to confront the issue and let go of the self-inflicted emotional pain and hurt.

Societal Implications - Attachment, Love and Flourishing Relationships

Societal implications of Attachment

Attachment is an emotional bond with another person. Social attachments play a critical role in adverse situation of human life. Social processes may serve a critical function in how people respond in trauma. Attachment is a deep and enduring emotional bond that connects one person to another across time and space. This bond starts from childhood and endures lifelong. Attachment theory is a psychological, evolutionary, and behavioral theory concerning relationships between people. It is thought to play a significant role in shaping one's life, personality, and happiness. Bowl by believed that the earliest bonds formed by children with their caregivers have a tremendous impact that continues throughout life. He suggested that attachment also serves to keep the infant close to the mother. The most important concept of attachment theory is that a young child needs to develop a relationship with at least one primary caregiver for social and emotional development because the caregiver feeds the child and provides nourishment. Attachment was characterized by clear behavioral and motivation patterns. When children are frightened, they seek help from their primary caregiver in order to receive both comfort and care. Attachment also serves to keep the infant close to the mother. Initially a child finds its mother or caregiver as its primary attachment figure and as it grows the attachment expand to siblings, peers, friends, teachers and so on. The central theme of attachment theory is that primary caregivers who are available and responsive to an infant's needs allow the child to develop a sense of security. The infant learns that the caregiver is dependable, which creates a secure base for the child. Ainsworth described three major styles of attachment: secure attachment, ambivalent-insecure attachment, and avoidant-insecure attachment. Later, researchers Main and Solomon (1986) added a fourth attachment style called disorganized-insecure attachment based on their own research. in developmental psychology, the theory that humans are born with a need to form a close emotional bond with a caregiver and that such a bond will develop during the first six months of a child's life if the caregiver is appropriately responsive.

The Stages of Attachment

Rudolph Schaffer and **Peggy Emerson** analyzed four distinct phases of attachment, as under:

1. **Pre-Attachment Stage**: From birth to 3 months, infants do not show any particular attachment to a specific caregiver. The infant's signals, such as crying and fussing, naturally attract the attention of the caregiver and the baby's positive responses encourage the caregiver to remain close.

2. **Indiscriminate Attachment:** Between 6 weeks of age to 7 months, infants begin to show preferences for primary and secondary caregivers. Infants develop trust that the caregiver will respond to their needs. While they still accept care from others, infants start distinguishing between familiar and unfamiliar people, responding more positively to the primary caregiver.

3. **Discriminate Attachment:** At this point, from about 7 to 11 months of age, infants show a strong attachment and preference for one specific individual. They will protest when separated from the primary attachment figure, and begin to display anxiety around strangers.

4. **Multiple Attachments:** After approximately 9 months of age, children begin to form strong emotional bonds with other caregivers beyond the primary attachment figure. This often includes a second parent, older siblings, and grandparents.

Factors that Influence Attachment

While this process may seem straightforward, there are some factors that can influence how and when attachments develop, including:

- **Opportunity for attachment**: Children, who do not have a primary care figure, such as those raised in orphanages, may fail to develop the sense of trust needed to form an attachment.

- **Quality care giving**: When caregivers respond quickly and consistently, children learn that they can depend on the people who are responsible for their care, which is the essential foundation for attachment. This is a vital factor.

Attachment Styles / Types of Attachments

There are four patterns of attachment, as under:

- **Ambivalent attachment**: These children become very distressed when a parent leaves. Ambivalent attachment style is considered uncommon. As a result of poor parental availability, these children cannot depend on their primary caregiver when they need them.

- **Avoidant attachment**: Children with an avoidant attachment tend to avoid parents or caregivers, showing no preference between a caregiver and a complete stranger. This attachment style might be a result of abusive or neglectful caregivers. Children who are punished for relying on a caregiver will learn to avoid seeking help in the future.

- **Disorganized attachment**: These children display a confusing mix of behavior, seeming disoriented, dazed, or confused. They may avoid or resist the parent. Lack of a clear attachment pattern is likely linked to inconsistent caregiver behavior. In such cases, parents may serve as both a source of comfort and fear, leading to disorganized behavior.

- **Secure attachment**: Children who can depend on their caregivers show distress when separated and joy when reunited. When frightened, securely attached children are comfortable seeking reassurance from caregivers. This is the most common attachment style.

Although attachment styles in adulthood are not necessarily the same as those seen in infancy, early attachments can have a serious impact on later relationships. Adults who were securely attached in childhood tend to have good self-esteem, strong romantic relationships, and the ability to self-disclose to others.

Children who are securely attached as infants tend to develop stronger self-esteem and better self-reliance as they grow older. These children also tend to be more independent, perform better in school, have successful social relationships, and experience less depression and anxiety.

Characteristics of Attachment

Bowlby believed that there are four distinguishing characteristics of attachment:

- **Proximity maintenance**: The desire to be near the people we are attached to.

- **Safe haven**: Returning to the attachment figure for comfort and safety in the face of a fear or threat.

- **Secure base**: The attachment figure acts as a base of security from which the child can explore the surrounding environment.

- **Separation distress**: Anxiety that occurs in the absence of the attachment figure.

John Bowlby theory of attachment

Attachment theory focuses on relationships and long-term bonds between people, including those between a parent and child and between romantic partners. The psychological theory of attachment was first described by John Bowlby. Bowlby's attachment theory rests on the idea that attaching with others is a fundamental human need. Bowlby argued that humans are born with a behavioral system dedicated to forming these attachment bonds and strategies based in the central nervous system. This attachment system is activated whenever the infant senses threat or danger, triggering feelings of distress and motivating behaviors to restore feelings of safety. John Bowlby believed that the relationship between the infant and its mother during the first five years of life was most crucial to socialization. According to Bowlby attachment is adaptive as it enhances the infant's chance of survival. Children come into the world biologically pre-programmed to form attachments with others, because this will help them to survive.

Bowl by also made three key propositions about attachment theory. First, he suggested that when children are raised with confidence that their primary caregiver will be available to them, they are less likely to experience fear than those who are raised without such conviction.

Secondly, Bowlby suggests that there is a critical period for developing at attachment (2.5 years). If an attachment has not developed during this time period then it may not happen well rest of the period of life. The expectations that are formed during that period tend to remain relatively unchanged for the rest of the person's life.Bowlby believed that the attachment system, as he and others called it, served two primary functions: to protect vulnerable individuals from potential threats or harm and to regulate negative emotions following threatening or harmful events.

Finally, he suggested that these expectations that are formed are directly tied to experience. In other words, children develop expectations that their caregivers will be responsive to their needs because, in their experience, their caregivers have been responsive in the past.

Bowlby's theory of attachment showed that infants placed in an unfamiliar situation and separated from their parents will generally react in one of three ways upon reunion with the parents:

1. **Secure attachment**: These infants showed distress upon separation but sought comfort and were easily comforted when the parents returned;

2. **Anxious-resistant attachment**: A smaller portion of infants experienced greater levels of distress and, upon reuniting with the parents, seemed both to seek comfort and to attempt to "punish" the parents for leaving.

3. **Avoidant attachment**: Infants in the third category showed no stress or minimal stress upon separation from the parents

and either ignored the parents upon reuniting or actively avoided the parents.

It makes intuitive sense that a child's attachment style is largely a function of the care giving the child receives in his or her early years. Those who received support and love from their caregivers are likely to be secure, while those who experienced inconsistency or negligence from their caregivers are likely to feel more anxiety surrounding their relationship with their parents.

Secure and Insecure Attachment

Secure attachment is typically related to healthier adjustment, where as insecure attachment is linked to various forms of maladjustments. Adolescents with secure attachment to both the parents have been found to have better emotional adjustment, to experience less loneliness, be more ego resilient, have fewer mental health problems such as anxiety, depression, inattention, conduct problems and delinquent activities, less experimentation with drugs and less frequent substance use. Adolescents with insecure attachment have lower levels of confidence, avoid problem solving, have more dysfunctional anger and have higher levels of internalizing symptoms compared with securely attached adolescents. Thus the quality of the child-parent attachment relationship has been linked with social competence, adjustment and maladjustment from early childhood through adolescence.

There are two distinct styles of coping with insecurity in the attachment relationship as under:

1. **Preoccupied**: Preoccupied attachments are characterized by a strong need for the caregiver in stressful and novel situations, difficulty in separating from the caregiver, and difficulty in deriving comfort from the caregiver when distressed. Preoccupied children have been found to be helpless, fearful, easily stressed by social situations, socially inept and emotionally under controlled, to possess internalizing problems such as withdrawal, anxiety and low self-esteem, and dependent with both peers and teachers, and to be passive, lacking in confidence and assertiveness. Adolescents with

preoccupied attachments have been found to report high personal distress, to feel socially incompetent, and to be perceived by peers as highly anxious.

2. **Avoidant**: Avoidant attachments are marked by limited affective commitment with the caregiver, including avoidance of the caregiver during exploration and reunion, and failure to seek the caregiver for assistance with coping. Avoidant attachments have been found to display the most dysfunctional anger while discussions with their mother and to be rated as most hostile by peer.

Causes of Insecure Attachment

There are many reasons why even a loving, conscientious parent may not be successful at creating a secure attachment bond with an infant. The causes of your insecure attachment could include:

1. **Having a young or inexperienced mother**, lacking in the necessary parenting skills.

2. **Your caregiver experienced depression** caused by isolation, lack of social support, or hormonal problems, for example, forcing them to withdraw from the care giving role.

3. **Your primary caregiver's addiction to alcohol or other drugs** reduced their ability to accurately interpret or respond to your physical or emotional needs.

4. **Traumatic experiences**, such as a serious illness or accident which interrupted the attachment process.

5. **Physical neglect**, such as poor nutrition, insufficient exercise, or neglect of medical issues.

6. **Emotional neglect or abuse**. For example, your caregiver paid little attention to you as a child, made scant effort to understand your feelings, or engaged in verbal abuse.

7. **Physical or sexual abuse**, whether physical injury or violation.

8. **Separation from your primary caregiver** due to illness, death, divorce, or adoption.

9. **Inconsistency in the primary caregiver**. You experienced a succession of nannies or staff at daycare centers, for example.

10. **Frequent moves or placements**. For example, you constantly changed environment due to spending your early years in orphanages or moving between foster homes.

Indian Perspective on Attachment

Developmental psychology in India has a relatively short history. Earliest works on Indian child development include the psychoanalytically-oriented account outlined by Kakar. The development of Indian childhood was emphasized by the mother-infant bond and the mother was supposed to key to the Indian child's development. Kakar's claims about men's roles in the Indian family are rooted in the traditional structural-functional of gender-linked roles and responsibilities. Indian men rarely cross the threshold of the kitchen, are devoted sons, hold the upper hand in the family, and expect their wife to do as home maker and devotion to family. Indian fathers are emotionally distant and largely uninvolved with young children. Maternal employment could be playing an important role in reducing sex role traditionalism. Indian mother are being the main source of early nurturance compared to others within the Indian family system.

But Indian society, now a day, is currently witnessing social and technological changes, putting pressure on family practices to deviate from the traditional norms of child-rearing. The changing scenario in the Indian society includes increase in nuclear compared to joined and extended type of family systems. However, multiple care-giving is still a relevant issue because mothers, especially when employed, relay on grandparents or alternate paid- help to be caregivers to the child. However, data on urban and semi-urban Indian families does not support that all adults who care for the Indian child are equally involved in early care-giving and social interactions. Moreover, while some of the care is exclusively carried out by the mother. Thus the Indian mother remains the child's primary caregiver care-giver with other female and male caregivers assuming complementary but nonequivalent roles in the child's intellectual and social development.

Implications of Attachment and Love for flourishing relationships

Attachment and love are necessary components of flourishing relationships, but they are not sufficient for the maintenance of such relationships. In this regard, attachment and love must be accompanied by purposeful positive relationship behaviors.The infant-caregiver attachment forms the foundation for future relationships; the adult attachment security is closely linked to healthy relationship development, the love that is considered a quality of relationships, and the purposeful positive relationship behaviors that sustain interpersonal connections over time. Sound relationships are built on a foundation of secure attachments and that they are maintained with love and purposeful positive relationship behaviors. Attachment is a dynamic force that connects children to their caregivers. Moreover, secure attachment provides the safe environment in which children can take chances, engage in learning activities, initiate new relationships, and grow into healthy life.

Attachment is a process that probably starts during the first moment of an infant's life. It is the emotional link that forms between a child and a caregiver, and it physically binds people together over time. John Bowlby identified numerous maladaptive parental behaviors and adaptive parental behaviors that were believed to be causally linked to functional behavior and emotional experiences of children.Suchadaptive and maladaptive parental's behaviors lead to the development of an attachment system that regulates the behaviors connecting infants and caregivers in physical and emotional space.

Relationship

Every human being is dependent upon others for their health and happiness. Relationship provides us with a tool for coping with anxiety, fear, sharing our concerns, social support, and intimacy. The relationships involved in our daily social interactions are very significant, but relationships involving friendship, romantic love and marriage are different and have a profound impact on our well-being throughout the life. Degree of intimacy is something that separates close relationships from casual relationships. It refers to the depth of understanding, trust, involvement, connection and whether or not the relationship is sexual.

Characteristics of relationships

1. Knowledge- mutual understanding based on reciprocal self-disclosure.
2. Trust- assumption that no harm will be done by the other person in the relationship
3. Caring- genuine concern for the other and ongoing monitoring and maintenance of relationship.
4. Interdependence- intertwining of lives and mutual influence
5. Mutuality- sense of "we-ness" and overlapping of lives.
6. Commitment- intention to stay in the relationship through its ups and downs.

Problems in a Relationship

Relationships can change over time and not every relationship is 100% healthy all the time. Times of stress, in particular, can lead to unhealthy behaviors. A relationship is unhealthy when certain behaviors are harmful to one or both individuals. Following are some examples of problems in relationship:

- Attempts to control your behaviors
- Avoiding one another
- Being afraid to share your opinions or thoughts
- Being pressured to quit the things you enjoy
- Criticizing what you do, who you spend time with, how you dress, etc.
- Feeling pressured to change who you are
- Feeling that spending time together is an obligation

- Lack of fairness when settling conflicts
- Lack of privacy or pressure to share every detail of your life with your partner
- Neglecting your own needs to put your partner first
- Poor communication
- Unequal control over shared resources including money and transportation
- Yelling

Some problems may be temporary and something that you can address together, either through self-help methods or by consulting a mental health professional. When it comes to more serious problems, such as abusive behaviors, your primary concern should be on maintaining your safety and security.

How to Build a Healthier Relationship

Toxic behaviors are often a sign that an unhealthy relationship should end. For other problems, there are many ways to fix weaknesses and build a healthier relationship.

1. **Show Appreciation:** Showing gratitude for a partner can be an important way to boost satisfaction in romantic relationships. Those who feel gratitude for one another feel closer to one another and tend to be more satisfied with their relationships.

2. **Keep Things Interesting:** There are some things that you can do to keep the romance alive over the long term as under:

   1. Make time for one another; schedule in dates or set aside time each week to focus on one another.

   2. Try new things together; take a class or try a new hobby that you can both enjoy

   3. Break out of the same old routine

   4. Look for ways to surprise each other

   5. Spend time apart once in a while

   6. Turn off digital devices and spend time focused only on one another

7. Find time for intimacy

Theories of Love

Love is much deeper, more intense, and includes a strong desire for physical intimacy and contact. People who are "in like mode" enjoy each other's company, while those who are "in love" care as much about the other person's needs as they do their own. There are several different theories of love to explain how it forms as well as how it endures

1. ***Biological Approaches:*** *Every human being have some biological need to express love like:* touching, hugging and kissing. In order to understand the brain's response to love, one must examine the brain and fully comprehend the myriad array of structures involved. One of the main structures involved with falling in love is the limbic system. The particular system is well known as being the part of the brain involved in emotional response. The limbic system is actually several structures combined, including the basal nuclei, the thalamus, and the hypothalamus. While all of these structures are vital, the hypothalamus is directly involved in both behavioral and sexual function. Combining these two important functions, one can see how the limbic system is so crucial to falling in love.

2. **Color Wheel Model of Love:** John Lee suggested that there are three primary styles of love color of the wheel as under:

   - **Eros**: The term *Eros* has taken from the Greek word meaning "passionate" or "erotic." Lee suggested that this type of love involves both physical and emotional passion. It represents love for an ideal person.

   - **Ludus**: *Ludus* comes from the Greek word meaning "game." This form of love is conceived as playful and fun but not necessarily serious. Those who exhibit this form of love are not ready for commitment and are not having of too much intimacy. So, it represents love as a game.

   - **Storge**: *Storge* has taken from the Greek meaning "natural affection." This form of love includes familial love between parents and children, siblings, and extended family members. This love can also develop out of friendship, where people who share interests and commitments gradually develop affection for one another. Therefore, it represents love as friendship.

3. **Attachment Theory of Love:** Romantic love is a biosocial process similar to how children form attachments with their parents. According to Hazan and Shaver's attachment theory of love, a person's attachment style is partially formed by the relationship they had with their parents in childhood. This same basic style then continues into adulthood, where it becomes part of their romantic relationships.

4. **The Triangular Theory of Love :** Love is the open hearted desire for human beings to attain happiness and well being. The capacity for love is a central component of all human societies. In developing the triangular theory of love, psychologist Robert Sternberg theorized that love is a mix of three components: (1) **passion**, or physical attractiveness and romantic drives; (2) **intimacy**, or feelings of closeness and connectedness, and (3) **commitment**, involving the decision to initiate and sustain a relationship. Various combinations of these three components yield eight forms of love. The most durable type of love is manifested when all three components passion, intimacy, and commitment are present at high levels and in balance across both partners.

5. **Compassionate love** is characterized by mutual respect, attachment, affection, and trust. This love usually develops out of feelings of mutual understanding and shared respect for one another.

6. **Passionate love** is characterized by intense emotions, sexual attraction, anxiety, and affection. When these intense emotions are reciprocated, people feel elated and fulfilled, while unreciprocated love leads to feelings of despondency and despair.

Hatfield suggests that passionate love arises when cultural

expectations encourage falling in love, when the person meets one's ideal love, and when one experiences heightened physiological arousal in the presence of the other person.

Passionate love is transitory usually lasting between 6 and 30 months.Ideally, passionate love leads to compassionate love, which is far more enduring.

Attachment and love flourish relationship between child and caregiver

Attachment is a process that probably starts during the first moment of an infant's life. It is the emotional link that forms between a child and a caregiver, and it physically binds people together over time. John Bowlby, identified that maladaptive parental have behaviors to their children like unplanned attempts to meet a child's needs but adaptive parental behaviors parents response to a child with smiling. The inconsistency in responses to children is associated with children's frustration and later anxiety. On the other hand, consistency in caregivers' responses to children is linked to children's contentment and later development of trust. Adaptive and maladaptive parental behaviors lead to the development of an attachment system that regulates the behaviors connecting infants and caregivers in physical and emotional space. A child with insecure attachment to a caregiver may have difficulty in cooperating with others and in regulating moods. These problems make existing relationships fragile and new relationships hard to build. Conversely, children with sound attachment systems become more appealing to their caregivers and other people.

The secure attachment pattern is characterized by a balance between exploration of the environment and contact with the caregiver. As the strange situation unfolds, the child will engage in more proximity-seeking and contact-maintaining behavior with the caregiver, exploring the environment only to return for comfort when necessary. Whereas, insecure patterns increases tension between the child and parent. Children with insecure-avoidant patterns avoid the caregiver when he or she is reintroduced into the situation, and those with the insecure-resistant/ambivalent pattern passively or actively demonstrate hostility toward the caregiver. Attachment is a dynamic force that connects children to their caregivers. Moreover, secure attachment provides the safe environment in which children can take chances, engage in learning activities, initiate new relationships, and grow into healthy, socially adept adults.

Flourishing Relationships

Flourishing is one of the most important key to improving the quality of life for people around the world.

Minding relationships: The minding theory of relationships (Harvey et al, 2002) describes how closeness in relationships may be enhanced. Minding refers to the reciprocal knowing process involving the non-stop, interrelated thoughts, feelings, and behaviors of persons in a relationship (Harvey et al., 2001). The five components of minding are as follows:

1. **Knowing and being known**: This relates to seeking to understand one's partner in terms of their dreams, fears vulnerabilities etc. This also involves giving more preference to knowing one's partner than focusing on one's personal information.

2. **Making relationship-enhancing attributions**: The best strategy would be to attribute positive behaviors to dispositional causes and negative behaviors to external causes. This also involves giving benefit of doubt to the partner.

3. **Accepting and respecting**: This involves empathy and social skills. Accepting the strengths and weaknesses of the partner is very important for the continued development of the relationship

4. **Maintaining reciprocity**: This relates to active participation of both the partners in relationship enhancement

5. **Continuity in minding**: this relates to persisting in mindfulness and planning to become closer to each other as the relationship grows

Questions

1. What is Empathy? Describe the signs and uses of Empathy.

2. Describe the types of Empathy. What is the impact of Empathy? Discuss.

3. What is Altruism? What are the characteristics of Altruism? Discuss.

4. Describe the categories and types of Altruism.

5. Define Altruism. What are the causes of Altruism? Describe its impact.

6. Define Gratitude. Describe the stages of Gratitude.

7. Discuss the Perspectives of Gratitude. What are the types of Gratitude? Describe.

8. What is Gratitude? Describe the signs and influence of Gratitude.

9. Describe the effects of Gratitude. How would you practice Gratitude?

10. Describe the impact of Gratitude.

11. Define Forgiveness. What are the benefits of Forgiveness?

12. Discuss the models of Forgiveness. Describe the steps to true Forgiveness.

13. Discuss Forgiveness as technique of positive living. What are the applications of Forgiveness?

14. Describe the stages of Attachment. What are factors that influence Attachment? Discuss.

15. Describe the types of Attachments. Discuss the characteristics of Attachment.

16. Discuss the John Bowl by theory of Attachment.

17. What are Secure and Insecure Attachment? Describe the causes of Attachment.

18. Discuss Indian Perspective on Attachment.

19. Discuss Attachment and Love for Flourishing Relationship.

20. Describe the characteristics of Relationship.

21. What are the problems in Relationship? How would you build a Healthier Relationship? Discuss.

22. Write notes of Flourishing Relationships.

❏

Chapter-VI

Positive Schooling

Introduction / Concept of Positive Psychology

The ultimate objective of education is imparting knowledge to students, enhancing their coping skills, helping them in building their character, and, finally, producing skilled and responsible citizens for nation building. Therefore, schools play an important role in achieving the objective of education and in shaping the career of a child. Everyone wants their children to be happy and to flourish. They want them to live out their dreams and reach their innate potential. But the challenge is to find the right education model and positive education system. Positive education is the combination of traditional education principles with the study of happiness and wellbeing. Positive schooling is defined as approach to education that incorporates student wellbeing and virtues as learning goals, besides academic achievement. A strength-based approach to positive schooling employs character strengths as a pathway to positive change and well-being.

Students bring all of life's ups and downs with them into the classroom, and in some cases this can lead to poor focus and disengagement. A learning environment that uses positive psychology focuses on giving all students a chance to build their resilience and learn to cope with and manage challenging situations. Positive psychology in the classroom can also have practical benefits. Students who feel supported and engaged will be more focused in class, will connect better with their teachers and classmates, and will achieve better academic outcomes. The aim of educational psychology is to help young people find their self-esteem, the meaning of life, and to gain self-confidence. In this dimension, positive psychology converges with the assumptions and practice of educational psychology. Positive education is an approach to education that draws emphasis of individual strengths and personal motivation to promote learning. A learning environment that uses positive psychology focuses on giving all students a chance to build their resilience and learn to cope with and manage challenging situations. Positive psychology provides one of the most powerful ways to build a positive learning environment. Seligman, one of the founders of positive psychology, has incorporated positive psychology into education models as a way to decrease depression in younger people and enhance their wellbeing and happiness by using his PERMA model. The PERMA model, created is one practical way to explore, explain and practice positive psychology.

Positive education is defined as positive character using the core character strengths that are represented in six virtues as under:

1. Wisdom and knowledge
2. Courage
3. Humanity
4. Justice
5. Temperance
6. Transcendence

The goal of positive education is to reveal children's combination of character strengths and to develop their ability to effectively engage those strengths.

Characteristics of Positive Classroom Environment

Following are the characteristics of positive classroom environment

- a safe, welcoming atmosphere
- a sense of belonging among students
- trust between students and the teacher
- willingness in students to ask questions, participate and take risks

- clear expectations, and fair and honest feedback, from the teacher.

PERMA's key elements of positive classroom

- **Positive emotions:** students can focus on things that make them feel good, like being recognized for quality work or having the chance to help a classmate.

- **Engagement:** students feel absorbed by their work because they find it challenging but achievable, and it explores new ideas in interesting ways.

- **Relationships:** students feel able to build strong connections with you, and with other students, through feedback and activities.

- **Meaning:** students understand the purpose of their work and why it's important for them to learn.

- **Achievement:** students receive encouraging and honest feedback on their work and feel a sense of accomplishment and success.

By focusing on each of these areas, you can build your classroom into a positive learning environment.

Components of Positive Schooling:

Schools play an increasingly important role in assisting youth to develop cognitive, social and emotional skills. Schooling has been conceptualized in many different ways and has multiple components to it including an emphasis on the role of technology in changing education, new pedagogies, curriculum, open learning spaces and reformed teacher training. schooling is the need for education to develop the whole-student through social, emotional, moral and intellectual development. The goal o f positive schooling is to turn all students into teachers who will pass down their wisdom and knowledge to others and teachers who will continue the ways of positive education. The major components of positive schooling are caring, trust, respect for diversity, goals, plans, motivation, hope and societal contributions. Goals, plans and motivation are three interrelated components, which are necessary for learning.

Coping Strategies in Positive Education

In academic life, students are exposed to a wide range of stressful situations which could negatively affect their academic achievement and their health. This stress is often caused by failure, the threat of failure or the belief that failure is inevitable. The reactions to these threats are both conscious and sub-conscious; we cannot fully control our behaviour in every respect. Most students identify academic pressure as the main reason for their stress. Chronic academic stress often leads to physical, emotional, and behavioral symptoms, such as frequent illnesses, depression, irritability, decreased academic performance, drug or alcohol experimentation, and cheating. Causes of academic stress include high-stakes tests, pressure from parents, overly demanding academic content, overbooked schedules, and pressure to gain admittance to prestigious colleges and universities, and conflicts with teachers. Learning becomes more difficult when students lack the necessary strategies to manage stress and anxiety. In an educational setting, coping strategies refer to the way in which learners predict, prepare, perceive, manage, react and alter their behaviour when stressed. Coping strategies means strategies that people use in stressful and challenging situations to manage their own stress and anxiety. Their primary goal is to avoid the perceived embarrassment caused by failure and the best way to achieve this. Students should manage stress by creating a positive meaning for it in terms of their personal growth and feeling. Students have to understand that positive stress and coping with negative stress can change them in a good way. Coping with stress is the attempt to manage or deal with stress. The importance of coping strategies is preventing harmful consequences.

Lazarus et al. defined coping as "the problem-solving efforts made by an individual when the demands of a given situation". It is a process by which people try to manage the demands in their lives and their resources in a stressful situation. Coping strategies are actions taken that are intended to reduce stress, such as expressing emotions, asking for help, or appraising the problem.

The most frequent consequences stress, which include:

1. Physical illness
2. Insufficient sleep
3. Anxiety and depression
4. Irritability or unusual emotionality or volatility
5. Decrease in academic performance
6. Social withdrawal
7. Drug or alcohol experimentation
8. Cheating.

Causes of Academic Stress

Different students respond to academic pressures in different ways. Parents, other students, and government policies, and the school, college and universities admissions process all play a role in increasing students' stress levels. Following is the most common causes of academic stress.

1. Developmentally inappropriate classrooms
2. High-stakes tests
3. Pressure from parents
4. Demanding academic content
5. Peer relationships
6. Fear of failure
7. Lack of preparation
8. Excessive homework
9. Overbooked schedules
10. Pressure to maintain high grades
11. Pressure to gain acceptance to prestigious colleges
12. Conflicts with teachers
13. Transitioning to secondary school
14. Poor diet and lack of sleep.

Student Strategies for Coping with Academic Stress:

Following strategies that can help students deal with their academic stress.

1. Eat well
2. Exercise
3. Sleep well at night
4. Don't use drugs, alcohol, or tobacco
5. Set realistic goals for yourself
6. Learn stress management skills, such as relaxation techniques and problem solving
7. Don't over-schedule activities
8. Find time to relax
9. Keep a schedule
10. Get organized
11. Be optimistic
12. Build resiliency;

Types of Coping Strategies

These are two approaches for coping strategies:

- **Problem-focused coping** involves handling stress by facing it head-on and taking action to resolve the underlying cause.
- **Emotion-focused coping** involves regulating your feelings and emotional response to the problem instead of addressing the problem.

Gainful Employment

Gainful employment refers to an employment situation where the employee receives steady work, payment from the employer and that allows for self-sufficiency. In psychology, gainful employment is a positive psychology concept that explores the benefits of work and employment. Gainful employment implies that an employee makes more than a living wage that covers their basic month-to-month expenses. Gainful employment refers to an employment condition where employee receives consistent work and payment from the employer.

Characteristics of gainful employment

Gainful employment consists of holding a job that:

1. provides a sense of engagement and involvement
2. allows one to find a sense of purpose in life via providing a product or service
3. leads to a sense of performing well and meeting goals
4. includes companionship with and loyalty to

Implications (Benefits) of Gainful Employments

1. **Working Conditions:** Gainful employment implies reasonable working conditions such as safe, clean, healthy, and professional environment and role that does not involve excessive physical demands or mental stress.

2. **Stability:** Gainful employment implies regular hours and some level of job security

3. **Risk:** Gainful employment implies a normal level of risk to the employee including things like financial risk, safety and health risk.

4. **Carrier path:** Gainful employment implies or builds or maintains marketable skill as the employee can reasonably expect to find employment with another employers in future

5. **Disposable Income:** Gainful employment implies that an employee gets more than a living wage that covers their basic month-to-month expenses.

Skill Development to Ensure Gainful Employment

Skilling our vast human resource will play significant role in ensuring gainful employment in following way

- Equip people with skills to adapt to changing technology and economic needs.
- Absorb large workforce from agriculture to manufacturing sector by enhancing productivity.
- Help people to take up entrepreneurship.

The Value of Self-Control

People with strong self-control have better careers. They are also less likely to have problems with overeating, overspending, smoking, alcohol or drug abuse, procrastination, and unethical behavior. People with high self-control are also more satisfied with their lives and experience their lives as more meaningful. Self-controlled people seem to be more successful. Although high self-control people are generally less likely to engage in illegal or antisocial activities like reckless driving or cheating than low self-control people, when they do engage in such activities. Self-control is the art of making the right choices without feeling conflicted. A self-controlled person focuses only on his / her goals and makes decisions keeping the end goals in mind. Self-control is the ability to regulate and alter your responses in order to avoid undesirable behaviours, increase desirable ones, and achieve long-term goals. Those who have possessing self-control can be important for health and well-being. Self-controlled people have habit such as exercising regularly, eating a balanced diet, being more productive, giving up bad habits, and saving money are just a few worthwhile ambitions that usually require self-control to achieve. The word Self-control is also known as discipline, determination, grit, willpower, and fortitude.

Characteristics of Self-Control

Psychologists typically characterized self-control as:[2]

- The ability to control behaviours in order to avoid temptations and to achieve goals.
- The ability to delay gratification and resist unwanted behaviours or urges
- A limited resource that can be depleted

Benefits of Self-Control

The benefits of self-control are not limited to academic performance. High levels of self-control during childhood predicted greater cardiovascular, respiratory, and dental health in adulthood, as well as improved financial status. Self-control can help leadership skills and live a happy and fulfilled life. The benefits of self-control are plentiful and essential for successful lives. Effective self-control has been linked to success in academics and occupations, as well as social wellness. Good mental and physical health, reduction in crime, and longer life spans are also linked to self-control. Here are some benefits of self-control:

1. **Decision-making Ability:** One of the benefits of self-control is that it makes decision-making easier. For instance, a person might love chocolate but high blood sugar levels will force them to exercise self-control and stay away from the chocolate bars, cookies, and desserts.

2. **Greater chances of Success:** A person who has self-control doesn't get distracted easily. This enables them to manage their time and resources better. They tend to make sustained and focused efforts toward their goals, which are more likely to result in success.

3. **Self-Control can beat temptations:** Self-control is the ability to beat temptation. Quite often, we can get tempted to do things that divert us from our goals and affect our quality of life.

4. **Self-Control can make you excel:** It helps students perform better in exams and stay mentally sharp. They are more focused on achieving their goals than their peers. Similarly, people with high amounts of self-control can channel their time and energy into being productive in the workplace, which leads to success at work.

5. **Better personal relationships:** Self-controlled people are not only in charge of their actions but they can regulate their emotions as well. They can control their anger or harmful emotions like jealousy or hatred. This helps them handle

personal relationships better than those who don't have much self-control.

Disadvantages of Self-Control

1. **Self-control can restrict emotional experiences:** Self-control persons are having less tempting desires. But this might also mean that these people have less intense emotional experiences; that is, they respond to situations in more neutral ways. For example, high self-control might prevent employees from fully enjoying positive career outcomes, such as promotions, raises, and outstanding performance appraisals.

2. **Self-control may lead to long-term regret:** When people reflect on their lives, they tend to regret too much self-control and missing out on the pleasures of life. This experience of regret emerges only after time has passed.

3. **Self-control can lead to increased workload:** People tend to rely on others with high self-control, and this might make the latter feel burdened.

4. **Self-control can lead to bias:** Policy makers often see complex social problems like overeating, overspending, smoking, alcohol or drug abuse, etc. as primarily self-controlproblems. However, this emphasis on self-control might obscure the social, economic, or political sources of these problems. This one-sided emphasis on self-control, also referred to as "puritanical bias," reflects an ideology that puts the blame for wrongdoing entirely on the individual and neglects the impact of broader societal factors.

Goals of Self-Controlled Person

Goals play an important role in decision making of self-controlled person. Such person often set goals to achieve a variety of objectives such as losing weight, saving money, and improving health. Goals are an important motivator.

Usually, self-controlled persons have following goal to achieve

1. exercising regularly,
2. eating a balanced diet,
3. being more productive,
4. giving up bad habits,
5. saving money

Rule of Goal Setting

Goal-setting as a psychological tool for increasing productivity involves five rules or criterion, known as the S-M-A-R-T rule.

- **S (Specific)** – They target a particular area of functioning and focus on building it.

- **M (Measurable)** -The results can be gauged quantitatively or at least indicated by some qualitative attributes. This helps in monitoring the progress after executing the plans.

- **A (Attainable/Achievable)** – The goals are targeted to suitable people and are individualized. They take into account the fact that no single rule suits all, and are flexible in that regard.

- **R (Realistic)** – They are practical and planned in a way that would be easy to implement in real life. The purpose of a smart goal is not just providing the plan, but also helping the person execute it.

- **T (Time-bound)** – An element of time makes the goal more focused. It also provides a time frame about task achievement.

Self-regulation

Self-regulation refers to the self-directive process through which learners transform their mental abilities into task related skills. Self-regulation is defined as direct thoughts, feelings, and actions, toward the attainment of one's goals. Physiological regulation means children demonstrate the emerging ability to regulate their physical processes in order to meet both their internal needs and external demands in accordance with social and cultural contexts. Self-regulation is control by oneself. Someone who has good emotional self-regulation has the ability to keep their emotions in check. They have a flexible range of emotional and behavioral responses that are well matched to the demands of their environment. The goal of Self-controlled person is to improve an individual's ability to self-regulate and to gain a sense of control over one's behavior and life. Self-regulation is the ability to control one's behavior, emotions, and thoughts in the pursuit of long-term goals. Self-regulation also involves the ability to rebound from disappointment and to act in a way consistent with your values. It is one of the five key components of emotional intelligence.

Behavioral Self-Regulation: Behavioral self-regulation is the ability to act in your long-term best interest, consistent with your deepest values. It allows us to feel one way but act another.

Emotional Self-Regulation: Emotional self-regulation involves control of or influence over emotions. Emotional self-regulation refers to the ability to manage disruptive emotions and impulses—in other words, to think before acting.

Components of Self-Regulation

There are four components of Self-regulation as under:

1. *Standards* of desirable behavior;
2. <u>Motivation</u> to meet standards;
3. *Monitoring* of situations and thoughts that precede breaking standards;
4. <u>Willpower</u> allowing one's internal strength to control urges.

These four components interact to determine our self-regulatory activity at any given moment.

According to <u>Albert Bandura</u> self-regulation is a continuously active process in which we:

1. Monitor our own behavior, the influences on our behavior, and the consequences of our behavior;
2. Judge our behavior in relation to our own personal standards and broader, more contextual standards;

3. React to our own behavior (i.e., what we think and how we feel about our behavior)

How Self-Regulation Develops

The ability of self-regulate in adult has roots in childhood. Self-regulate is an important skill that children learn both for emotional maturity and, later, for social connections. A toddler who throws tantrums grows into a child who learns how to tolerate uncomfortable feelings without throwing a fit, and later into an adult who is able to control impulses to act based on uncomfortable feelings.

Qualities of Self-Regulators

People who are adept at self-regulating tend to be able to:[4]

- ct in accordance with their values
- Calm themselves when upset
- Cheer themselves when feeling down
- Maintain open communication
- Persist through difficult times
- Put forth their best effort
- Remain flexible and adapting to situations
- See the good in others
- Stay clear about their intentions
- Take control of situations when necessary
- View challenges as opportunities

Questions

1. Write a Positive Schooling? What are the characteristics of Positive Classroom environment?

2. Explain PERMA'S key elements of positive classroom.

3. Describe the components of positive schooling. What are the coping strategies in positive education?

4. Discuss the causes of Academic stress. Describe the student strategies for coping with Academic Stress.

5. What are the causes of Academic Stress? Describe the types of coping strategies.

6. Describe the characteristics of Gainful employment. What are the implications (Benefits) of Gainful employment? Discuss

7. Describe the skill development to ensure gainful employment.

8. Describe the characteristics of self-control.

9. What are the advantage (benefits) and disadvantage of self – control?

10. Describe the goals of self –controlled person

11. Describe the rule of goal setting of self-control.

12. What are the components of self-regulation? How dose self-regulation develops? Explain.

13. Describe the Qualities of self-regulations.

❏